OSWALD JACOBY, who introduces this book, is the most famous all-round player of games combining skill and chance in the world, and an author of leading works on poker, gin rummy, canasta, bridge, and backgammon. He has won four world backgammon championships, and in 1978 won three major tournaments—the best record in the world that year.

His wife, MARY ZITA JACOBY, is a backgammon player and teacher of the top rank. She has taught backgammon for more than 15 years, lectures on backgammon throughout the country, and established herself as the world's leading woman backgammon player by winning several major tournaments.

Their son, JAMES JACOBY, is well known for his bridge exploits, including three world championships, in addition to such bestselling books as *Instant Bridge*. He now devotes increasing time to backgammon and has won numerous tournaments, including the 1978 Children's Cancer Fund Tournament.

The New York Times
BOOK OF BACKGAMMON

by
JAMES OSWALD
and
MARY ZITA JACOBY

Introduction by Oswald Jacoby

A PLUME BOOK
NEW AMERICAN LIBRARY
TIMES MIRROR
NEW YORK AND SCARBOROUGH, ONTARIO

PLUME TRADEMARK REG. U.S. PAT. OFF. AND FOREIGN COUNTRIES
REGISTERED TRADEMARK—MARCA REGISTRADA
HECHO EN FORGE VILLAGE, MASS., U.S.A.

SIGNET, SIGNET CLASSICS, MENTOR, PLUME and
MERIDIAN BOOKS are published *in the United States* by
The New American Library, Inc.,
1301 Avenue of the Americas, New York, New York 10019,
in Canada by The New American Library of Canada Limited,
81 Mack Avenue, Scarborough, Ontario M1L 1M8.

First Plume Printing, October, 1974

8   9   10   11   12   13

Printed in The United States of America

CONTENTS

FOREWORD by Oswald Jacoby   vii

PREFACE   ix

LESSON I   So You Want to Play Backgammon   1

LESSON II   The Running Game   15

LESSON III   The First Move   25

LESSON IV   The Reply to the First Move   45

LESSON V   Let's Play Some Backgammon
                    (The Early Game)   65

LESSON VI   The Arithmetic of Backgammon   79

LESSON VII   Doubles and Redoubles   89

LESSON VIII   Let's Play Some More Backgammon
                    (The Middle Game)   95

LESSON IX   Finishing the Running Game   105

LESSON X   Finishing One-Sided Games   121

LESSON XI   Back Games and Special Problems   133

LESSON XII   Chouettes and Settlements   145

APPENDIX A   Pip Count   155

APPENDIX B   The Laws of Backgammon   161

GLOSSARY   171

FOREWORD

Mary Zita Jacoby may or may not be the best woman back-gammon player in the world but she certainly is the best teacher —male or female.

James Oswald Jacoby is principally known as a bridge player. He is the only man under forty to ever acquire over 10,000 master points and, in addition, has managed to pick up three world championships.

In spite of this, backgammon is his favorite game. He has done well in the few tournaments he has had a chance to play in, and in my slightly prejudiced opinion is now as good at the game as anybody, anywhere.

In the last year Mary Zita has been teaching backgammon class after backgammon class. She needed lessons to do this teaching and Jim and I helped her prepare a set.

It occurred to me that there was material in these lessons for a book. I wanted to write it but my wife and son put their feet down and said that I had done enough writing.

Then they went ahead and produced this book—a series of lessons that will enable beginners to learn the game quickly, that will help good players become experts, and even give the greatest experts a chance to add to their knowledge of the game!

I am proud of them and believe firmly that they have written the best backgammon book of all time.

Oswald Jacoby
Dallas, Texas

PREFACE

This book is designed not only to enable the beginner to become a good backgammon player, but also to enable the good backgammon player to become an excellent player. It is presented in the form of twelve lessons.

While written with the beginner in mind, every lesson has points that good players will do well to pick up if they wish to improve their game. As for the top backgammon experts, they won't agree with everything in this book but we expect they all will read it —if only to see how we disagree with them. Of course, they also disagree with each other; you can't be an expert at anything and not have definite opinions.

In our search for ways to simplify the game for the average player we have formulated some rules that even the greatest experts will do well to learn. The most important of these concerns the Doubling Number, an invention which is described in the lesson on doubles and redoubles. Next is the rule for positioning one's last men. The opening moves recommended here represent the opinion of many of our top players but, as you would expect, not all.

We wish to express our sincere thanks to: Captain William H. Benson, U.S.N. (Ret.), who worked extensively with us on the entire book; Prince Alexis Obolensky, who is largely responsible for popularizing the game; the other backgammon experts whose brains we have picked; and, finally, Oswald Jacoby—the current backgammon champion of the world—who also happens to be our father and husband, respectively.

James Oswald Jacoby
Richardson, Texas

Mary Zita Jacoby
Dallas, Texas

August, 1973

The New York Times

BOOK OF BACKGAMMON

Lesson I

SO YOU WANT TO PLAY BACKGAMMON

Learning a game is similar to learning a language. You not only must extend your vocabulary by adding new words and their meanings, but also must learn how to organize the new words into coherent and useful patterns. Even if you have played back-gammon previously we urge you not to skip any of this lesson. It is quite likely that you are unfamiliar with some of the fine—but therefore the more important—points discussed.

To start at the beginning—backgammon is basically a two-handed game. It is suggested, however, that you obtain a back-gammon set and play against yourself as you go through these lessons. There is no question that following this suggestion will result in improving your understanding of the game. You will need certain equipment to play the game: a backgammon board, thirty men (fifteen of one color and fifteen of another color), and a pair of dice. A second pair of dice, two dice cups, and a doubling cube come with most sets. You should always use the dice cups. They frequently are designed with a narrow ridge on the inner side of the lip which acts to toss the dice about as they are thrown and to insure, as far as possible, an honest roll of the dice. The beginner has no need for the doubling cube. Its use will be discussed in Lesson VI.

The board is designed with twenty-four triangular playing posi-tions which are colored alternately. These playing positions, called "points," are divided by a blank space extending across the board into two groups of twelve points each. We have numbered the different points as shown in Diagram I-1. Further, we

Diagram I-1

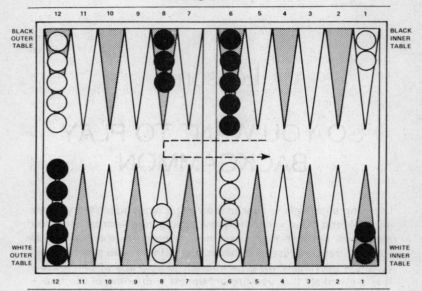

have selected white and black as the colors of the men. We thus have white points one to twelve and black points one to twelve. These two groups of twelve points are subdivided by the bar into two sets of six each. The name "bar" derives from the fact that most backgammon boards fold into a box with one side along this dividing line. As a result, when the box is opened for play there is actually a bar dividing the points into sets of six each. The board is thus divided into four parts which (as indicated in Diagram I-1) are named "White Inner Table," "Black Inner Table," "White Outer Table," and "Black Outer Table." The word "board" is used interchangeably with the word "table" by some players; we thus have "White Inner Board," etc.

Before play is begun the thirty men are placed upon the board in the positions shown in this diagram. During the play you move your men around the board from your adversary's inner table to his outer table, to your own outer table, and then to your own inner table. That is to say, the white men move in the direction

of the arrow in Diagram I-1 and the black men move in the opposite direction. Of course, this arrow, the table names, and the
point numbers will not appear on your board. They are put on
the diagrams merely for your convenience. Throughout this book
you will be White, playing the white men.

Backgammon is an old game. Certainly it is older than all card
games and possibly older even than chess. It is, after all, a dice
game and dice have been used since the dawn of civilization.
Backgammon sets are made of all types of materials and quality. They range from very cheap to very expensive. While the
quality of your game depends in no way upon the quality of
your set, the amount of satisfaction you derive from playing with
it may. Once you have learned the game, it is time to consider
buying a reasonably good set. But do not go overboard as a
starter, thinking it will make the game easier to play.

The two players roll their dice alternately. Your objective in
backgammon is to move your men around the board (subject
to certain restrictions on play imposed by the laws) in accordance with the numbers uppermost on the two dice that you roll
when it is your turn to play. There is some luck in backgammon
but it is by no means all luck. There is also a lot of skill involved.
In fact there is so much skill involved that nine of the eighteen
major backgammon tournaments played since such events became popular have been won by three men.* There is enough
luck in it so that three of the other nine winners have been rather
poor players who just happened to get into a lucky streak
of the dice.

You start a play by placing your dice in a cup, shaking it, and
rolling the dice out onto the space to your right of the bar. If
you roll before your adversary has completed his play you must
rethrow the dice. If your dice do not come to rest flat upon
the table (that is, if they are cocked) they must also be rethrown.
Once the dice have come to rest you should leave them alone
while you advance your men the exact number of points they
indicate. The men are never moved backwards. You may advance
any man the number of points indicated by one die and a second
man the number of points indicated by the other die, or you may
advance any one man for the total number of points the dice
indicate. A man can only be advanced to "an open point," that

*Publisher's note: Walter Cooke has won two. Tim Holland has won three. Oswald
Jacoby has won four.

is, to a point which is not occupied by two, or more, of your opponent's men. In other words, you may advance a man to any point which is unoccupied, to one which has at most one of your opponent's men on it (as will be discussed shortly), or to one on which one or more of your own men sit. When a double is thrown you must make four plays of that number. These plays may be made by advancing one, two, three, or four separate men as you choose—the only condition being that the final combination of advances must total four moves of the number on the dice. Note that in moving a man more than the number of points indicated by a single die it must be possible for that man to touch down temporarily upon an open point. As an example, suppose that your opponent (Black) starts the game (we will return to opening plays shortly) with a 3-1 and advances one of the men on his eight point to his five point with the 3 and uses the 1 to advance a man from his six point to the same five point. See Diagram I-2. When you move a second man to a point upon

Diagram I-2

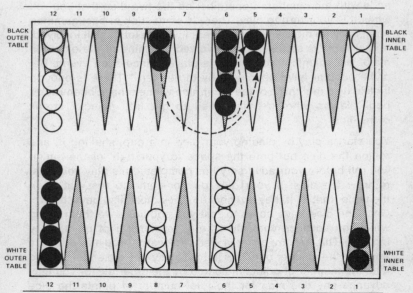

which you already have one man you are said to "make that point." Such points are very helpful to you—they are available for you to use but, as long as you keep at least two men on a point, you deny the use of that point to the enemy. Points upon which your opponent has two or more men act to impede your progress in a similar manner.

Suppose you now roll double 5. You cannot advance either of your "back men" (the two men you have on Black's one point). Regardless of the fact that Black's eleven point is open, the fact that he has more than one man on his six point prevents either of these men from advancing. They have no open point to touch down on as they move forward. On the other hand, if instead of a double 5 you had thrown a 6-4 you could, if you so desired, advance one of your back men to Black's eleven point since that man could use the 6 to touch down at the open black seven point (which is known as the "bar point") while en route. When you have finished moving your men **and** have picked up your dice you have completed your play and it is your adversary's turn to roll.

As a matter of interest note that you start the game controlling your own six and eight points and Black's one and twelve points. Black's men occupy points symmetrically opposed to yours. He has control of his six and eight points and your one and twelve points. There is no limit to the number of your own men that you may place upon any point but you cannot place one of your men, even temporarily, on a point controlled by your opponent—that is, on a point which he has made by occupying it with two or more of his men.

In addition to the above, there are several other requirements which must be met when it is your turn to play. You must play both of the numbers that you roll (all four numbers in the case of doublets) when at all possible. You may play either number first, but you cannot select one number and play it in such a manner that it becomes impossible to play the other one. In other words, you must play both numbers if you can do so. If you can play either of two numbers (but cannot play both numbers) you must play the larger one.

Let us assume that you did roll a 6-4 and did advance one of your back men to Black's eleven point as shown in Diagram I-3. A single man on a point is known as a "blot." You now have blots on Black's one and eleven points. Blots are vulnerable to attack. If your opponent should happen to throw a number which permits him to move one of his men to the point occupied by

Diagram I-3

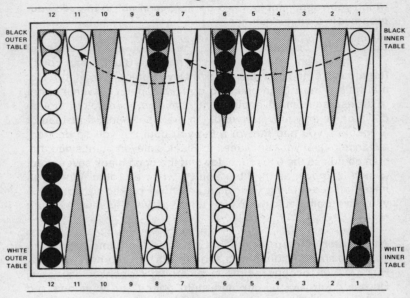

Diagram I-4

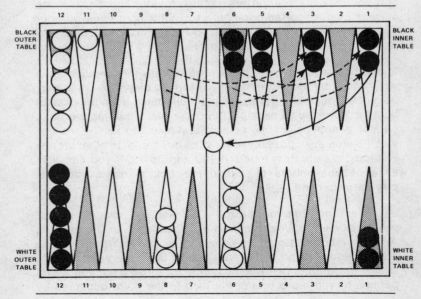

one of your blots (in this example he needs a 2 to advance a man to the black eleven point) and if he chooses to make this move, he will be said to have "hit your blot." When he has hit your blot he picks up your man and "places it on the bar." Suppose, instead of throwing a 2, Black throws double 5 (see Diagram I-4). Double 5 is not usually much of a roll except as a freight mover: it does get men around the board. But right now it has become deadly. He will use two of his 5's to hit your blot on his one point (and simultaneously make this point) with two men on his six point, and the other two 5's to make his three point (with the two men left on his eight point). Black now controls blocks on his one, three, five, and six points—the only open points in his inner table are the two and four points—and you have a man on the bar plus a blot on the black eleven point!

Whenever you have one or more men on the bar the laws place a severe restriction on your play. You must bring all the men that you have on the bar into your opponent's inner table before you can move any other man. This isn't much of a restriction in the starting position (Diagram I-1). The only point your opponent holds in his inner table is the six point, so you can play any number from the bar except double 6. Once he makes a second point, such as the five point, he blocks off three more rolls (double 5 and 6-5). Why do we say three more rolls? Because any regular roll such as 6-5 is actually two different rolls (6 with one die and 5 with the other die or 5 with the first die and 6 with the second die). If he makes a third point in his inner table, that cuts out five more possibilities and leaves you with just twenty-seven playable rolls out of the thirty-six that are possible. A fourth point made leaves you with just twenty playable rolls. A fifth point made leaves just eleven. If he has all six points made you can't play at all until he breaks one of them.

Thus it is not a matter of life and death to expose a blot when your opponent holds one, two, or even three points in his inner table—but it is when he holds more than three. Therefore, the time to take chances with blots is early in the game. You may have to later on, but if you do you should be fully aware of the danger.

In the example we are looking at (Diagram I-4), you exposed two blots when your opponent held two points in his inner table. He has rolled double 5, hit one of your blots, and made two more points in his inner table. He now holds four points and is said to have made a "four point board."

You must roll a 2 or 4 to play at all. If you roll some usually good roll such as double 1, you lose your whole play and are in dire straits. You have a second blot exposed on the black eleven point; if your enemy hits it you will have two men on the bar and there will be a good chance he will make the other two points in his inner table before you can enter them both. If he does he will have closed you out until such time as he gets around to bearing off his men (see below).

Now let's look at Diagram I-5. We don't show all of the men here

Diagram I-5

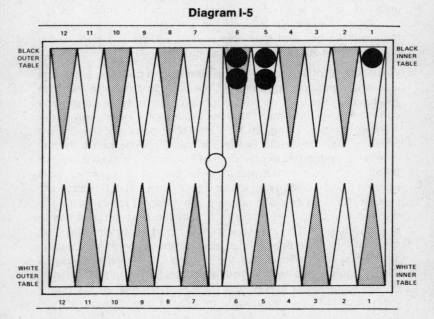

because the important considerations have to do with your man on the bar and the black men in their inner table. You roll 3-1. You can enter on either the one or the three point. In general you will come in on the one point in order to hit his blot, and play the 3 by advancing your man to the black four point or by moving one of your other men three points. There are, however, situations where you will enter with the 3, use the 1 for some purpose other than entering, and refuse to hit the blot at all.

Fundamental strategy requires that you pay special attention to blots (both yours and Black's). You don't want to hit a blot merely because it is there, but you always want to consider the possibility. You don't want to expose a blot for the sheer joy of living dangerously but you don't want to walk around wearing suspenders and a belt and carrying safety pins in your pockets. The more points you have made the more mobile your position and the less mobile your opponent's. You can make a point by moving two men to it but it is far easier to make a point by just adding one man to a blot you already have there.

If you have to leave a blot when your opponent has made several points in his inner table, leave your man where he is exposed to the smallest number of shots. In general, when open to a direct shot (when you can be hit with one of the numbers from 1 to 6) the closer you are to the danger the less the chance of being hit; while when open to an indirect, or long, shot (7 or more) the further away the safer. Also, the chance of being hit by any indirect shot is less than the chance of being hit by any direct shot.

A second, and more important, guideline is that when you must expose a blot, expose it on the point that will be of most value to you if the blot lives. (See Lesson IV, page 55, Diagram 14, as a simple example.)

As already mentioned, once play has begun the players roll and play alternately. How do you determine who plays first? Obviously, you could cut cards, toss a coin, roll high dice, or use any other method you wish to separate the "firsts" from the "seconds." Backgammon rules provide for an easy, straightforward way to accomplish this. After the board has been set up and the seats chosen, each player rolls a single die. If there is a tie the two dice are picked up and rerolled. The player rolling the higher number makes the first move by advancing his men just as though he had won the toss of a coin and rolled both dice himself.

We stated earlier that, "Your objective in backgammon is to move your men around the board." We would have been more accurate if we had said, "Your object in backgammon is, first, to move your men around the board until you have **all** of them in your own inner table and, second, to "bear them off" before your enemy is able to "bear off" all of his men. If you succeed in bearing off all of your men before your opponent bears off all of his men you have won the game and, if you are playing for a stake, you have won that stake. If when you bear off your last man your opponent has not borne off a single man you have won a gammon and the stake, if any, is doubled. Further, if when you bear off your last man your opponent not only has not borne off a single man but has one or more men in your inner table or on the bar, you have won a backgammon and the stake, if any, is tripled.

It is now apparent that the rules governing play must cover three different possibilities, namely, forward movement of the men, entering from the bar, and bearing off. We have discussed the first two of these and it now remains to discuss the third.

Assume your men are positioned as shown in Diagram I-6. In this situation, where the enemy has no men in your inner table

Diagram I-6

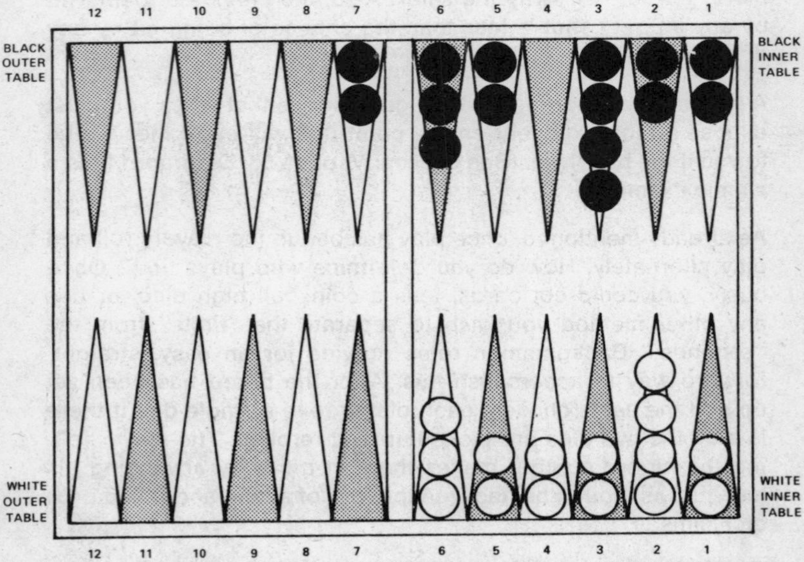

or on the bar, the position of his men has no bearing whatsoever on your play. You simply "bear off" (that is, remove from the board) your men as rapidly as the rules will permit. You may play either number first. Having thrown the dice, you may bear off a man on a point corresponding to the number uppermost on a die or you may advance a man the number of points indicated by that number. Of course, both numbers must be played. At times this may prove to be a serious disadvantage. In the event you roll a number which is, at the time you play it, higher than the number of any point upon which you have men remaining you must bear off a man from your highest numbered occupied point.

Returning now to Diagram I-6, assume that you roll double 5. You have two men on the five point so you bear them off as two of your four plays. For the remaining two plays you have no choice. You must move two of your men from your six point to the one point. You have no other legal play available at this point. You cannot bear a man off from the four point with a 5 when you have a man on your six point. You could, of course, have moved three men from your six point and borne off one of your men on the five point but this would not make sense. You want to bear your men off as rapidly as possible.

Diagram I-7

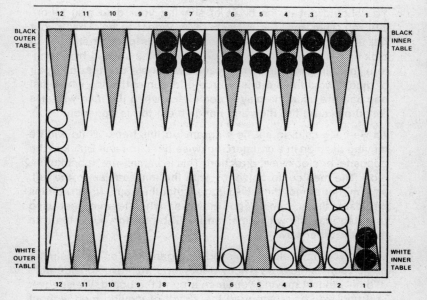

Take a look at Diagram I-7. You are well along in the process of bearing off and Black still has two men left on your one point. At your last roll you were forced to leave a blot (notice that lone

man on your six point). Obviously, Black failed to hit it and now
you want to get that blot out of trouble right away. You are
surely going to win the game if Black never hits one of your blots
but you are quite likely to lose if he does hit one. You roll 6-3.
Your first thought is to use the 6 to bear off that man on your six
point. Then you will have to play the 3 and the only way you can
play it would be to bear off a man from the three point and leave
the other one exposed as a blot. Black will have another chance
to hit you.

Can you protect yourself? Yes, you can! You are allowed to play
either number first, so start your play by using the 3 to move
that man from the six point to the three point. Then you can
use the 6 to bear off one of the men on your four point. This
play may be slightly confusing, but it is proper and legal.

We have by no means gone into all of the intricacies of bearing off
—we have only barely covered the laws governing it. We'll return
to it in Lesson X.

You should get in the habit of shaking your dice well before
you roll them, but it is even more important to hold back your
roll until your opponent has completed his play by starting to
pick up his dice. Argument after argument is caused by premature rolls. Incidentally, while very few people use just one pair
of dice it would avoid this source of argument, since when just
one pair are used the play is completed when the man who has
rolled picks up the dice and hands them to his opponent.

As we have said, in all the diagrams in this book White will be
moving his men in a counterclockwise direction and Black in the
opposite, or clockwise, direction. This is immaterial in backgammon. The men could be set up with the inner tables to the left.
As a matter of fact the laws suggest that the home (inner) tables
be nearer the source of light. However, when learning get used
to going just one way. Later on it will be up to you to learn to
move the other way.

Unless you have already played backgammon, or some similar
game such as the Navy's acey-deucy, you will have considerable
difficulty in just moving your men around the board. We suggest
that until you have acquired the knack of moving men without
counting 1, 2, 3, 4, 5, etc., that you just roll and move men around
the board. Note that a move of exactly six always brings a man
from a point in one table to the corresponding point in the next

table; that an even number moves a man to a point of the same color as the point he just left while an odd number moves a man to a point of the opposite color.

So much for the principal rules governing play. In subsequent lessons we shall examine the options open to you under various conditions, and develop your appreciation of the fine points involved as well as fundamental strategy. In general, after you have thrown your dice and before you play, think a moment. Look to see if you can make a point or hit a blot. You may not want to do either but make sure you haven't overlooked the possibility. Don't play too safe but, at the same time, don't expose blots for the sheer joy of gambling. Get your back men off and running at the earliest possible opportunity and impede the progress of your opponent's back men as much as possible.

Lesson II

THE RUNNING GAME

If you have followed our suggestion in Lesson I you will have spent some time in just moving your men around the board to familiarize yourself with how they move. You will probably have played some games right to the end and will have seen that at some point in the play all the white and black men will have passed each other. As soon as this occurs you are said to be in a "running game." In the early and middle stages of a game you don't get into a running game by accident. If you do get there, at some time or other either you or your opponent has deliberately moved into that position.

Why does a player do this? Because, when his estimate of the existing situation shows that he is closer to winning than his opponent, he will want to eliminate the possibility of having to leave a blot for his opponent to hit and will, therefore, break contact when he can.

Why are we discussng the running game before giving the proper opening moves and replies to them? Because we want you to know something about swimming before you get into the water. If you disagree with this, skip to Lessons III and IV; but if you want to get the most value out of them, read this lesson first.

Diagram II-1 shows a typical running game position. There is still some contact between your men on Black's twelve point and his men on your twelve point but there is no real chance that either of you will ever have to expose a blot to the other. Which of you has the advantage here? It is your roll and that is in your

Diagram II-1

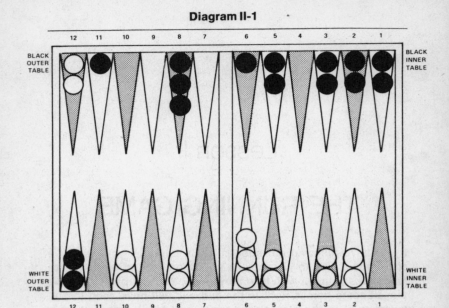

favor but if you look the position over carefully you will see that Black has a slightly better game.

How do you come to this conclusion? In this position it is a cinch to count how many pips you are ahead or behind. A pip is one of those little spots on the dice. If you roll a 6 you advance a man six pips. If you roll double 4 you advance one to four men a total of sixteen pips.

Your pip count is the total number of pips you would have to roll (assuming no waste motion) to bring all of your men around to your inner table and then bear them off. Obviously, there is going to be some wastage but in most positions you can just assume that this will affect your opponent as much as it will affect you.

You don't need to make total pip counts to see how far you are ahead or behind. You can count the net difference if you wish. Now back to our position to demonstrate this. You have the same number of men in your inner table as Black has in his and if you moved two of the men on your six point forward to your one point (a total move of ten pips) your inner boards would be identical. The positions in the outer tables would also be identical if you took one of your men on your ten point and moved it one pip back to the eleven point and moved the other man on your ten point two pips forward to your eight point.

Hence you are $10 + 2 - 1 = 11$ pips behind, but it is your roll. You could roll double 6 and be thirteen pips ahead or 2-1 and still be eight pips behind, but you don't know what you are going to roll.

Your average roll, when you allow for the extra moves with doublets, is 8-1/6 pips.

How did this position develop? Prior to his last roll two of the black men now on the black eight point were on your bar point. He rolled double 5 and moved tentatively to this position.

How do you make a tentative move? You move and leave your dice on the table. It is not necessary to say you are moving tentatively but it is good form to do so. Anyway Black did this and finally picked up his dice to show he had made his play.

Did Black make a pip count before picking up his dice? Maybe he did, but probably he just saw that he could not afford to leave those two men back on your bar point where it would be very difficult to get them away safely later on.

How should the play go from here on? Each player should endeavor to bring his men into his inner table as quickly as possible and to bear them off in that same manner. Since it is White's roll and his outside men are in about the same position as Black's, White is likely to get the first men off. Later on Black's inner table position will let him bear men off with a 1 while White's won't.

Most running games do not develop as such for quite a while. Still it is possible to get into one after only two moves by each player. Look at Diagram II-2. Each player has started with two rolls of 6-5 and brought his two back men out. The player about to roll has a minuscule advantage and is said to be a half roll ahead.

This is not going to be a very interesting game but there will be a best way to play most rolls and we will actually play it in Lesson IX to show some running game techniques.

You got into the preceding running game without any effort on anyone's part. Other running game positions may be reached this way or because one player tries to work into one.

Diagram II-2

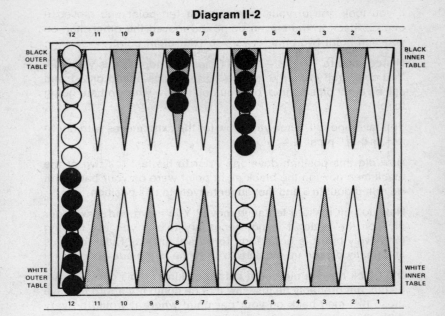

Why does he do this? Because in his opinion he will have the best of the game once there are no worries about blots being hit. How does he know that he will have the best of it? The expert way is by means of a pip count. In positions like that shown in Diagram II-1 it is easy to count the net difference. In most other positions it will be more difficult. Appendix A shows how to make an accurate pip count. Look at it now if you wish, but don't work on it yet.

Some backgammon teachers have recommended a 4-3-2-1 count to make a quick running game estimate (4 for each man in the adverse inner table; 3 for each man in the adverse outer table; 2 for each man in your own outer table; and 1 for each man in your own inner table).

We are great believers in the 4-3-2-1 count in bridge but it doesn't work well in backgammon. Take the position shown in Diagram II-3 as an example.

Your count is nine for the three men on the black twelve point, eight for your four men on your eight point, and eight for the eight men you have in your inner table, for a total of twenty-five.

Diagram II-3

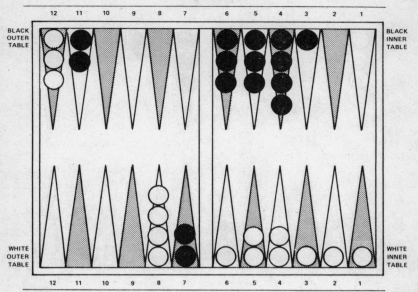

Black's count is six for his two men on your bar point, four for his two men on his own eleven point, and eleven for the eleven men in his inner table, for a total of twenty-one.

Now put the backgammon player's eye to work. You note that it takes just one pip to move your men from the black twelve point to your outer table while it will take Black six pips to get his men from your bar point to his outer table; that it takes just two pips to move your men from your eight point to your inner table while it will take Black five pips to get his men from his eleven point to his inner table. You also note that your men in the inner table are more advanced than Black's. You arrive at the conclusion that at the present moment the positions are about even—with possibly a slight edge in your favor.

Your backgammon player's eye has worked better than the 4-3-2-1 count, but it hasn't told the whole story. Actually you are nine pips ahead and it is your roll.

It is also apparent that the position shown in Diagram II-3 is by no means a running game. There is still plenty of contact. The two black men on your bar point and your three men on the

Diagram II-4

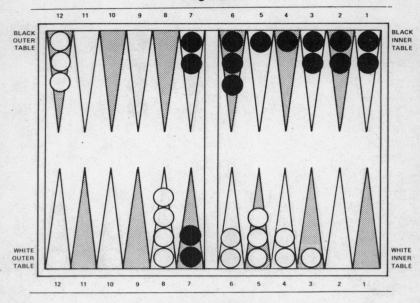

Diagram II-5

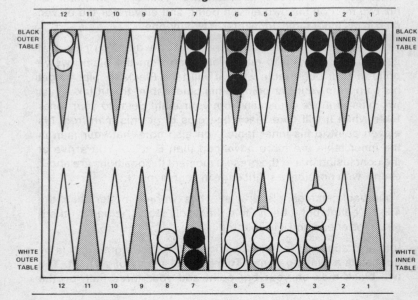

black twelve point must pass one another and, until they do, you will have contact.

Then why do we show this position at all in a lesson on the running game? Because it is your roll and you roll double 5. You have already analyzed the position and seen that it is about even. The double 5 puts you well ahead. You simply move your three men from the black twelve point (two to your eight point; one to your three point) and start a running game. In addition to being ahead, you have another advantage: you can expect to get the first man off. Your six men outside your inner table are on your eight point—each is just two pips from home. Both of Black's men on your bar point are twelve pips from home and the two men he has on his eleven point are five pips away.

Diagram II-4 shows a situation somewhat similar to that in Diagram II-3. Your inside men have been moved back a trifle. Also, Black's men have been moved forward somewhat. The two men that were on his eleven point have been advanced to his bar point and the men in his inner table have been advanced so that the resulting positions will be about equal after you have played your double 5.

If you want to maintain contact you move three men to your three point to produce the position shown in Diagram II-5. If you want to shift to a running game (which is still the proper play for you to make) you simply advance your three men from Black's twelve point.

There are two reasons for this. The first is that while your running game will be almost even (Black will have a slight edge because it is his roll) you will probably get the first men off. The second is that if you maintain contact you are more likely to have to leave a blot than your opponent. In a fairly even position the man who has to give his opponent a shot at a blot becomes a decided underdog.

Now let us look at two more situations, those in Diagrams II-6 and II-7. It is your roll and you have rolled double 5. What should you do?

In this first case, Diagram II-6, it would be very foolish to run. Not only will you be very far behind in the resulting running game but, if you do wait, you are extremely likely to get a shot at a black blot. You will even get cracks at two blots if he throws a 5-1, 4-2, or 4-1.

Diagram II-6

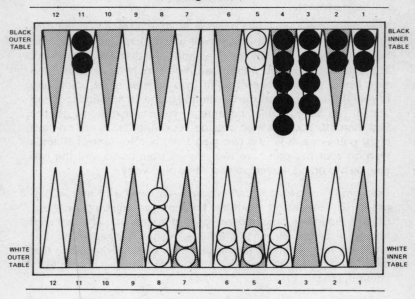

Diagram II-7

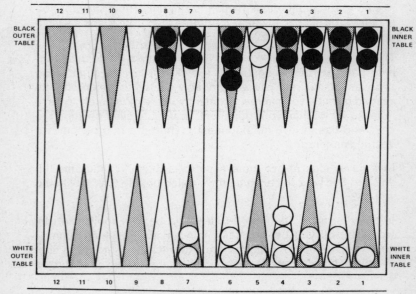

In the second case, Diagram II-7, there is no point in waiting. As far as the probability of blots is concerned, you will have all the worst of it if you wait. On the other hand, if you run with your two men on the black five point you will be only slightly behind in the running game.

We are going to keep coming back to the running game in almost every lesson that follows. You must have a game plan at all times. That game plan should be to try to get into a running game when you are ahead, to get further behind in an effort to maintain contact when you are behind, and to maintain all options when you are slightly ahead or slightly behind. In other words, be ready to get off and running with big dice and to sit back and wait with little numbers.

Lesson III

THE FIRST MOVE

The player who wins the first move starts the game. It is an advantage; not much of an advantage to be sure, but an advantage.

Except in some way-out variations of backgammon you don't start with a double number, so we are going to discuss the fifteen possible regular rolls here and let the play of opening doublets go until later on.

In Lesson I we recommended that after rolling, and before playing, you should always look to see if: (a) you can hit a blot, or (b) you can make a point.

You can't hit a blot on the first play: your opponent's men are all safe on points which he controls, but you do have five rolls that allow you to make a point. These are:

6-1   You can make your bar point by moving one man from the black twelve point with the 6 and one man from your eight point with the 1. See Diagram III-1.

3-1   You can make your five point by moving one man from your eight point with the 3 and one man from your six point with the 1. See Diagram III-2.

4-2   You can make your four point by moving one man from your eight point with the 4 and one man from your six point with the 2. See Diagram III-3.

Diagram III-1

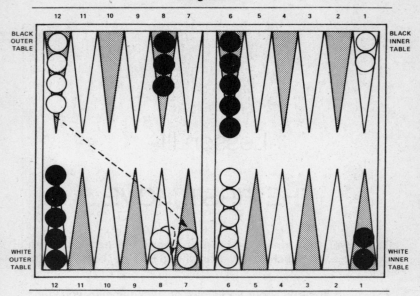

Diagram III-2

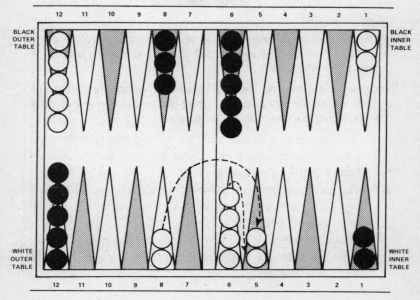

Diagram III-3

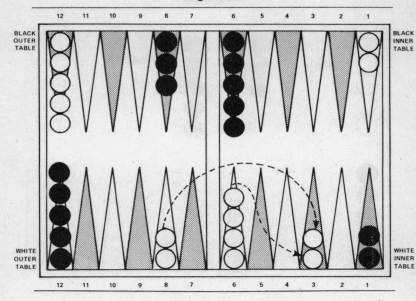

Diagram III-4

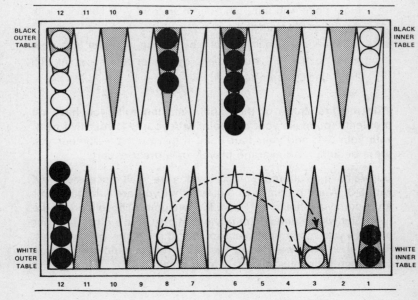

Diagram III-5

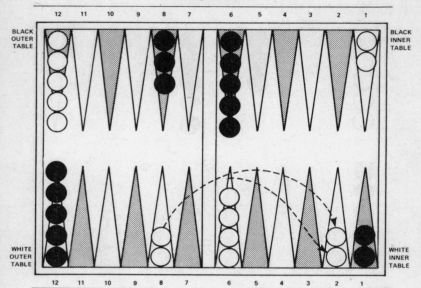

5-3 You can make your three point by moving one man from your eight point with the 5 and one man from your six point with the 3. See Diagram III-4.

6-4 You can make your two point by moving one man from your eight point with the 6 and one man from your six point with the 4. See Diagram III-5.

With the first three of these point-making rolls you have no problem. You make your bar point with your 6-1; your five point with your 3-1; and your four point with your 4-2—whether you are a beginner, an average player, or a great expert.

But we have an alternate choice, which we shall discuss shortly, with 5-3. When it comes to 6-4, whether you are a beginner or an expert, you should **not** make the two point. Those men on the two point will be almost entirely out of play. It is a cinch for your adversary to move past them to your three, four, or five point. Remember what we said in Lesson I—you should not make a point merely because it is there for the making.

Basic Opening Moves

6-5   This is known as "lover's leap." Move one of your back m[en]
from the black one point to the black twelve point, where he
joins the five men already there. This is a good roll, since it
starts you well on your way to a successful game. See Diagram III-6.

Diagram III-6

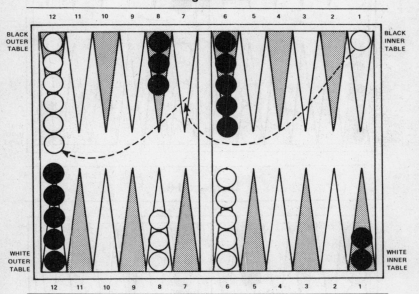

6-4   Move one of your back men from the black one point to the
black eleven point. He is exposed to a direct 2 but you have
lost little if he is hit and, if he is not hit, he is in a beautiful
position to move to your outer table on your next roll. Do not
make the two point with 6-4. See Diagram III-7.

6-3   Move one of your back men from the black one point to the
black ten point. There is no way to avoid leaving a blot no
matter how you play the roll. See Diagram III-8.

6-2   Again we run with a back man from the black one point. There
is no way to play this number safely. See Diagram III-9.

Diagram III-7

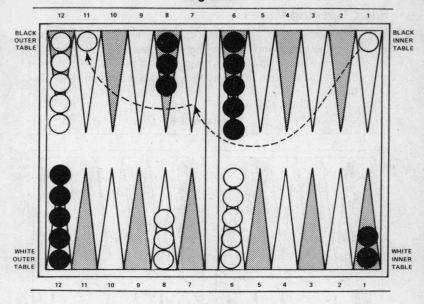

Diagram III-8

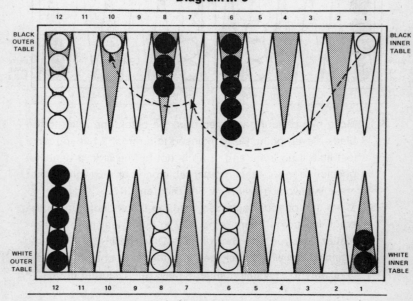

Diagram III-9

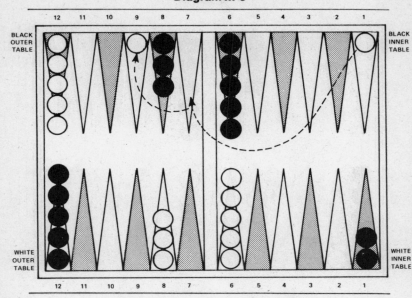

Diagram III-10

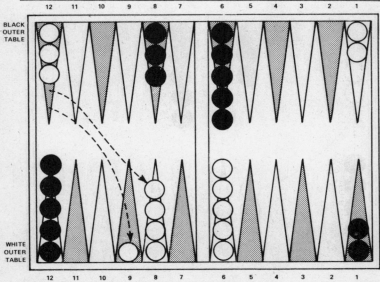

Diagram III-11

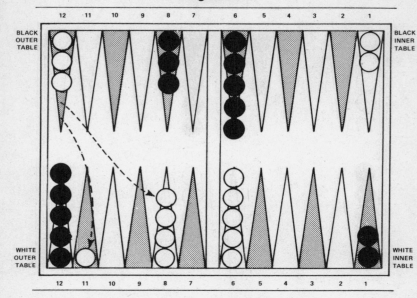

Diagram III-12

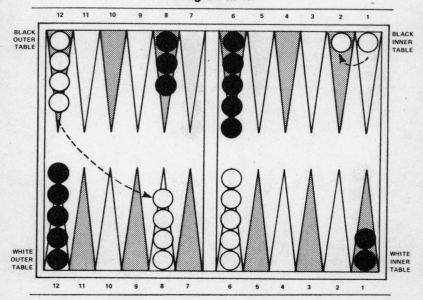

Diagram III-13

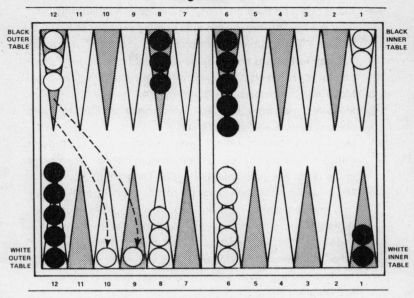

Diagram III-14

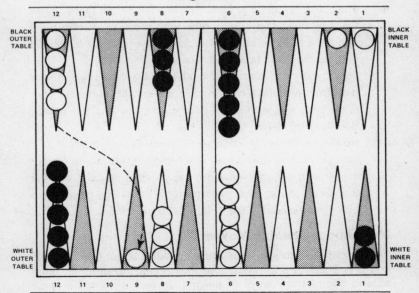

6-1   Make your bar point. See Diagram III-1.

5-4   Move two men from the black twelve point to your eight and
      nine points. The man on the nine point is exposed to 5-3, 6-2,
      double 4, and double 2, but don't worry about this. It is a risk
      you can well afford since you have put that man in good posi-
      tion for your next turn. See Diagram III-10.

5-3   Make your three point. See Diagram III-4.

5-2   Move two men from the black twelve point to your eight and
      eleven points. See Diagram III-11.

5-1   Move a man from the black twelve point to your eight point
      with the 5 and one of your back men from the black one point
      to the black two point with the 1. See Diagram III-12.

4-3   Move two of your men from the black twelve point to your
      nine and ten points. You are exposing two blots to indirect
      shots but your opponent cannot hit both of them. In fact, the
      odds are well over two to one that he won't be able to hit
      either of them. If he doesn't, you will have two valuable
      builders bearing on those very important five and bar points.
      See Diagram III-13.

4-2   Make your four point. See Diagram III-3.

4-1   This move is similar to the move with the 5-1, in that you use
      the 4 to move one of your men from the black twelve point
      and the 1 to move one of your back men from the black one
      point to the black two point. See Diagram III-14.

3-2   This is the same kind of move as with 4-3. Move two of your
      men from the black twelve point around the corner to your
      outer table where they will bear on the five and bar points.
      See Diagram III-15.

3-1   No problem here! Make your five point. See Diagram III-2.

2-1   This move is similar to that of 5-1 and 4-1. Move one of your
      men from the black twelve point to your eleven point with the
      2 and one of your back men from the black one point to the
      black two point with the 1. See Diagram III-16.

More About Opening Moves

You do not have to spend any time thinking about 6-5, 6-1, 4-2,
and 3-1. These are all good first moves and no one has been
able to suggest any ways of playing them that compare at all

Diagram III-15

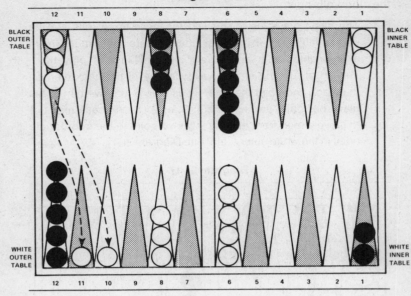

Diagram III-16

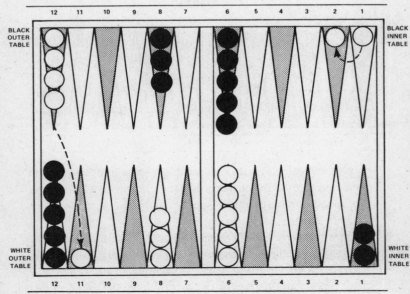

favorably with the standard ones. Let's take a second look at the other rolls now.

6-4   The basic plays just discussed for these three rolls are the
6-3   traditional plays. In the last fifteen years the experts have
6-2   experimented with an entirely different kind of play here.
      Instead of running all the way with one of the back men on
      the black one point they merely use the 6 to move him to the
      black bar point and use the 4, 3, or 2 (as the case may be)
      to move a man from the black twelve point to the appropriate
      point in the white outer table. See Diagram III-17.

Diagram III-17

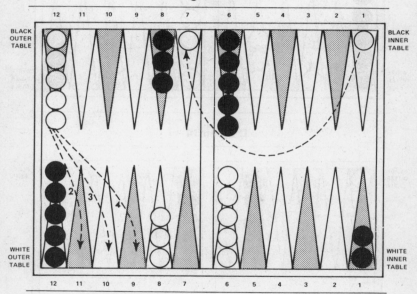

This alternate play has considerable merit with 6-2 and some merit with 6-3. But it has practically no merit with 6-4; its proponents have practically abandoned it, so our recommendation to you is not to use it at all.

6-2   There happens to be a special play with 6-2. It is decidedly
      an attacking play and one that we have always favored. It is
      to move a man from the black twelve point all the way to your
      five point. See Diagram III-18. We are delighted to report that

Diagram III-18

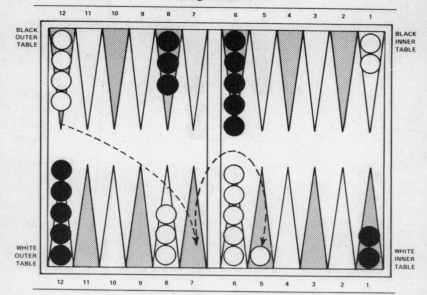

it has gained almost universal expert acceptance today and we recommend that you experiment with this play as soon as you get out of the beginner class.

5-4   Stick with the basic play shown in Diagram III-10. The alternate one, which is to move one of your back men from the black one point to the black ten point, is not recommended.

5-3   The basic play shown in Diagram III-4 is best. For a while the experts tried an alternate play, which was to move two men from the black twelve point to their eight and ten points. See Diagram III-19. A few still make this alternate play but most of the others, including the writers, have gone back to making the three point.

5-2   The basic play shown in Diagram III-11 is the only good play here but you may want to try a couple of others. We will discuss them here but they really aren't worth trying.

The first bad play is to move to the position shown in Diagram III-20. When Oswald Jacoby first learned to play backgammon over forty years ago he was taught to move a man from the black twelve point to his own six point. The instructor

Diagram III-19

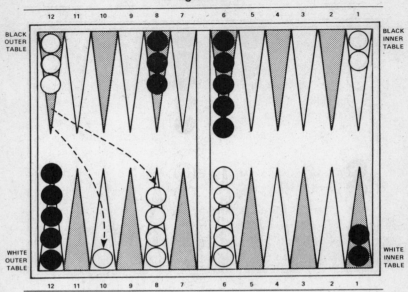

Diagram III-20

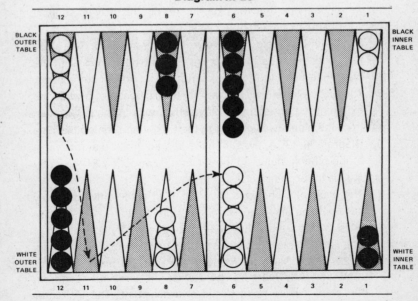

said, "You are advancing a man with complete safety." He learned to beat the instructor with regularity and one reason he beat him was that it didn't take him long to see that this kind of play was for the birds.

At first he experimented with what turned out to be another bad way to play 5-2. This ineffective way was to move one of the back men from the black one point to the black three point with the 2 and one of the men from the black twelve point to his own eight point with the 5. See Diagram III-21.

Diagram III-21

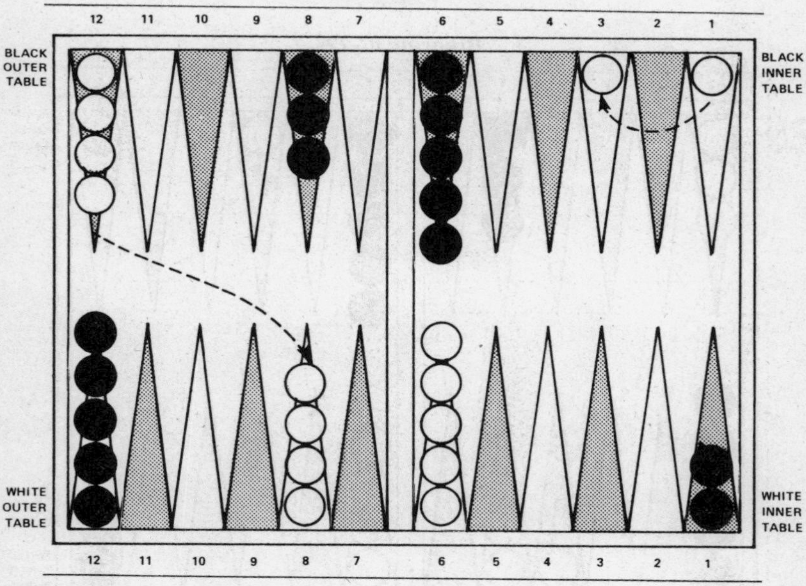

There was nothing wrong with the move of the 5. It was the split of the two back men to the three and one points that caused trouble. If his opponent rolled double 5 he would hit both blots while making his one and three points. Jacoby would have to bring two men back in from the bar against a three point board. One time in four he would do this and have a playable, but poor, game. The rest of the time he

would bring neither, or just one, in and have an almost
hopeless game!

5-1   The alternate play here is to use your 1 to expose a man on
your own five point. It has some merit but we much prefer the
standard use of the 1—move a back man from the black one
point to the black two point as shown in Diagram III-12.

4-3   The basic play shown in Diagram III-13 is still recommended
but there are several others that have some merit. The best of
these is to use the 4 to move a man from the black twelve
point to your nine point and the 3 to move a back man from
the black one point to the black four point. See Diagram
III-22.

Diagram III-22

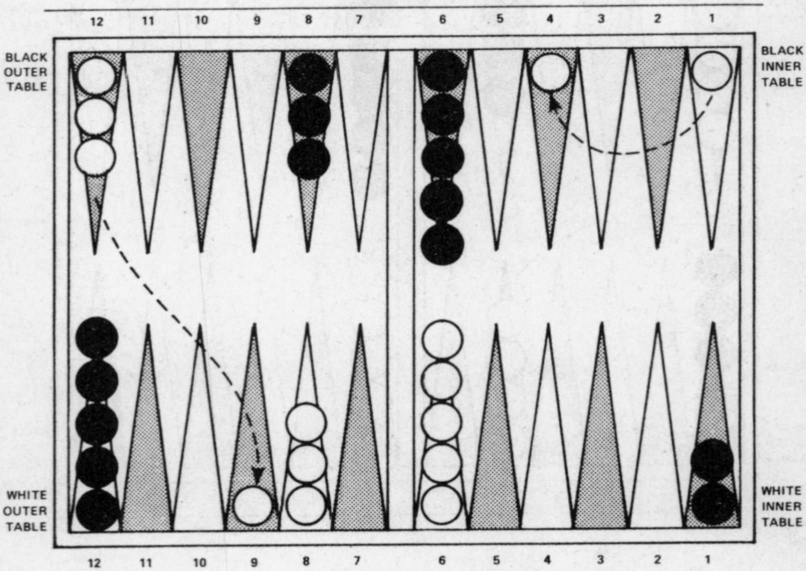

How about the play of moving a man to your own ten point
with the 3 and one of your back men from the black one point
to the black five point with the 4? We do consider it, but we
reject it! Try to avoid exposing a blot on your opponent's
five point. It is bad enough if he makes this valuable point;

it is terrible if he makes it and puts one of your men on the
bar at the same time.

4-1   The basic play is the best. An alternate used occasionally by
      players who like to attack recklessly is to use the 4 as in the
      basic play and the 1 to expose a blot on the five point. See
      Diagram III-23. When this play works it is wonderful but the

Diagram III-23

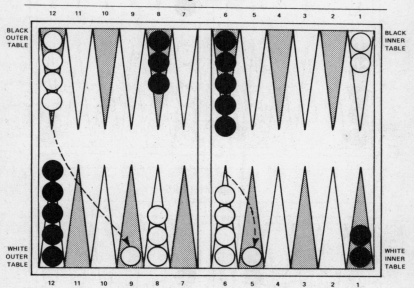

trouble with it is that, in addition to the many rolls that will
hit your blot on the five point, 6-2 or 5-3 will hit your blot on
the nine point. Also, with double 2 he can hit both blots (but
will probably settle for just hitting one of them); with double
4 he *will* hit both blots.

3-2   The same general principles apply as with 4-3. Do not con-
      sider the absolutely safe play of moving a man from the black
      twelve point to your eight point. There is, however, an ac-
      ceptable alternate play which is to use 2 as before (by mov-
      ing a man from the black twelve point to your eleven point)

Diagram III-24

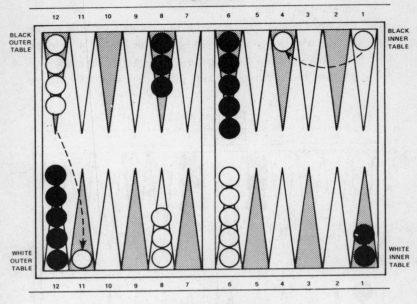

Diagram III-25

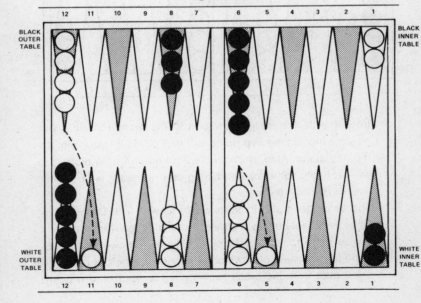

and the 3 to move a back man from the black one point to the black four point. See Diagram III-24.

2-1   As with 5-1 and 4-1 the alternate play is to use the 1 to expose a blot on your five point. See Diagram III-25. As with the others it is not the sort of alternate you want to use as a steady diet.

Lesson IV

THE REPLY TO THE FIRST MOVE

Your reply to the first move, as well as your reply to all subsequent moves, has to be based in large measure on what your opponent has already played. Let's see how you play each of the six doublets in case you are lucky enough to roll one of them.

Double 1

The best opening roll. It gives you a tremendous position right off the bat. Move two men from your eight point to your bar point and two men from your six point to your five point. Diagram IV-1 shows the position after Black has started with 3-1 and you have replied with double 1.

He has made his five point but you have made your five point and your bar point. Unless he rolls 6-1, 5-2, or 4-3 and hits your blot, you have a very good chance to have four points in a row at your next turn.

If your opponent has rolled 5-1, 4-1, or 2-1 and split his back men you don't make this play. The blot you would have to leave on the eight point would be too vulnerable. Instead you play double 1 like 3-1 to produce the good position shown in Diagram IV-2.

Diagram IV-1

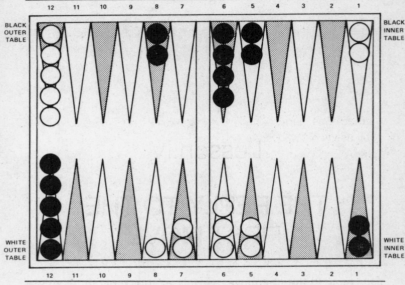

Diagram IV-2

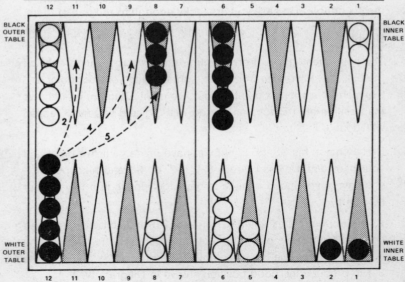

Double 2

Irrespective of what Black's first play has been, use two of your 2's to make your four point. If you can hit a blot with the others, do so; otherwise, move two men from the black twelve point to your eleven point. Diagram IV-3 shows the play after Black has started with 5-4. (Note that you could have used all four 2's to hit his blot but the point-making play is far superior.)

If Black has started with 6-1 you make a slightly different play. You still use two 2's to make your four point, but now you use the other two to move your two back men from the black one point to the black three point.

Double 3

There are more attractive ways to play this fine roll than any other. The reason is that any of your fifteen men can make effective moves of three pips. In general the best way to play it is to make the three and five points in your inner table. Diagram IV-4 shows the position after Black has started with 4-3 and you have made this play. Note that you could have hit the blot on his ten point but you did not.

Suppose Black had started with a 6-3 and moved a man to your ten point. You should use two of your 3's to point on that blot and the other two to make your five point. See Diagram IV-5.

Diagram IV-6 shows how you should play double 3 after Black has started with 5-1, 4-1, or 2-1 and split his back men. You did not make your five point because that would leave a blot on your eight point exposed to either a 6 or a 7.

Double 4

It has been said that you can't play a double 4 badly. This isn't entirely true. An idiot could move four men from his six point to his two point or some other move as nonsensical, but there are any number of good moves.

The best way in most positions is to move two of your back men from the black one point to the black five point and two of your men from the black twelve point to your nine point. Diagram IV-7 shows

Diagram IV-3

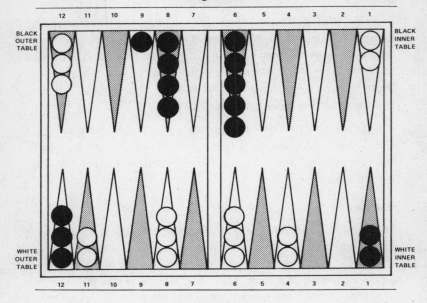

Diagram IV-4

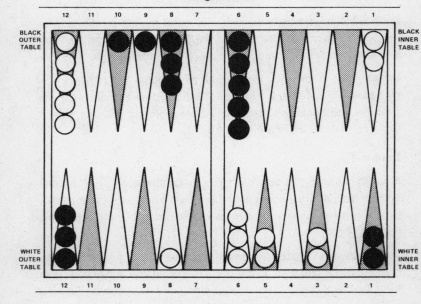

Diagram IV-5

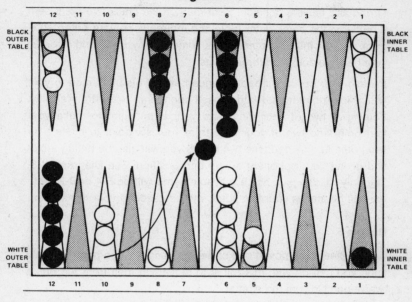

Diagram IV-6

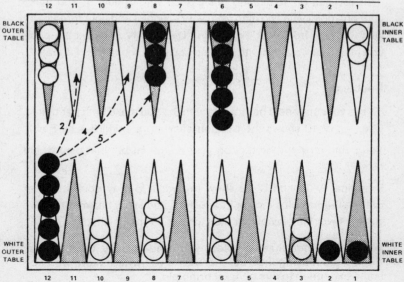

the position after Black has started with a 6-1. You are in a very strong and flexible position. Your men on the black five point bear directly on the black outer table and indirectly on your outer table. Your men on the nine point block some enemy plays and threaten your bar, five, four, and three points.

In case your opponent has advanced one of his back men to your two or four point he has laid himself open to an even stronger play. You move two of your men from your eight point to make your four point and two of your men from your six point to make your two point. In making these two points you will also be hitting a blot and giving your opponent a very bad position. See Diagram IV-8. The only rolls to give him a playable game will be 5-4 or 3-2. With the first he makes your five point; with the second your three point.

Double 5

Unless Black has moved one of the men on your one point the only thing you can do with this roll is to move two men from the black twelve point to your three point.

This is a fairly good move, but if Black has moved one of those back men you can do something really good with double 5. You make your one point with two men from your six point and your three point with two men from your eight point. Diagram IV-9 shows the position after Black started with 6-4 and you have replied with double 5.

Double 6

Unless your opponent has started with 6-1 you make both bar points. Diagram IV-10 shows the position after an opening 6-4 by Black.

You could have hit the blot on your one point but that play would be silly.

Diagrams IV-11 and IV-12 show two ways to play double 6 after Black's 6-1 has blocked your back men. Each play has merit but we slightly favor the play of four men to your bar point (Diagram IV-11).

With rolls other than doublets you tend to play the same as if you were moving first, but there is no roll where there won't be some exception to this general principle.

Diagram IV-7

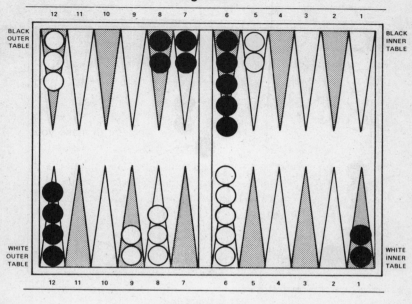

Diagram IV-8

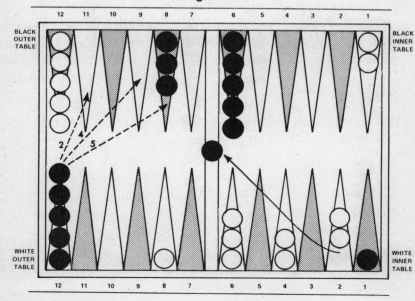

Diagram IV-9

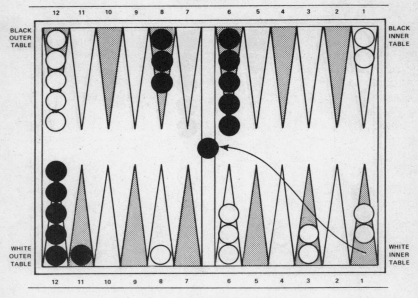

Diagram IV-10

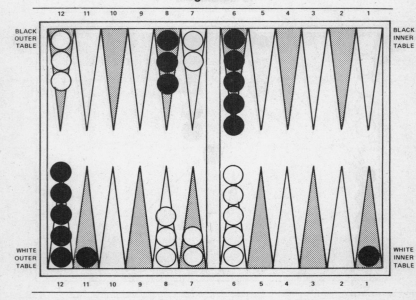

Diagram IV-11

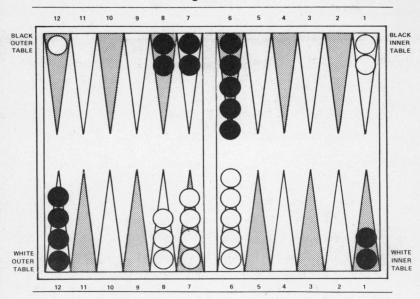

Diagram IV-12

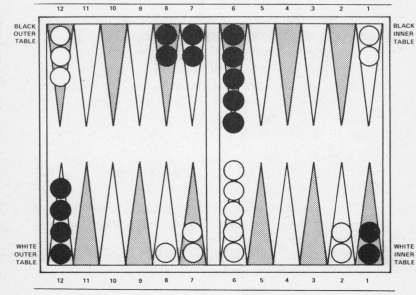

⌐ see if your opponent's first play has put a blot where you ⌐t it or if it has made your normal play either impossible or ⌐ractive. If these conditions do not apply, make your normal ⌐. Now let's look at some of the exceptions.

6-5   Lover's leap cannot be made if your opponent has made his bar point with a 6-1. In fact, except for nonsense moves, you are restricted to one of the two plays shown in Diagrams IV-13 and IV-14.

We strongly recommend the play shown in Diagram IV-14. Your blot is exposed to any 6, or to any combination which adds up to 6, but if it is not hit you will be in a fine position to make your bar point at your next turn. Remember, when you must expose a blot try to expose it where it will do some good if allowed to live.

In case your opponent started with 6-4, 6-3, or 6-2 and used the 6 to move a back man from your one point to your bar point you have a very good way to play 6-5. See Diagram IV-15. You have used the 6 to hit the man on the bar point and the 5 to hit the man on the one point. He has to bring two men in from the bar and even if he hits the blot on your one point you expect to make your bar point at your next turn.

6-4   If your opponent has moved a man into your outer table you
6-3   don't want to make the basic move with either of these plays since your blot in his outer table will be exposed to two direct shots. Of course, if you can hit the blot in your outer table you do so but, if you can't, you solve your problem as shown in Diagrams IV-16 and IV-17. In both cases Black has started with a 6-4.

In Diagram IV-16 you have used the 6-4 to make your two point. Not a happy choice, but the best one available. In Diagram IV-17 you have used 6-3 to move a man from the black twelve point to your four point. This attacking play may pay dividends.

6-2   If Black started with 6-4 and brought one of his back men to your eleven point, hit him with the 2 and use the 6 to move

Diagram IV-13

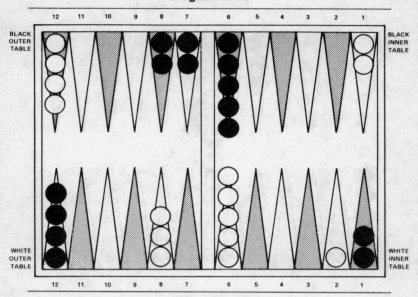

Diagram IV-14

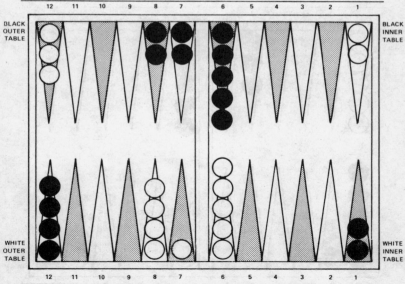

Diagram IV-15

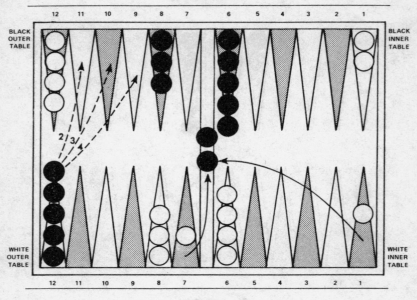

Diagram IV-16

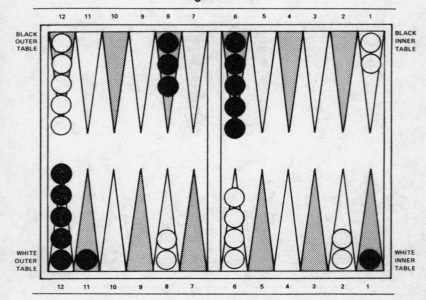

Diagram IV-17

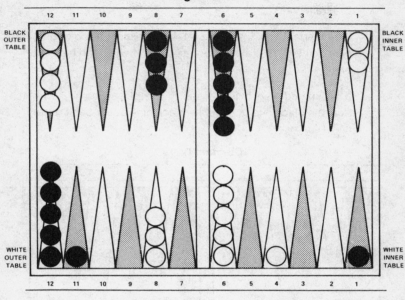

Diagram IV-18

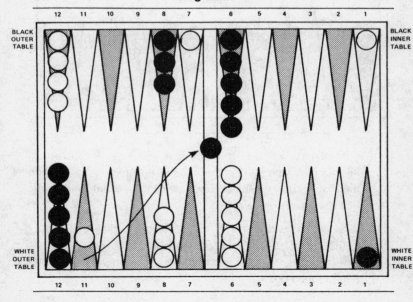

a man from the black one point to the black bar point. See Diagram IV-13.

If he started with 5-4, 4-3, or 4-1 and exposed a blot on his nine point, hit that blot with one of your men on the black one point.

If he started with 5-1 and split his back men bring a man from the black one point to the black nine point. See Diagram IV-19.

Diagram IV-19

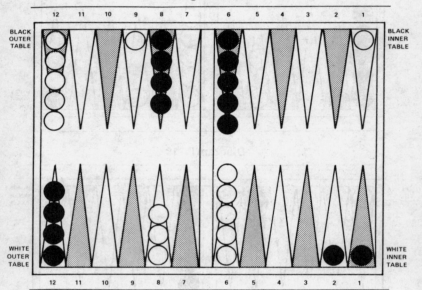

If he started with 3-2 and moved a man to your four point, hit that man with your 2 and use the 6 to move one of your back men from the black one point to the black bar point. See Diagram IV-20.

If he started with 2-1 and made the basic play you are in trouble. The best of a lot of bad plays is to move to your eleven point with the 2 and to the black bar point with the 6. See Diagram IV-21.

Diagram IV-20

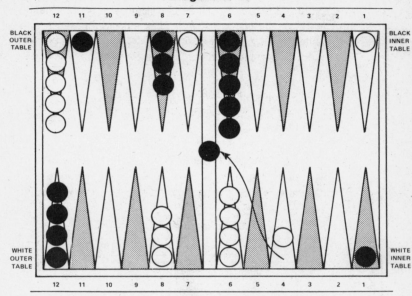

Diagram IV-21

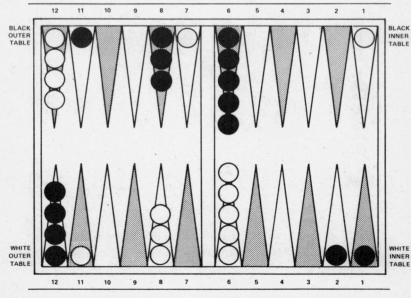

Incidentally, the combination of a Black roll of 2-1 followed by a roll of 6-3 by you is just as bad. Here you should make the same type of play. Move your back man to the black bar point with the 6 and a man from the black twelve point to your ten point with the 3.

6-1   No change.

5-4   Make the basic play unless Black has already exposed a man on his ten point, in which case you hit him with a man from the black one point.

5-3   Make the three point unless:

(a) Black has exposed a man on your ten point, in which case you hit him with the 3 and move a man to your eight point with the 5. See Diagram IV-22.

Diagram IV-22

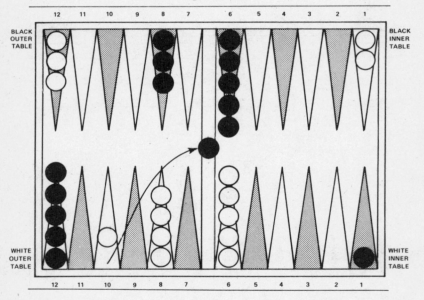

(b) Black has exposed a blot on his nine point, in which case you hit that blot with one of your men on the black one point.

Diagram IV-23

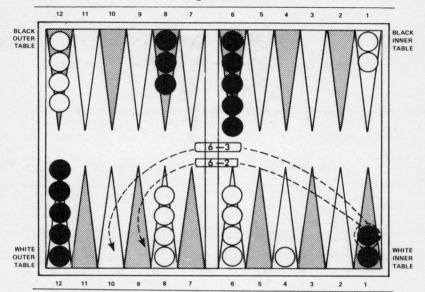

5-2 Unless Black has moved a man from your one point to your nine or ten point, make the basic play. If he has done this, play the 5 normally but use the 2 to expose a blot on your four point. See Diagram IV-23.

5-1 No change.

4-3 If you can hit a blot in your outer table or in the black inner table, do so. If Black has split his back men make the play shown in Diagram IV-24. Here Black has played 5-1, so you use the 4 to move a man from the black twelve point to your nine point and the 3 to move one of your back men from the black one point to the black four point. You don't expose two blots in your outer table because there are too many combination shots which will hit one or the other of them. Otherwise, make the basic play.

4-2 No change unless you can hit a blot worth hitting.

4-1 There is one important exception here. If Black has moved one of his back men to your two point, hit both blots. See Diagram IV-25.

Diagram IV-24

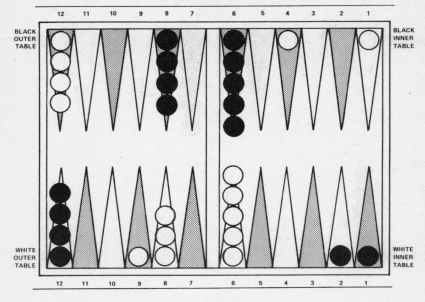

Diagram IV-25

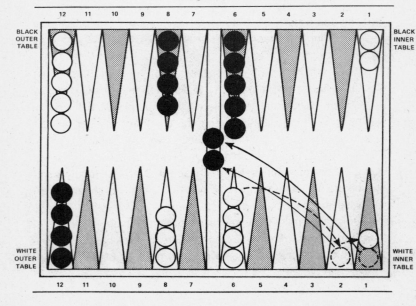

Diagram IV-26

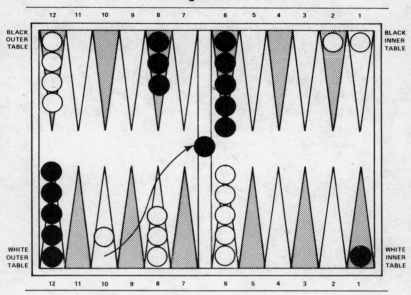

Diagram IV-27

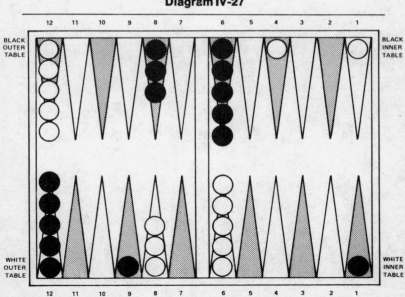

3-2   The same principles apply here as in the case of a 4-3 roll.

3-1   If Black has exposed a man on your ten point use the 3 to hit that man with one of your men on the back twelve point and use the 1 to split your two back men. See Diagram IV-26. Otherwise, just make your five point.

2-1   If Black has exposed a blot on your ten point, use the whole roll to hit it with one of the men from the black twelve point. If he has exposed a man on your nine point you should move a man from the black one point to the black four point. See Diagram IV-27. Otherwise, make the basic play.

Lesson V

LET'S PLAY SOME BACKGAMMON THE EARLY GAME

You are now ready to play a little backgammon and to see why you make certain early moves.

Game Number 1

Black starts with 6-5. You reply 3-1; he replies 6-4; and you roll 5-1. The first plays are obvious. Black's second play was to run with his second back man to your eleven point. You had hoped to roll a 2 so as to hit that blot but instead you rolled 5-1 to reach the position shown in Diagram V-1.

It is apparent from this diagram that you used the 5 of your 5-1 to advance a man from the black twelve point to your eight point and the 1 to split your two back men. Why did you make this split?

The reason is that Black has moved a total of twenty-one pips in his first two plays and brought both of his back men out. You have only been able to move ten pips with your two rolls. Not only is Black ahead in a potential running game but he has a fair start toward getting into one. The chances are that he will have to expose a blot in his outer table on one of his next few

Diagram V-1

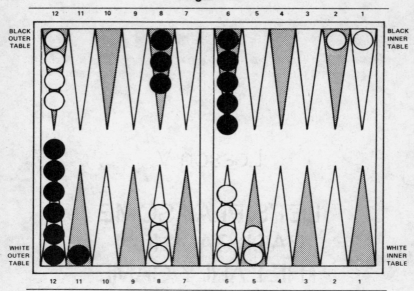

Diagram V-2

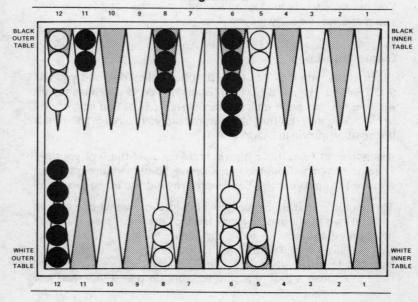

rolls. With your back men split you have twice the hitting potential against his outer table. You have exposed two blots but they are on points he really does not want to make this early in the game.

Black rolls 3-2, a nice quiet roll since it enables him to make his eleven point with a man from your twelve point and the blot on your eleven point. You roll 4-3 which is now a very good roll since it enables you to make the black five point and bring up the position shown in Diagram V-2.

Black has the better of the game but you can't help that. He has rolled very well. Your rolls have been inferior but you have made his five point and the two men there will be a thorn in his flesh for a long time.

Black rolls 6-4. This gives him a chance to make his bar point but he doesn't make it because this would leave a blot on his eleven point directly exposed to your men on his five point. Instead Black simply moves a man from your twelve point to his three point. You roll 4-2 and make your four point.

Your game plan is to hit a blot and make Black start a man from the bar. If this happens every extra point you have made will hurt him. If you never hit a blot you will lose the game unless you suddenly start rolling doublets. You are now in the position shown in Diagram V-3.

Black rolls double 4. As we have said, it is hard to play double 4 badly—there are any number of good ways to play this roll. Black decides to move two men from your twelve point to his nine point and two men from his eleven point to his bar point. You roll another 4-2 and move a man from Black's twelve point to your bar point, which brings us to the position shown in Diagram V-4.

Only five plays have been made by each player, but the early game is over. Black has rolled higher numbers, including one large doublet, and is way ahead of you in case a running game develops. His game plan must be to get into a running game; yours to maintain as much contact as possible. In other words, he will want to get those two men off your twelve point into safety in his side of the board; you will want to stay back with your men on his five point and hope to be able to hit a blot with one of them.

Early play is over. We will get back to this game in Lesson VIII.

Diagram V-3

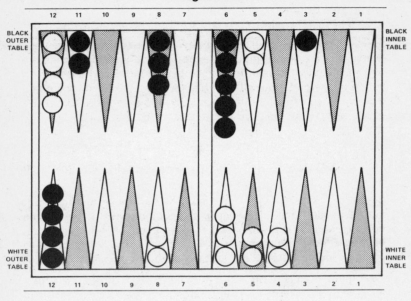

Diagram V-4

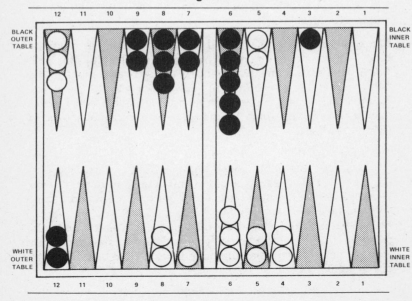

Game Number 2

You start with 5-2 and make the standard play of one man to your eight point and one man to your eleven point. Black rolls 6-4 and hits your blot on your eleven point. Your second roll is 5-4. You bring your man in from the bar with the 5 and use the 4 to move one of your back men from the black one point to the black five point to join the man you just placed there. Black rolls 4-3 and moves the man from your eleven point with the 4 and one of his men from your twelve point with the 3 to produce the position shown in Diagram V-5.

Diagram V-5

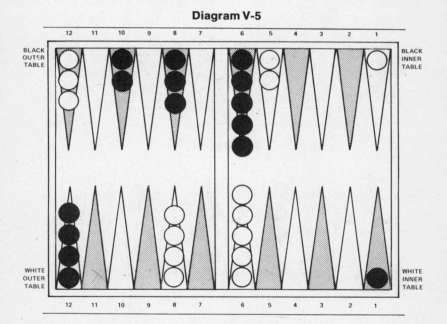

You have lost ground, since one of your men has been sent back fourteen pips from your eleven point to the bar but you have a sound defensive position.

You roll 3-1 and make your five point. Black rolls 5-4 and can't do anything at all good with it. His back man can't move because you have blocked off a move of either a 4 or a 5. He does the best he can and moves a man from your twelve point to his four point.

Diagram V-6

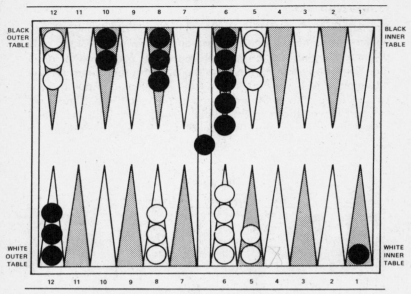

Diagram V-7

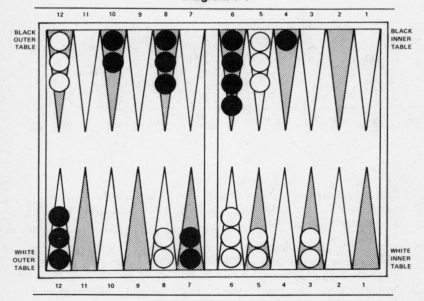

You roll another 3-1 and use the 3 to hit his blot on the four point and the 1 to continue on with the same man to leave you with three men on the black five point and no blots anywhere on the board. See Diagram V-6.

You have made up lost ground in case you get into a running game and also have the better position, since you hold both five points.

Black rolls 4-2. He brings the man on the bar in on your four point with the 4 and moves a man to his own four point with the 2. This last blot means nothing right now, since you have nothing that will hit it.

You roll 5-3 and make your three point. Black rolls 6-3 and finds a nice way to play this normally poor roll. He makes your bar point to produce the position shown in Diagram V-7.

Your backgammon player's eye tells you that the running game position is about even. An accurate pip count (see Appendix A) makes your total 149 and Black's total 147, but it is your roll. Furthermore you are a long way from getting into a running game.

Your immediate aim should be to get Black to expose a blot and to hit that blot. Black's immediate aim should be to make some more points in his inner table and then hope to hit a blot in the event that you expose one.

You roll 6-3. You could play safe by moving a man from the black twelve point to your four point but you should not do this. You don't need to play safe right now: Black holds only one point in his inner table. Instead you move a man from the black five point to your eleven point. Black can hit this man with any 4, 3-1 or double 2.

Will he? Not if he knows what he is doing—unless he is lucky enough to roll double 4. He has an even game if he plays safe. He is likely to lose immediately if he gambles.

Black does roll 4-3. He looks longingly at your blot but then proceeds to move a man from his eight point to join his blot on his four point with the 4 and a man around the corner to his own ten point with the 3.

You roll a 6-1 and move your blot all the way to your four point. You exposed him for one roll; there is no need to leave him exposed. Black rolls 6-4 and uses the 6 to move a man from the ten point to his own four point and the 4 to move a man from his six point to his two point.

You roll double 6 and move the two men from the black five point to your eight point. Black rolls 3-1 and makes his five point to produce the position shown in Diagram V-8.

Diagram V-8

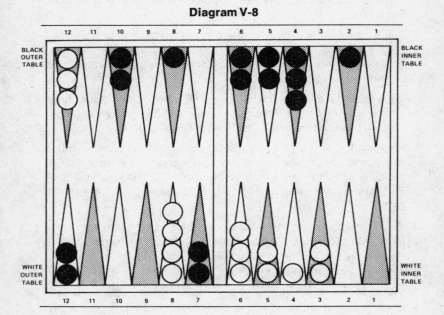

The early play is over since your whole plan is to get into a running game; Black's is to maintain contact in the hope of hitting a blot. We will return to this game in Lesson VIII.

Game Number 3

You start with 6-4 and bring a back man from the black one point to the black eleven point. Black replies with double 2. He uses two of the 2's to hit your blot on the eleven point and the other two to make his four point. You roll 5-1.

You have two ways to play this roll. Both are bad. One way is to use the 5 to bring your man in from the bar and the 1 to move the other man in the black inner table to the black two point. This produces the position shown in Diagram V-9. The other way is to use the 1 to bring your man in from the bar and the 5 to move

Diagram V-9

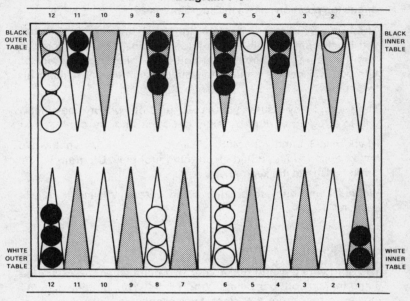

Diagram V-9a

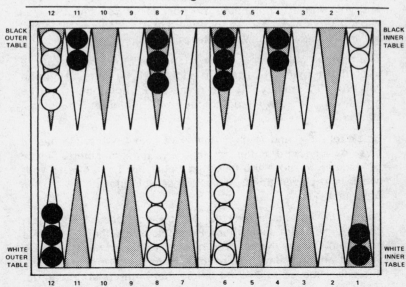

a man from the black twelve point to your eight point. This produces the position shown in Diagram V-9a.

The first play is an effort to get right back into the game. Black will hit the man on his five point if he can. If he can point on him the game will probably end quickly. If he doesn't point on him you will have a chance to equalize matters by making his five point.

The second play insures you a bad game but will probably allow you to struggle on and possibly get back into the contest.

Black rolls 3-1 and you roll 5-4. Diagram V-10 shows what would have happened if you had elected the first play. Diagram V-10a, if you had made the second one.

We will come back to position 10 in Lesson VII and to 10a in Lesson VIII.

Game Number 4

You start with 3-1 and make your five point. Black rolls double 6 and makes both bar points. You roll 4-1. You can play safe by moving a man from the black twelve point to your eight point but this would be poor tactics. Black has jumped out in front and you want to complicate the position, if you can. So, you use the 1 to move a back man forward in Black's inner table and the 4 to expose a blot in your outer board.

You have no objection to Black hitting this blot. You can afford to start that man over again. In addition, if he does hit him he will probably leave you some come-back shots and it will be greatly to your advantage to thus get a blot-hitting contest started.

Black rolls 5-4 and is immediately in mild trouble. He has to give you a shot no matter how he plays these numbers. Finally he decides to move the two men from your bar point to your twelve and eleven points. This exposes his blot to any 2. See Diagram V-11.

You roll 5-4 and make your four point. Black rolls 6-3 and again has to leave a blot somewhere. He elects to use the 6 to move a man from your twelve point to his bar point and the 3 to move the blot on your eleven point forward to his own eleven point. It is only exposed to 6-4 and 6-3 so that is the best he can do.

Diagram V-10

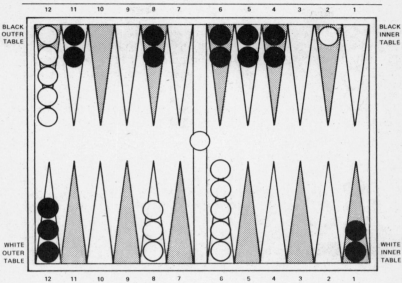

Diagram V-10a

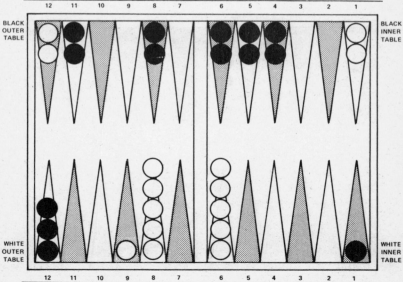

Diagram V-11

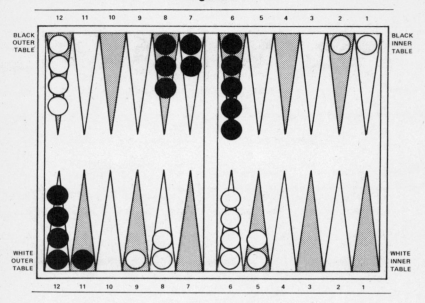

Diagram V-12

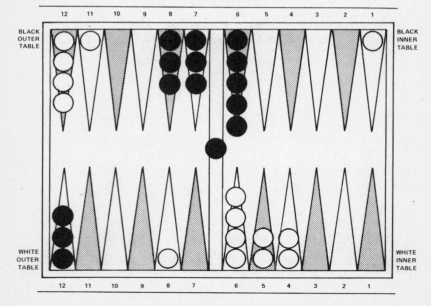

You roll 6-3 and proceed to hit that blot with your man on the black two point. He rolls 5-4 and can't come in. The position is now as shown in Diagram V-12.

You have a slight advantage but you are not ready to double as yet (more on doubles in Lesson VII). You roll 5-1 and consider your play. You decide to move the blot on the black eleven point over to your nine point with the 5 and a man from your six point to your five point with the 1. Why didn't you simply make your eight point instead of voluntarily leaving two blots? Because your two blots are only exposed to 6-3, 6-2, and 5-3 and if Black doesn't hit one of them you are in an excellent position to make another point in your board and to really hamper the movement of that man now on your bar.

Black rolls a 5-2. He has to come in with the 2 and he uses the 5 to hit your blot on his one point. See the position in Diagram V-13.

Isn't this a poor play—to move down to his one point this early in the game and to be leaving a blot at the same time? It is a poor play but it is his last gasp. If he simply moved a man from your twelve point to his eight point you would probably point on that man on your two point. This play will keep you busy since

Diagram V-13

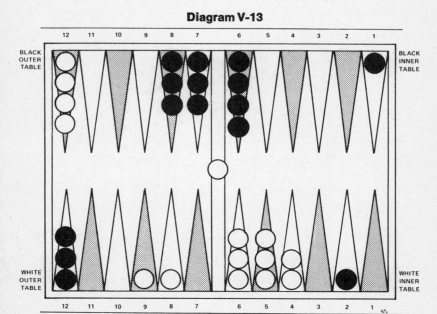

Diagram V-14

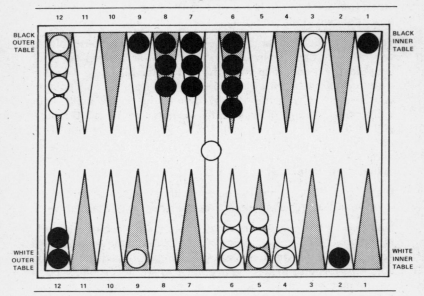

you will have to use part of your roll to bring your man in from the bar.

You roll 6-3 and have to use the 3 to bring your man in from the bar and your best play with the 6 is to hit the blot on your two point. If Black hadn't hit you on his one point at his last turn to play you would have been able to make that two point.

Black rolls 4-2. He hits your blot on your two point with the 2 and moves a man to his nine point with the 4. This produces the position shown in Diagram V-14, which we will come back to in Lesson VIII.

Lesson VI

THE ARITHMETIC OF BACKGAMMON

Let's look at an apparently simple backgammon position. See Diagram VI-1. You are in mighty good shape—your opponent has a man on the bar and you are bearing off.

Diagram VI-1

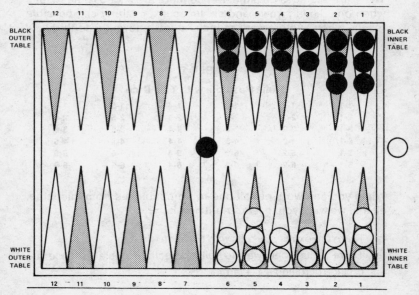

Then trouble rears its ugly head. You roll double 5. You have a choice between bearing off three men and moving one man from your six point to your one point or bearing two men off and moving both men from your six point to your one point. In either case you must leave a blot. Which play do you make?

Is that extra man off going to make any difference in the final result of the game? Possibly, one time in several hundred! For all practical purposes you are going to win if your blot survives and lose if he is hit. It's as simple as that!

Hunch players gaze at the stars and ask, "Will my opponent throw a 6, or will he throw a 5?" Then they mentally toss a coin and make their play. Backgammon players don't waste time on the stars or on hunches. They leave the blot on the five point because in that position he can only be hit with any 5. On the other hand, a blot on the six point can be hit, not only with any 6, **but with a 5-1!**

We'll come back to this position in a little while and tell you just how much better the right play is. Meanwhile we want to develop a few tables to show you how to figure all one-roll and some two-roll problems.

There are six faces on a die. Hence there are six possible results when one die is thrown and six times six, or thirty-six, possible results when two dice are rolled. Table 1 shows these thirty-six possibilities.

TABLE 1
Rolls Possible with Two Dice

1-1	1-2	1-3	1-4	1-5	1-6
2-1	2-2	2-3	2-4	2-5	2-6
3-1	3-2	3-3	3-4	3-5	3-6
4-1	4-2	4-3	4-4	4-5	4-6
5-1	5-2	5-3	5-4	5-5	5-6
6-1	6-2	6-3	6-4	6-5	6-6

While you can work out all one-roll probabilities from this table, all that we want you to learn right now is:

(a) There are exactly 36 rolls with two dice.
(b) There is just one way to roll a specific doublet—hence the chance of rolling a 4-4 is 1 in 36.

(c) There are two ways to roll any ordinary number—hence the chance of rolling a 5-3 is 2 in 36.

(d) There are eleven ways for a specified number to be rolled— hence the chance of rolling a 3 is 11 in 36.

Table 2 is derived from Table 1.

TABLE 2

Number of open points	Number of rolls which will allow you to bring in from the bar	
	One man	Two men
1	11	1
2	20	4
3	27	9
4	32	16
5	35	25

Once you know that the number 11 represents the number of rolls that will include a specific number on at least one die you can derive the rest of column two by adding 9 for a second open point; 7 for a third one; 5 for the fourth; 3 for the fifth; and finally one more to give a total of 36 ways to enter an open board.

Why do you start by adding 9 to 11? Aren't there 11 ways to roll any number? Of course there are, but you can count any given roll only once. Suppose the open points are 3 and 1. Your 11 ways to roll a 3 include 3-1 and 1-3—and so do your 11 ways to roll a 1. You can't count them twice, so you just add 9 more for your second open point. Similarly, when you have a third open point—say the 5—you just add 7 because you have already counted 5-3, 3-5, 5-1, and 1-5.

In order to derive column three, just note that when you have to bring in two men the number of successful rolls is the square of the number of open points—1 × 1 = 1 with one point open; 2 × 2 = 4 with two points open; et cetera.

Blots are like death and taxes. They can't be avoided. A game without a blot occurs once in a blue moon. When your opponent has closed (that is, he has two or more men on a point) only one or two points in his inner table, you expect to bring a hit blot right back in. It doesn't always happen—everyone has some bad luck. Anyway, in the early game if you do expose a blot you want to expose it where it will do some good if it is not hit. Later on, when a hit blot may well mean the loss of the game you will want to know the exact chances that it will be hit. This probability will, of course, vary with the distance between the blot and the opponent's man threatening him. See Table 3.

TABLE 3

Distance between blot and threat	Rolls which can hit blot with		Total number of ways to hit blot
	single die	combination of both dice	
24		Double 6	1
20 or 15		Double 5	1
16		Double 4	1
12		Double 6, 4, and 3	3
11		6-5	2
10		6-4, double 5	3
9		6-3, 5-4, double 3	5
8		6-2, 5-3, double 4 and 2	6
7		6-1, 5-2, 4-3	6
6	Any 6	5-1, 4-2, double 3 and 2	17
5	Any 5	4-1, 3-2	15
4	Any 4	3-1, double 2 and 1	15
3	Any 3	2-1, double 1	14
2	Any 2	Double 1	12
1	Any 1		11

Columns two and three show the actual rolls which will hit your blot for each of the possible distances. Column four gives the total number of ways that your blot can be hit.

Get into the habit of counting the actual rolls which will hit you whenever that knowledge is important. Most of the time these simple rules will suffice:

1. Any indirect shot (distance 7 or more) is better than any direct shot (distance 6 or less).
2. If you expose to a direct shot, the *closer* the better. The number of ways that you can be hit will vary from 11 to 17.
3. If you expose to an indirect shot, the *further away* the better. The number of ways you can be hit vary from 6 to 1.

At times it is convenient to refer to points which are under the control of one of the two players (that is, they are occupied by more than one man) as blocks—they prevent, or block, the use of that point by the other player.

It is important to note that Table 3 is based upon the assumption that there are no intervening blocks which impede the attacker's progress. Since the number of ways a blot can be hit depends not only upon the distance between the threat and the blot, but also upon the number of intervening blocks and upon their location, it is not practical to cover every possibility. This complication will not bother you in the least provided you get into the habit of counting the number of ways a blot can be hit. All you need to remember is that there is just one way to roll a doublet, two ways to roll any ordinary number, and eleven ways to roll any specific number with a single die.

Now let us go back to Diagram VI-1 and your roll of double 5. If you expose a blot on your five point it can only be hit by a direct 5—eleven different ways. Your men on the one, two, three, and four points have blocked out all combination shots. If you expose your blot on the six point it is open to a hit by any direct 6 (eleven different ways) and also to a 5-1 combination roll—that is, to a total count of thirteen different ways. Note that your blocks on the one, two, three, and four points have eliminated all other combinations.

On the average you are going to lose eleven games out of thirty-six when you leave your blot on the five point and thirteen games out of thirty-six when you leave your blot on the six point. Why lose an extra two games in thirty-six?

Now let's look at Diagrams IV-11 and IV-12, reproduced here as Diagrams VI-2 and VI-3. In Diagram VI-2 your blot is exposed to twelve different rolls—any 1 by one of the men on your twelve point and double 4 by one of his back men on your one point. Note that your men on your bar point block the back men from hitting him with a double 6 or double 3.

In Diagram VI-3 the blot on your eight point is exposed only to 5-2 and 4-3 (four different rolls). Here your men on the two and bar points prevent him from hitting your blot with a 6-1. Twelve ways are a lot more than four, but there are two considerations which make the play shown in Diagram VI-2 preferable. One is that it won't be a tragedy if your blot is hit in this position. The other, and really your primary consideration at the moment, is that the overall position with three points made in a row (Diagram VI-2) is far superior to your position in Diagram VI-3.

Here is a rather unusual position. See Diagram VI-4. Your last roll was 6-5 which you used to move a man from the black ten point to your four point. Black then rolled 3-2 and could not hit your blot. You proceed to roll 4-1. You are not happy about this

Diagram VI-2

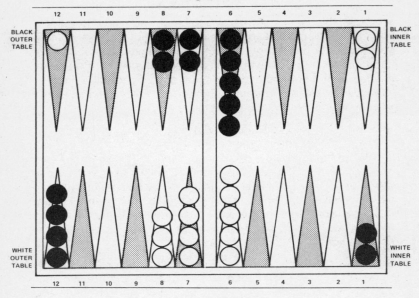

Diagram VI-3

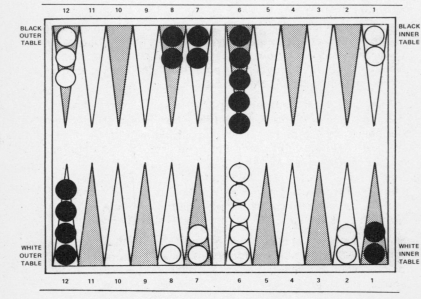

Diagram VI-4

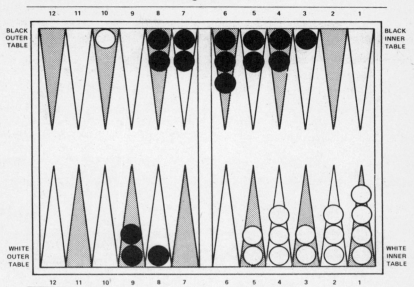

roll. You should not really be surprised that you were not able
to pass Black's men. There were sixteen different rolls which
would have left you in difficulty (5-1, 4-2, 4-1, 3-2, 3-1, 2-1, double
6, double 3, double 2, double 1). Your first thought is to leave
that man on the black ten point where he is and move up in your
inner table, but you decide to make an accurate count. There
are seventeen different ways one of the men on your nine point
can hit him (the eleven 6's plus 5-1, 4-2, double 3, and double 2).
In addition the man on your eight point can hit you with 5-2
or 4-3. Thus, if you leave your blot where it is, it will be exposed
to twenty-one shots.

Now suppose you move him right up to your ten point. He is now
exposed to a direct shot by any 1 or any 2. There are twenty different ways of throwing one of two specific numbers (11 + 9).
So, you find that your man is in slightly less danger close-up
than well back. An advanced player would not have bothered
with all this computation. He would see that if he brought the man
forward, and the blot was not hit, he would almost surely win
the game; if he left him back on the black ten point, and he lived,
there would still remain the problem of getting him past Black's
sentinels.

Diagram VI-5

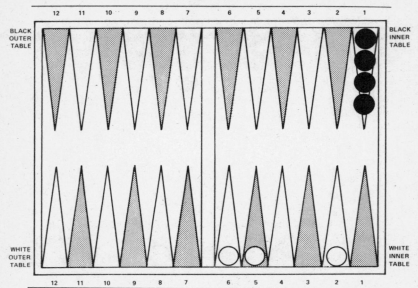

Let's take a look at a typical end game situation. See Diagram VI-5. You roll 3-2. Obviously, you use the 2 to bear off the man on the two point. How do you play the 3? Do you leave the remaining two men on the six and the two points or on the five and the three points? Does it make any difference? It won't if Black ends the game on his next roll by throwing a doublet!

Otherwise, it will! If you have your men on the six and two points you will get them off on your next roll with any 6 except 6-1 (nine different rolls) and with any double 5, 4, 3, or 2 (four more rolls) for a total of thirteen different rolls.

If you have your men on the five and three points you will get them both off with any 6 except 6-1 and 6-2 (seven different rolls), plus any 5 except 5-1 and 5-2 (five additional rolls, not seven, because you have already counted 6-5 among your 6's), plus double 4 or 3 (two more rolls) for a total of fourteen different rolls. Not much difference you say! Isn't it worthwhile to win one more game out of thirty-six when it costs you nothing?

Similar calculations can be made for each of the possible end game positions where you have only one or two men left to bear off. The first three columns of Table 4 show the results of such calculations. The fourth column gives your probability ("chance" or "likelihood" if you prefer either of these terms) of winning. Any time you know the number of rolls favorable to a given event all that you need to do to get the probability of its occurring is to divide by the number of possible ways, thirty-six, and multiply by 100 to convert it to a percentage. The last column is the result of further calculations involving two rolls.

You should learn to work out the figures in column three on your own. After a little practice this will become fairly easy and, therefore, there is no need to memorize it.

In instances where you can't end the game but will be down to one or two men after completing your play you will usually be able to choose how to leave your men. In this connection the

TABLE 4

Probability of Bearing Off the Last One or Two Men in One or Two Rolls

Total points to go	Points on which your man or men are located	In one roll you have the following		In two rolls you have the following probability of winning (percent)
		Number of winning rolls	Probability of winning (percent)	
2	2	36	100	100
	Both on 1	36	100	100
3	3	36	100	100
	2 and 1	36	100	100
4	4	34	94	100
	3 and 1	34	94	100
	Both on 2	26	72	100
5	5	31	86	100
	4 and 1	29	81	100
	3 and 2	25	69	100
6	6	27	75	100
	5 and 1	23	64	100
	4 and 2	23	64	100
	Both on 3	17	47	100
7	5 and 2	19	53	99+
	4 and 3	17	47	99+
	6 and 1	15	42	99+
8	5 and 3	14	39	99
	6 and 2	13	36	99
	Both on 4	11	31	98
9	5 and 4	10	28	96
	6 and 3	10	28	97
10	6 and 4	8	22	93
	Both on 5	6	17	92
11	6 and 5	6	17	88
12	Both on 6	4	11	78

following short series of rules will solve all of your problems quickly:

(a) *Whenever possible, always leave only one man.*

(b) When you must leave two men never leave them on the same point; place the man that will be farther away on the five point (first choice), four point (second choice), or six point (third choice).

As for column five just note that you are an overwhelming favorite to get two men off in two rolls no matter how far back they are placed in your board.

Lesson VII

DOUBLES AND REDOUBLES

It is now necessary to discuss the doubling cube mentioned in Lesson I. Physically the doubling cube is an overgrown die with the numbers 2, 4, 8, 16, 32, and 64 on its six faces.

Backgammon was played for thousands of years without the doubling cube. Then, sometime in the twenties, an unsung, unremembered genius began using it and thus transformed a rather uninteresting game into one of the most fascinating games there is.

Whether you play for money, marbles, or chalk, the doubling feature speeds up and enlivens the game. Once the value of a single unit is agreed upon, the first double raises the "count" (the number of units you are playing for at the moment) from 1 to 2; the next double will raise the count from 2 to 4; the next, from 4 to 8; and so on. Doubles are made in two ways:

(a) *Automatically:* Each tie in the opening throw doubles the previous count. Automatic doubles are not played in tournaments and, if you agree to play them, be sure you limit their number. Beware of the man who wants to play unlimited automatic doubles. Remember that four doubles increase the count from one to sixteen and not from one to four.

(b) *Voluntarily:* Either player may make the first voluntary (or optional) double. After that the right to double the previous count (that is, to redouble) alternates, being always with the man who accepted the previous double.

A double, or redouble, may be offered only when it is the player's turn to play and before he has thrown the dice. It may be accepted or it may be declined. A refusal terminates the game and the refusing player loses whatever the count was before the double was offered.

At the start of the game the doubling cube is placed alongside the board, approximately halfway between the two sides, with the number 32 or 64 up. (The cube is then turned to 2 if there is an automatic double, to 4 if there are two automatic doubles, etc.)

When a player wants to offer the first voluntary double he says, "Double," and, turning the doubling cube to the next higher number (that is, from 64 to 2, 2 to 4, etc.), moves it toward his opponent.

If the opponent accepts the double he moves the cube to his side of the board. If he refuses the double the game is over.

Redoubles are made in a similar manner.

When the doubling cube is on your side of the board you are said to "own the cube." Possession of the cube is a very real advantage. You are the only one who can redouble—the count cannot be further increased unless you desire it!

It is very important to realize that there are positions which warrant a first voluntary double (this moves the cube from the center of the table to your opponent's side) but which do not warrant a redouble (this moves the cube from your side of the table to your opponent's).

Doubling situations fall naturally into one of four main classes:

1. *Positional doubles,* those doubles based upon the fact that your position is sounder than your opponent's.
2. *Running game doubles,* those doubles based upon the fact that you are in a running game (or near running game) and your men are further advanced than your opponent's men.
3. *General doubles,* those doubles based upon a combination of the preceding two classes.
4. *End game doubles,* those doubles based upon your position, relative to that of your opponent, in the last stages of bearing off.

When should you double? Anytime you feel that, if you were to get to the same position a thousand times, you would win more points by doubling than by playing on.

When should you accept a correct double? Any time you feel that, if you were doubled a thousand times in the same position, your net loss if you accepted all of the doubles would be less than if you refused them.

When should you refuse a double? When you expect to lose more by accepting than by refusing.

Your experience is the only thing that can help you with doubles in Classes 1 and 3. For doubles in Class 2 we are going to give you a rather simple rule of thumb (providing you are willing to make an accurate pip count of both your own position and that of your opponent) which will place you immediately in the expert class as far as these doubles are concerned.

It will be work to learn how to make these pip counts but, if you have not already done so, we strongly recommend that you turn to Appendix A and take time to learn how to count the positions. This ability will repay you many times over for the effort expended in learning.

In a running game situation when you are ahead—should you double? When you are behind—should you refuse a double if Black offers one? If you have learned to make a pip count of your own and your opponent's position, you can work out the difference in the two counts and, with this information, determine the doubling number. This doubling number will answer both of these questions for you.

The doubling number is determined by dividing the lower of the two total pip counts by the difference in the two counts. You do not have to work this out to three decimals, or even to one decimal—all you need to know is what two natural numbers (what two integers) it lies between. Suppose your pip count is 106 and that Black's pip count is 120. Your lead is 14 pips. The

TABLE 5
Doubling Number
Range in which you double, redouble, or refuse a double

	Always	Sometimes	Never
Double	Under 8	8 to 10	Over 10
Redouble	Under 6	6 to 8	Over 8
Refuse a double	Under 5	5 to 6	Over 6

doubling number is 106 divided by 14. It is more than 7 and less than 8.

Once you know the doubling number all that you need to do is to look at the preceding table and act in accordance with it! In the example just given your doubling number was between 7 and 8. Table 5 shows that you should offer the first double since you always do this when the doubling number is less than 8.

How about offering a redouble? The range for consideration is 6 to 8 and, since you are closer to 8 than to 6, you probably won't redouble. Then why do you consider it at all? Because you may know that your opponent is a pessimist in running game situations and is likely to refuse the double. If you expect him to accept, wait a roll or two—thus keeping the cube on your side for the moment.

If you want to try to approximate by means of the backgammon player's eye and your general experience, you can do so; if you really want to know how to handle running game doubles, learn how to make pip counts and to use the doubling number.

Diagram VII-1

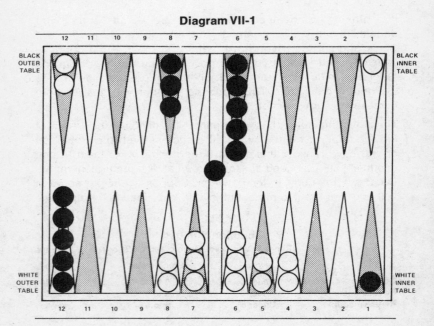

Diagram VII-2

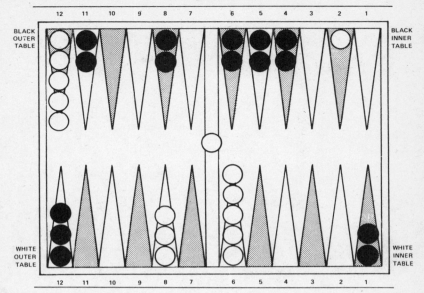

Class 1 (Positional) doubles usually represent early game problems and are complicated by gammon possibilities. Thus, a position may be so strong that you don't want to double because you know that your opponent will refuse. Diagram VII-1 shows one such position.

You don't need any experience at all to see that the worst that can happen to you in this position is that you make a poor roll and Black replies with 3-2 to make the three point in your inner table. In that case you can still double and Black will still refuse. On the other hand, if you have just a little more good luck you will be gammoning him.

Don't double—just roll!

Diagram VII-2 repeats Diagram V-10. You have just failed to bring a man in from the bar and Black doubles you. Was he right to double you? Yes, he was. His position is very strong, yours is bad. Then why doesn't he play on for a gammon? Because he has only three rolls that will crush you. They are double 6, double 4, and double 3. If he doesn't get one of them and you roll any 2, or 3-1, or double 1, your position will be good enough for you to take a double. Right now it isn't that good and you refuse.

We will discuss Class 3 doubles in the next lesson where we carry forward the games we started in Lesson IV. Class 4 doubles will be discussed in Lesson X.

Lesson VIII

LET'S PLAY SOME MORE
BACKGAMMON
(THE MIDDLE GAME)

Just when does the middle game begin and end? There is no formula for this in backgammon any more than there is in chess, but for purposes of this book it will begin:

(a) When the position is such that a hit blot is likely to determine the result of the game, or

(b) When the first double is accepted.

It will end:

(a) When a running game position is reached, or

(b) When the first man is borne off, or

(c) When one player closes his board (has made all six points in his inner table) against an adverse man, or men, on the bar.

It is entirely possible to go from the early game directly into a running game. In Lesson II we discussed a game in which the first two rolls of each player were 6-5 and each player moved his back men from his opponent's one point to his opponent's twelve point. After only four rolls (two by each player) they were in a running game situation—the early game was over and the middle game had never existed!

Diagram VIII-1

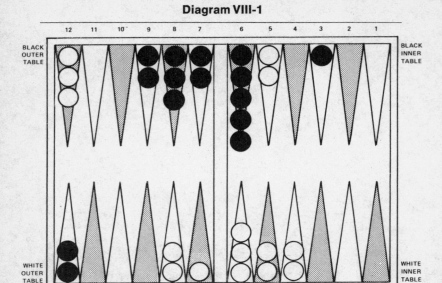

In Diagram V-4 (repeated here for convenience as Diagram VIII-1) we return to Game Number 1 where each player has made only five moves. Yet the whole game plan has been determined and we are in a middle game situation.

It is Black's roll, but instead of rolling he doubles. Is it correct to do this? Should you accept?

Black clearly has an advantage since he has outrolled you considerably. His position is sound and his only real problem is to get his two men on your twelve point safely across to his side of the table.

Your position is also sound: your men on his five point are a potential threat against his men that must pass them. You are not fully in a running game but the position should be counted.

A quick use of the backgammon player's eye shows that, if the two white men on the black five point were advanced twelve points each to the white eight point, the game would be almost exactly even. In other words, if you as White could be given an extra double 6, it would be an even game.

If you have followed our advice in Lesson VII and learned how to make a pip count you will see that Black's count is 115 and your count 138 (with a difference of 23 pips), so that the doubling number is 115/23 or exactly 5.

Hence, if it were just a running game situation you should refuse the double, but the slight chance that you can hit a blot and turn the game around makes it a proper take and you accept.

Black's next roll is 6-4 and you wish you had given up. He has moved those two men on your twelve point to a safe position in his outer table and also has rolled an above average number. You come back with 6-5 and use the 6 to move a man from the black twelve point to your own bar point and the 5 to move a man from your eight point to your three point. You have gained one pip and are now only twenty-two pips behind but your position was worsened materially.

Block now rolls 3-2 and moves two men to his six point (one man from his nine point and one man from his eight point). You roll double 6 and all of a sudden things look brighter. You

Diagram VIII-2

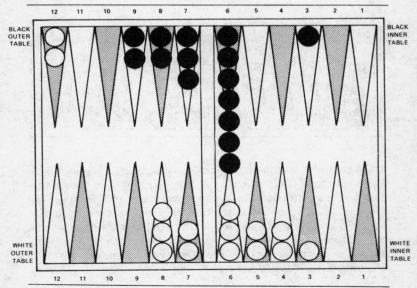

will be only three pips behind after you play this double 6 and
you decide to move your two back men from the black five point
to your own eight point to produce the position shown in Diagram VIII-2.

Why is this the proper play for you to make when you will still
be behind in the running game? Because those two men on the
black five point would have become a liability if left there. It is
better to get out and hope to pick up those three pips in the
next few rolls. You are now in a running game, which we will get
back to in Lesson IX.

Diagram VIII-3

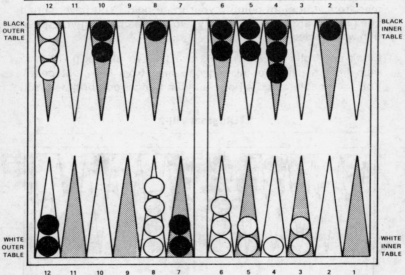

In Diagram V-8 (repeated here for convenience as Diagram VIII-
3) we return to Game Number 2. It is your roll and your backgammon player's eye tells you that you have an advantage, so
there is no need to make a pip count. You are not going to
double because, while you will want to get into a running game
and will do your best to do so, there are plenty of problems
ahead. You may be lucky and never leave a blot, but the odds
are that you will have to leave one.

You roll 5-4 and move a man from the black twelve point to your four point. Black rolls 3-2 and moves a man from his ten point to his five point. You roll 6-5 and move a man from your eight point to your two point with the 6 and use the 5 to move a man from your six point to your one point. Black rolls 4-3 and moves a man from his ten point to his three point to bring up the position shown in Diagram VIII-4.

Why did you use the 5 in your last roll to move a man from your six point to your one point when you could have moved a man from your eight point to your three point?

Because your game plan in this position is to keep from giving Black a shot. You want to keep as many men outside your inner table as possible so as to allow you to play 6's safely.

Diagram VIII-4

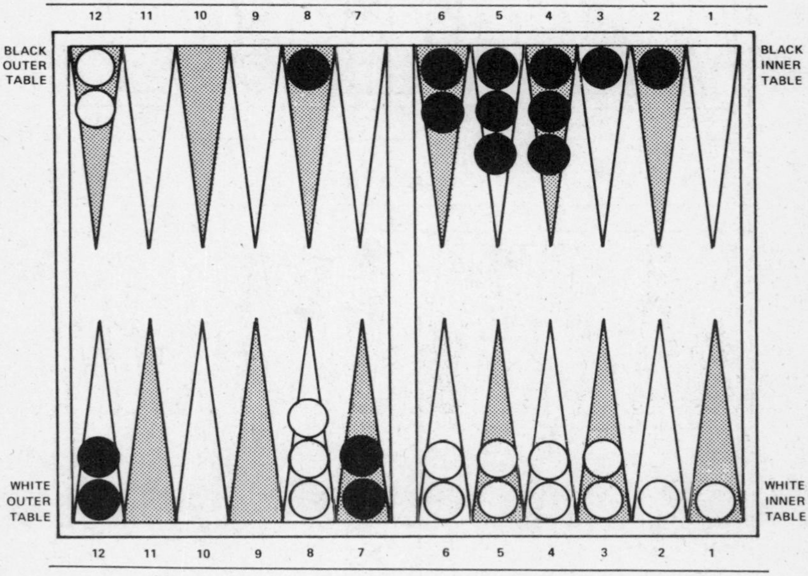

It is evident that you lead by a country mile in the potential running game and some players might even double at this point, on the theory that there is a chance not to leave a blot and that, even if one is left, the odds are that it will not be hit.

Diagram VIII-5

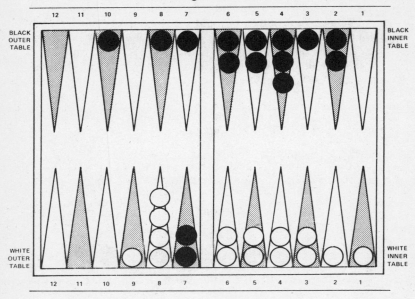

Diagram VIII-6

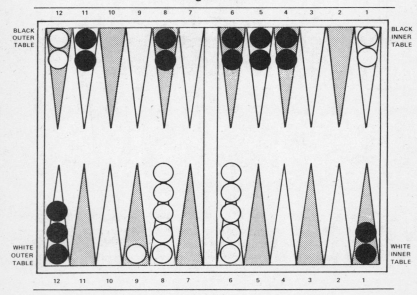

Of course, Black would take a double if it were offered.

You don't double and proceed to roll 5-4. Our recommendation here is that you have the tooth out immediately. Move the two men on the black twelve point forward to your eight and nine points.

The odds are 25 to 11 that Black won't hit your blot and, if he misses, you will be able to double immediately. If he misses with double 4, 5, or 6, he will have a proper take of your double; otherwise, the game is over.

Furthermore, unless he hits you with double 2 (which will allow him to cover his blots on his two and three points) you will have plenty of return action going for you. Black rolls double 3 and moves the men on your twelve point to his bar point and ten point with three of the 3's and uses the fourth 3 to move a man from his five point to his two point, thus producing the position shown in Diagram VIII-5.

We now return to Game Number 3. Diagram V-10a is reproduced here as Diagram VIII-6. Black doubles and you decide to accept. Not that this acceptance is recommended: your position is very

Diagram VIII-7

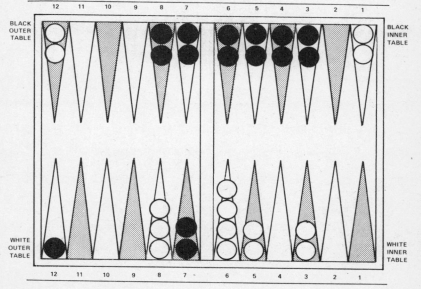

unsound, but you do hold his one point and hope springs eternal in the human breast.

Black rolls 6-3 and moves the men from his eleven point to his eight and five points. You roll 6-5 and decide to use this roll to make your three point with the blot on your nine point and one of the men on your eight point. Black rolls double 6 and makes both bar points. He doesn't worry about leaving a blot on your twelve point. He has your two back men on his one point practically blocked and anticipates no trouble if his blot is hit.

You roll 3-1 and should not bother with his blot at all. Just make your five point. Black rolls 5-2 and completes his prime (makes six points in a row) by moving two men to his three point from his eight and five points. See Diagram VIII-7 (the same position shown as Diagram X-1, Lesson X).

Now back to Game Number 4. Diagram V-14 is reproduced as Diagram VIII-8. Black has been kept alive, but still is in a bad position. Your only bad roll is double 6, which you won't be able

Diagram VIII-8

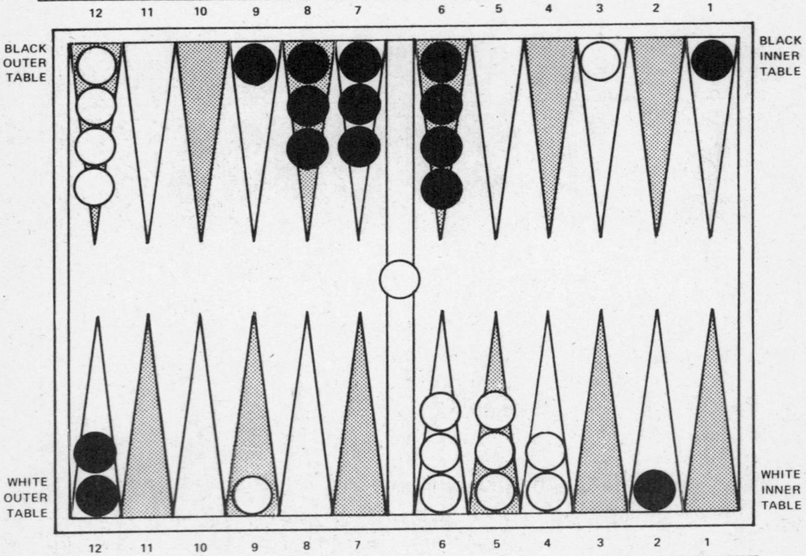

to play at all on account of your man on the bar. There are quite a few crushing rolls and you think about doubling but decide not to on the theory that it rarely pays to double when you have a man on the bar.

You roll double 4. This is not one of your best rolls but it plays nicely. You bring your man in from the bar; move two men from the black twelve point to your nine point and hit his blot on your two point with your last 4. Black rolls 6-3; brings his man on the bar to your three point with the 3 and hits your blot on his three point with the 6. See Diagram VIII-9. You are back on the

Diagram VIII-9

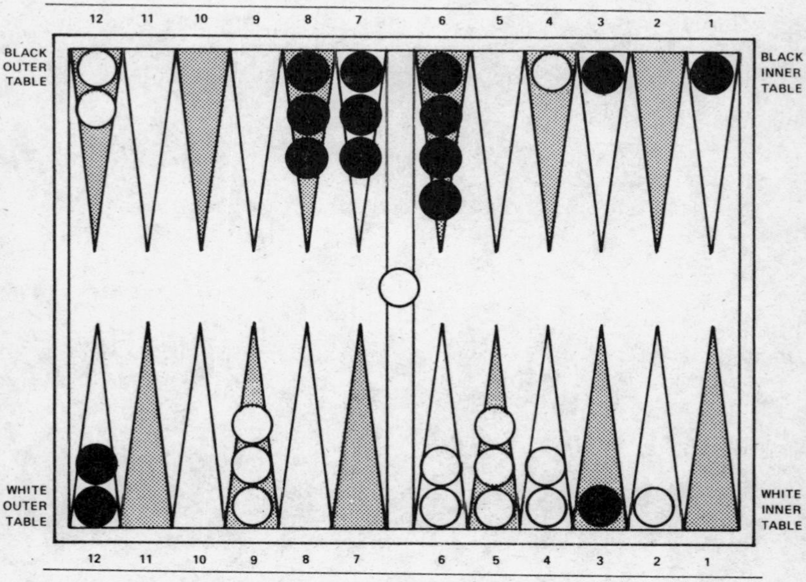

bar, but Black has two blots exposed in his home board. You decide to double him. Black really should not accept, but he sees that if you miss his blots in his inner table and he can get that man on your three point to safety, he will be well ahead in the running game—so he accepts.

He sure wishes he hadn't because you proceed to roll double 3. You hit his blot on his three point as you enter your man from the bar with the first 3; cover your blot on your two point with the second 3; hit his blot on your three point with the last two 3's. Black rolls 4-2 and can't bring either man in from the bar. We will return to this game in Lesson X. See Diagram X-6.

Lesson IX

FINISHING THE RUNNING GAME

In Lesson II we discussed a game where both players rolled 6-5 on their first two rolls to arrive at the position shown in Diagram II-2 (repeated as Diagram IX-1) as an example of how it was possible for the early game to be extremely short and the middle game nonexistent. In continuing this game now we shall see how to play a long running game. It is your move and that gives you a slight edge. Your game plan and Black's will be the same. You will want to get your men into your home table as quickly as possible. At the same time, while you won't want to bring them all onto the six point, you won't want to waste too much time in getting them in. Accordingly, you will bring men to the five and four points but not try for the lower-numbered points. Black will be using the same tactics and neither of you will consider doubling for a while unless one of you really outrolls his opponent.

Your first three rolls in order are 5-2, 4-3, and 6-2. Black's are 6-1, 4-2, and double 3.

You bring two men around the corner with each of your first two rolls; on the third roll you can not repeat this procedure because this will leave you with a blot on the black twelve point. Your 6 is easy. You move a man from the black twelve point to your bar point. The 2 is also easy. You continue with that same man to your five point.

Diagram IX-1

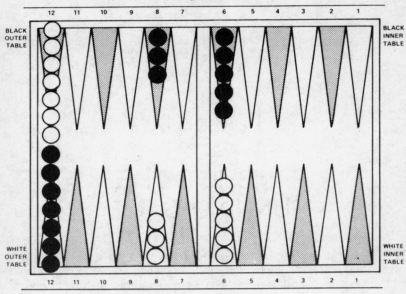

Diagram IX-2

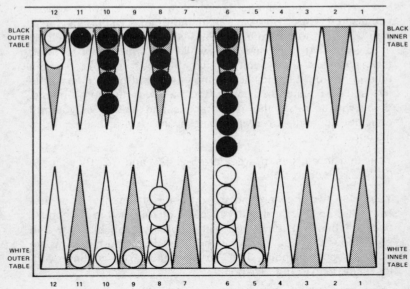

Black plays his 6-1 by moving a man from your twelve point to his six point. He brings two men around from your twelve point with the 4-2 and clears it with double 3, to bring about the position shown in Diagram IX-2. There is no need to make a pip count here but there is a little trick of the trade to tell you exactly how you stand. Three rolls back you were even. Both of your first rolls were 7's. Still even. You gained one pip on the next roll. 7 against 6. You lost four pips the next roll—12 for Black against 8 for you—so Black is now three pips ahead.

You roll 5-3. You could bring your last two men around the corner, but decide to bring two men to your five point. Black rolls 6-4. He decides to move a man from his ten point to his four point and the man on his nine point to his five point. He now has a five-pip lead.

You roll double 2 and use two of the 2's to bring your last two men around the corner to your eleven point and the remaining two 2's to move two men from your eight point to your six point. Black rolls double 4. He brings two men to his six point and two men to his four point. He is now thirteen pips to the good.

You roll 6-3 and bring two men to your five point. Black rolls 5-4 and brings the last man from the ten point to his five point and

Diagram IX-3

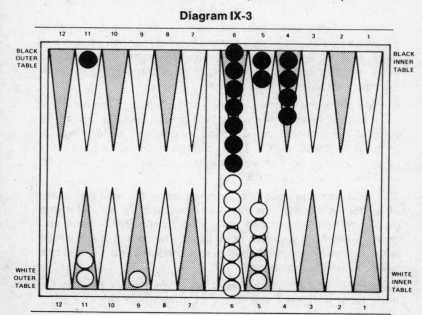

the last man from his eight point to his four point to bring up the position shown in Diagram IX-3.

You roll 3-2 and bring a man from your eleven point in to your six point.

Black doubles. What do you do?

If you have been counting along you know that you are eight pips behind. If you haven't you can check it quickly. Outside your inner table you are nine pips to the bad. In the inner table you have three extra men on your five point against Black's four men on his four point, so you are one pip ahead there for a total of eight to the bad. Black's pip count is $11 + 48 + 10 + 16 = 85$.

The doubling number (85 divided by 8) is over 10. Black does have the better of the game but his advantage is not enough to warrant the double, so you accept.

Black rolls double 5. He moves the man from his eleven point to his one point and uses the remaining two 5's to bear off the two men on his five point. You roll 6-5 and bring in your last two men to your five and four points. Black's lead is up to seventeen pips and, if he doubled you now (the doubling number is 65 divided by 17 or less than 4), you would refuse—but he doubled the last roll and has to play on. You "own the cube"!

He rolls 2-1, the worst possible number. He bears off his man on the one point and moves a man from his four point to his two point. You roll 5-3. You bear off a man from your five point and move a man from your six point to your three point to leave the position shown in Diagram IX-4.

Black's pip count is now sixty-two and his lead is twelve. If he were to double you now you would surely take the double in spite of the fact that the doubling number (62 divided by 12) is just the least bit over 5. The reason is that Black's position is so poor. He has no man on any odd-numbered point, hence he can't bear off a man with a 5, 3, or 1.

This disadvantage becomes apparent when his next roll is another double 5. He brings four men from his six point to his one point. You roll 6-3 and bear off a man from your six point and move a man from your five point to your two point. Black's lead is up to twenty-three pips, but all is not lost for you. He still has twelve men left on the board.

Black now rolls 4-3 and moves a man from the six point to his three point with the 3 and bears off a man from the four point with the 4. See Diagram IX-5.

Diagram IX-4

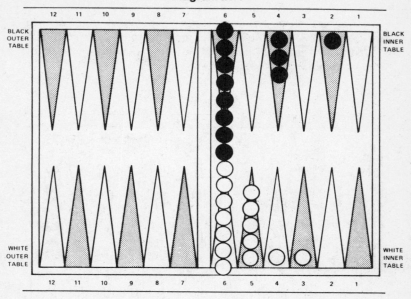

Diagram IX-5

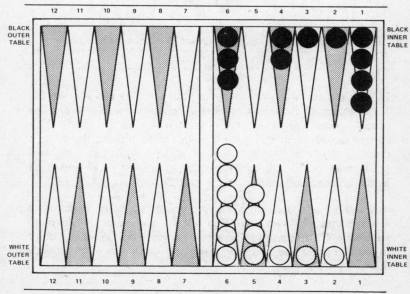

You roll double 3 and bear off two men from your six point. Black rolls 5-2 and can do nothing better than move a man from the six point to the one point and bear off the man from the two point. You roll 5-2 and bear off two men. He rolls another 5-2 and moves a man from his six point to his one point and another from his four to his two point. See Diagram IX-6.

Diagram IX-6

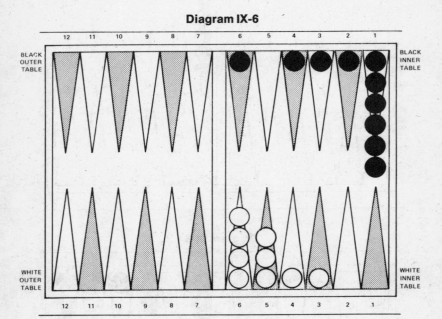

Black's pip count is twenty-one to your forty-six but you are out of the pip count stage now and in the **"counting of rolls to end the game"** stage. You have only nine men left on the board. You can miss once and still get off in five rolls without throwing a doublet. Black is also in a five-roll situation but one miss will put him up to six. You do figure to miss at least twice and don't even consider a double.

You roll 5-1 and bear off a man from your six point. Black rolls 4-1 and bears off two men. You roll 6-3 and bear off two men. He rolls 5-4. He uses the 5 to move his last man on his six point to his one point and bears off the man from his three point with the 4.

Diagram IX-7

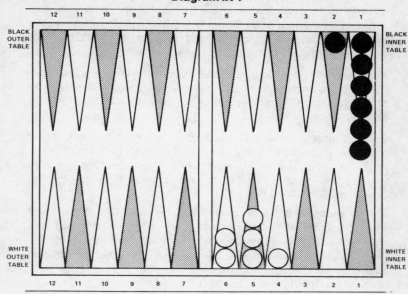

Diagram IX-8

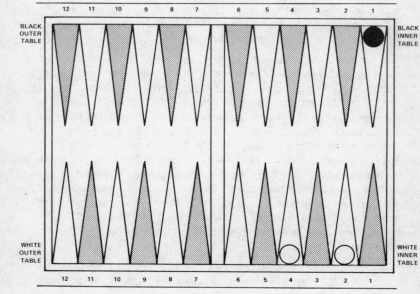

You are now in the position shown in Diagram IX-7 and, if Black doesn't throw a doublet, you have an excellent chance to win. You can miss twice and still get off in four rolls. Your next rolls are 6-3; 4-1; and 6-5. Black rolls 6-4; 5-4; and 6-2. Nice big rolls but 2-1 would have been just as good for him each time.

You are now in the position shown in Diagram IX-8. It is your roll. The cube is on your side and it is clearly to your advantage to turn it to four. (Remember Black doubled to two several rolls back.)

No guarantee goes with this redouble. You have thirteen losing rolls and twenty-three winning rolls. If this position were to occur thirty-six times you would expect to win ten more games than you would lose $(23 - 13 = 10)$ and it is certainly a paying proposition to increase the stake.

Should Black take this redouble? Yes, he should! In those same thirty-six games if he had refused every redouble he would lose $36 \times 2 = 72$ units. If he took every redouble he would lose 23 $\times 4 = 92$ units and win $13 \times 4 = 52$ units for a net loss of just 40 units. You don't get rich losing 40 units but you don't go broke quite as fast as when you lose 72 units.

It is also worthy of note to observe that, if Black had waited one more roll before making his unsound double, you would have given up the game and he would be a point to the good instead of sweating out a poor four-point game.

We return now to Game Number 1. In Diagram VIII-2, repeated here as Diagram IX-9, it is Black's roll. He has a three-pip lead, but the doubling cube is on your side. He rolls 5-2 and moves a man from his nine point to his four point with the 5 and a man from his bar point to his five point with the 2, in order to bring men to the open points in his inner table. You roll 6-4 and bring your two men around the corner. He rolls 5-1 and moves a man from his bar point to his two point with the 5 and from his six point to his five point with the 1. He could have brought a man in but decided to improve his board. You roll 6-1 and bring your man on the nine point to the three point with the 6 and a man from your bar point to your six point with the 1. Black rolls 3-2 and brings two men in to his five point to produce the position in Diagram IX-10.

A quick pip count shows that you are still four pips behind, but it is your roll. To all intents and purposes the game is even except that you own the cube.

Diagram IX-9

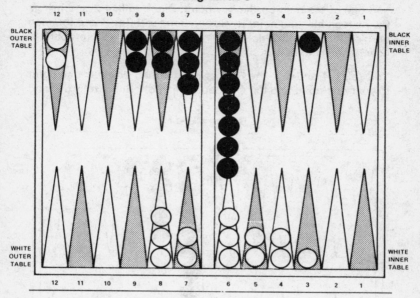

Diagram IX-10

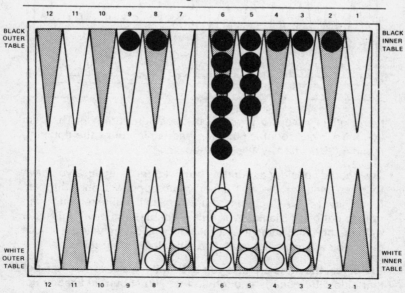

You roll double 4 and bring in the three men on your eight point and one of the men on the bar point. Black rolls 4-2 and brings the man on his nine point to his five point with the 4 and the man on his eight point to his six point with the 2. Your pip count is now 70 and your lead is six pips.

You roll 6-4 and use the 6 to bring the man on your bar point to your one point and the 4 to bear a man off. Black rolls 5-2 and

Diagram IX-11

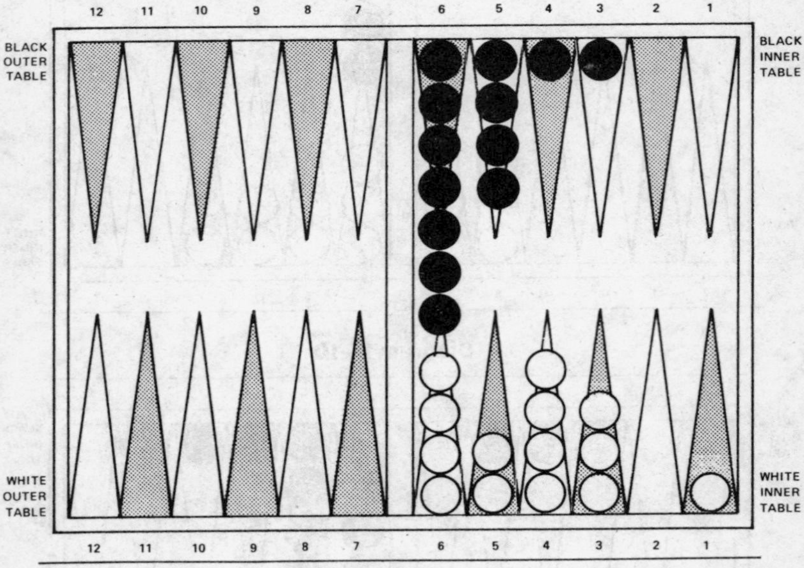

bears off two men to produce the position shown in Diagram IX-11. Your pip count is 60; your lead is nine pips; the doubling number (60 divided by 9) is between 6 and 7.

You should consider a redouble but not offer it because you have fourteen men on the board and your opponent only thirteen. If you never roll a doublet and never miss it will take you seven rolls to get off. If Black never rolls a doublet and never misses it will take him that same seven rolls. Now suppose you each miss once: you will need eight rolls; he will still get off in seven.

Of course, the odds are that you both will miss several times but that little difference is enough so that you should not redouble.

Diagram IX-12

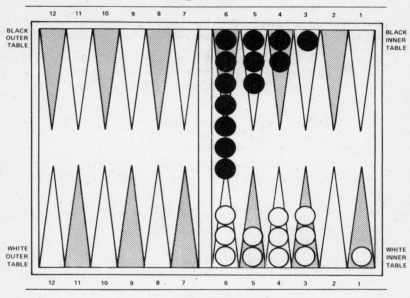

Diagram IX-13

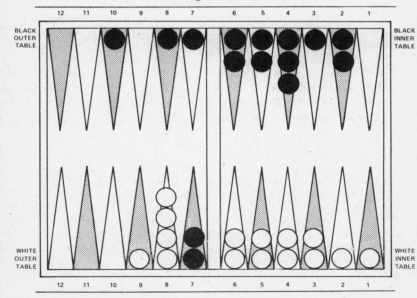

You roll 6-4 and bear off two men. Black rolls 5-2. He makes his best play, which is to use the 5 to bear off a man from the five point and the 2 to move a man from his six point to his four point to produce the position in Diagram IX-12.

Your pip count is 50; your lead is twelve pips; the doubling number (50 divided by 12) is less than 5. In addition each of you is down to twelve men. You should double and Black should refuse the double.

Diagram IX-13 is carried over from Lesson VIII (Game Number 2). Black has just played double 3. Why didn't he do something about his two men on your bar point? Because they represent all the contact left. If your next roll is double 2 or double 6, you will have to leave him a shot right away; in addition, the shot may still come later.

You make a quick pip count to see that yours is 80 and your lead is twenty-two pips. The doubling number (80 divided by 22) is less than 4 and you double.

Should Black accept. No, he shouldn't. There is a chance that he will get a shot but, even if he does get it, he still will have to hit your blot.

Nevertheless, Black does accept and you proceed to roll double 6! You bring the man on your nine point to your three point and three men from your eight point to your two point. Why did you leave the blot on your eight point, rather than on your nine point? It is that matter of giving yourself the best chance to win. The blot on the eight point can be hit by any 1 (11 different rolls). If left on the nine point it can be hit by any 2 and by double 1 (12 different rolls). Remember, when a direct shot is involved, the closer your blot to the threat, the better.

Black rolls 4-2 and moves a man from his bar point to his five point with the 2 and a man from his ten point to his six point with the 4. He does not move the men on your bar point because you just might roll double 1 (after all you did roll double 6 at the wrong time!) and not be able to move that man on your eight point to safety.

Actually you roll 6-2. We won't bother to finish this game. Black might win but he is so far behind that it is pointless for us to play it out.

When to Give and Take End Game Doubles

Diagram IX-8 showed a one-roll position. You were going to win the game or lose it on your next roll since Black was sure to get his last man off if he got a chance to play.

We pointed out that you should double and Black should accept. If your men were on the four and one points instead of on the four and two points, you would have an even stronger double. In fact so strong a double that Black should not accept it. You would win with any one of twenty-nine rolls and lose with only seven (3-2, 3-1, 2-1, and double 1).

If this position were reached thirty-six times and Black took all redoubles he would lose 29×4 (remember you are redoubling from 2 to 4) $= 116$ units and win just $7 \times 4 = 28$ units for a net loss of 88 units. If he refused all thirty-six redoubles he would lose only 72 units.

There must be some point at which it is equally undesirable to refuse or to accept a double. This point is when the doubler's chance of winning is exactly 75% (27 out of 36 in a one-roll position).

Remember this figure. Take end game doubles, no matter how distasteful, if you have better than a 25% chance to pull the game out; refuse them and save money if your chance is less than 25%; let your conscience be your guide when right on the mark.

Counting Rolls instead of Pips

Suppose you and your opponent have six men left apiece and that they are all on the one point. The pip count is even, but you shouldn't bother with it. If no one rolls a doublet, you will be off in three rolls and he will be sitting with two men. If you roll a doublet at either of your first two turns it doesn't matter what he does. You have won. Thus, the only way he can win is for you to roll two ordinary numbers while he rolls a doublet at one of his only two rolls.

If you want exact figures, your chance of winning the game is 1021 divided by 1296, or 78.8%. This is above the 75% mark so you should double and he should refuse to accept your double.

How about eight men against eight men—with all the men on the one point? This is a four-roll position with doublets reducing it to three, or even two.

This position also illustrates the great value of possession of the cube. Suppose you own the cube. If you don't double you have an 88% chance to win the game since at your next turn you will be able to double and end the game unless you roll an ordinary number and your opponent rolls a doublet. In addition, if this last event does happen—and you have retained possession of the cube—you will be able to play the game out to the end and may be able to come back with a doublet of your own.

Now suppose you do double. Your chance to win has gone down to 73% from 88% because your opponent will get to play the game to the end and because if he should get into a redoubling position, you may not be able to finish the game.

Should you redouble in spite of this difference? Yes. Take a hundred games. If you don't redouble, you will win 88 of them and lose 12 for a net gain of 76 units. If you redouble, and your opponent accepts, you will win 73 games and lose 27 for a net gain of 46 games—but the stake will be doubled so your actual gain will be 92 units.

Should your opponent take the redouble? Of course he should. His chance of winning is 27% which is slightly above the 25% mark. He will lose 92 units if he takes a hundred doubles, which is eight units less than the 100 he would lose by refusing.

With ten against ten (all on the one point) you should double, but should not redouble. In other words, you can afford to move the cube from the middle of the table to your opponent's side, but you cannot afford to move it all the way from your side to his. Of course, he should accept.

With twelve against twelve (a six-roll situation) a double is slightly optimistic.

In Diagram IX-14 you are in a six-roll position. Black just might need seven rolls to get off but this chance is not worth considering. What is worth considering is that if Black rolls double 2 or double 3 he will only be able to bear off three men. This will leave him with nine men and he will still need five more regular rolls to get all his men off. In other words, he will not gain anything from a double 2 or from a double 3.

Diagram IX-14

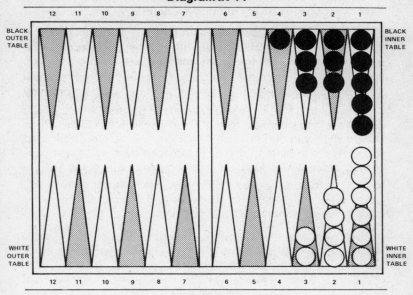

Diagram IX-15

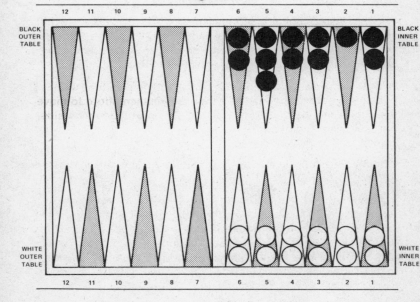

This difference is enough to warrant your offering a first double. It is not enough to warrant offering a redouble.

In Diagram IX-15 you have two men on each of the six points in your inner table; Black has a slightly poorer position since he has three men on his five point and only one man on his two point.

At first glance this looks like a time to count rolls, but it isn't. You are not in a six-, or even a seven-, roll position although you do have a good chance to get off in seven rolls. Instead you should stick with the pip count. Your count is 42 pips; your lead is 3 pips; the doubling number (42 divided by 3) is 14 and your correct procedure is to roll. Do not double at this point.

Lesson X

FINISHING ONE-SIDED GAMES

The position shown in Diagram X-1 is carried over from Game Number 3 in Lesson VIII. The game is one-sided and you are on the wrong end.

You proceed to roll 6-1. You can hit the blot on your twelve point but this would be very bad tactics. Your main interest right now is just to avoid being gammoned. If you hit that blot you will not only be delaying Black's movement of his last men around the board, but you will be creating complications that may result in more of your men being trapped on the black one point or on the bar.

You also don't want to use the 1 to split your men on the one point. If you do split them you give Black a chance to close his board with two of your men on the bar.

Two men back on the one point may get you gammoned—two men on the bar are quite likely to lead to that unpleasant result. So you play a man from your eight point to your two point with the 6 and from your six point to your five point with the 1.

Black rolls 5-4 and moves the men from your bar point to your eleven and twelve points. He doesn't mind leaving a blot because he wants you to hit that blot. You roll 6-3 and bring your men around the corner. Black rolls 6-5 to produce the position in Diagram X-2.

Diagram X-1

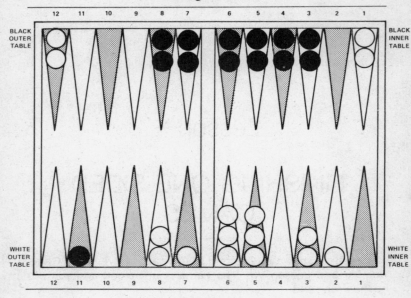

Diagram X-2

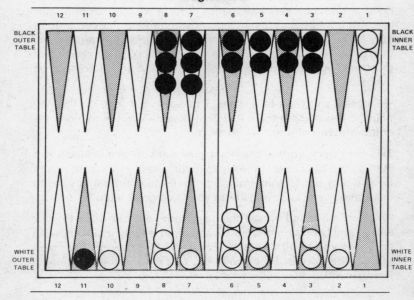

You roll another 6-1. The 6 is easy to play. Move the man on your ten point to your four point. You probably start to use the 1 to make your four point but there is a special play for you to make here. Move the man on your bar point to your six point.

You aren't going to get a chance to hurt Black for some time. He may expose a blot on his two point but it won't do you any good to hit it. Eventually he will make his two point and bring all his men into his home table. Then he may give you a shot and, if you hit that blot, you will have a good chance to win the game provided you have been able to retain your six point.

In order to retain your six point you hope you won't have to play damaging high rolls. The highest number you can roll is a 6. Once you get all your men in your home board you just don't have to play that high number at all. Therefore, get your men home right away. The four point will take care of itself later on.

A few more rolls bring you to the position in Diagram X-3. You have managed to hold your board but Black has come in very well and has no immediate bad roll. He does roll 6-1. He bears a man off with the 6 and, if he is an average player, will undoubt-

Diagram X-3

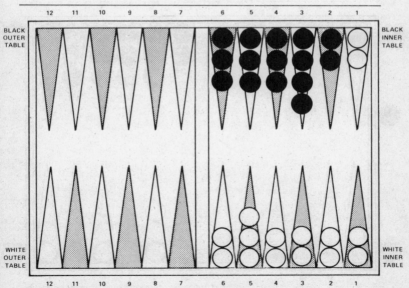

Diagram X-4

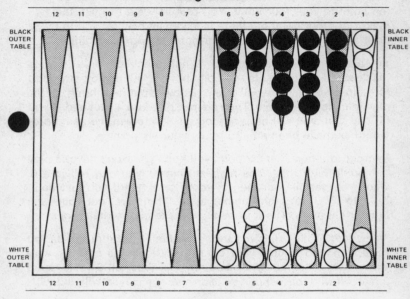

Diagram X-5

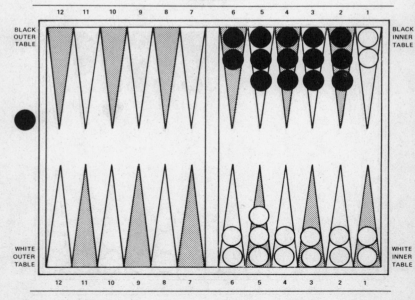

edly use the 1 to move a man from the five point to the four point to produce the position in Diagram X-4.

His reason for this move is that he will be able to play any doublet with complete safety and the average player has learned to guard against positions where the roll of a doublet may force him to expose a blot.

But the expert will move a man from the three point to the two point to produce the position in Diagram X-5 instead. In this position he will have to leave a blot if he throws 6-5, double 6, or double 5, but he will be able to play any of the other thirty-two rolls with complete safety.

Now go back to position X-4. All doublets are safe but one blot must be left with a 5-4 and two blots if the dice show 6-5. There are still thirty-two safe rolls but of the four bad rolls, two will leave two blots.

A player is unhappy when he must leave one blot, but he is miserable when he must leave two!

Diagram X-6 shows the continuation of Game Number 4 in Lesson VIII. Black has just failed to bring either of his two men in

Diagram X-6

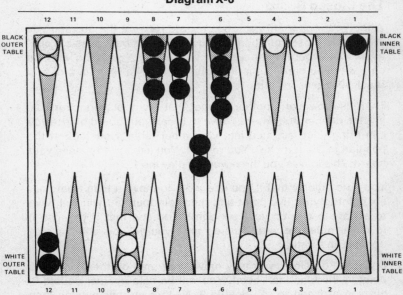

from the bar. You roll 6-2. The six is easy. You cover the blot on your three point. You use the 2 to move the man on the black three point to the five point. The reason for this is to guard against the possibility that you will roll a couple of double 5's and not be able to move that man out of the black inner board.

Black fails to come in. You roll 5-2. Move from the black four to the black nine point with the 5 and from your nine point to your bar point with the 2.

Black rolls 5-1 and brings one man in. You roll double 4. Use three 4's to hit the blot on your one point with a man from the black twelve and the other 4 to move the man on the black five point to the black nine point.

Black fails to come in. You roll 5-4 and move the man on the black twelve point to your four point.

You hope Black won't roll a 6, but the only roll that can really embarrass you is double 6. Actually Black rolls 5-1 and once more brings a man onto the board.

We'll leave the game here. You expect to close your one point and win a gammon. See Diagram X-7.

The Closed Board

When your opponent has one or more men on the bar and you are able to close your board, you are in your best possible situation. You expect to win a game, or possibly a gammon, and the only way you can lose is if you are forced to leave a blot and Black succeeds in hitting it.

There is, however, another danger that many players overlook. It is the danger that you will have to break your board before you can bring your last men into your inner table. Now look at the position in Diagram X-8. You roll 4-1. You use the 4 to close your board. This leaves you three ways to play the 1.

You note quickly that if you use the 1 to move a man from your six point to your five point and then roll double 6 you will have to expose a blot on your six point. You see that if you use it to move either of your outside men you will be able to play double 6 in safety.

If you are careless, you may move your man on the black nine point to the black ten point. You will be safe against double 6, but you proceed to roll double 3. Neither of your outside men

Diagram X-7

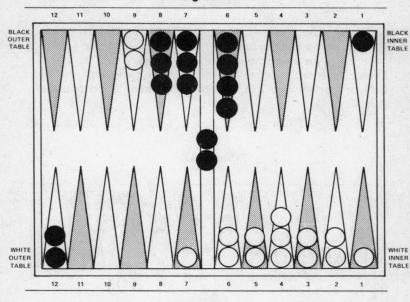

Diagram X-8

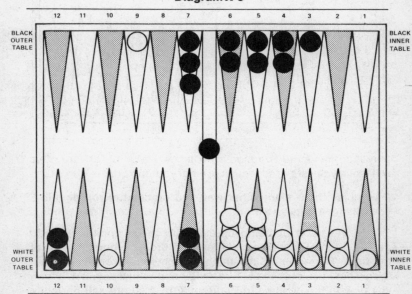

will be movable and you will be forced to give up two points in
your board.

A careful player will see this possibility and will move his man
on his own ten point to his nine point. Double 4 will be a bad roll
but he will be able to play it and break only one point in his
board. He doesn't want to have to do this but it is better to break
only one point than to break two and there is no absolutely
safe play.

When in the position of Diagram X-9 you roll 5-1. Your only safe

Diagram X-9

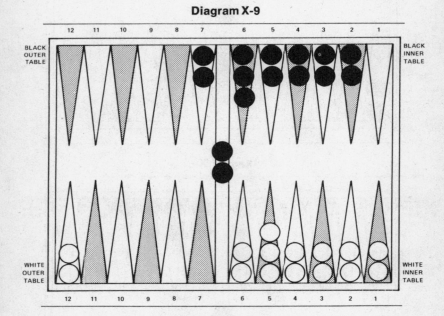

play is to move the two men on your twelve point forward. This
will leave you safe irrespective of what your next roll is.

If you play the 5-1 any other way and proceed to roll double 6
you will have to leave a blot.

Get in the habit of being careful with these apparently sure
games. With practice you will learn to protect yourself most of
the time. There is no such thing as complete protection, however. Thus, you play the 5-1 correctly and follow with 6-4, which
you play to the position in Diagram X-10. You are still perfectly

Diagram X-10

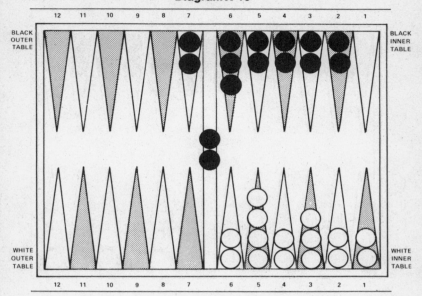

Diagram X-11

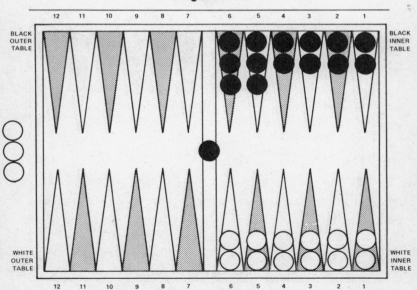

Diagram X-12

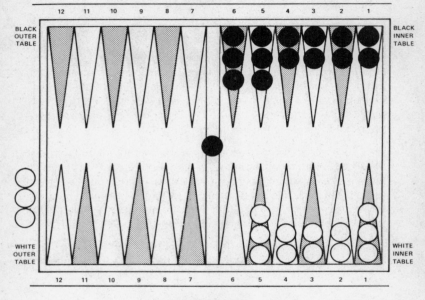

Diagram X-13

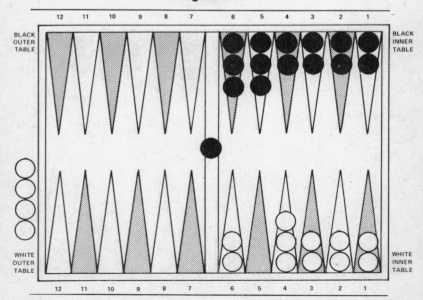

safe—but your next roll is 6-1. You must bear off a man with the 6 and move the other man on the six point to your five point with the 1. Now if you follow that roll with double 6, or double 5, you will have to leave a blot.

As you break your board in this and similar positions your game plan should be to break first from the six point, then from the five point, and so on. Diagram X-11 illustrates just about the only exception to this rule. You roll 5-1 and can either break your six point to produce the position in Diagram X-12 or break your five point to produce the position in Diagram X-13.

Let's look at these two positions from the standpoint of your next roll. In either position if you roll double 6, 5, or 4, you must leave a blot. Now look at the ordinary rolls. In position X-12, if you roll 6-5, 6-4, 6-3, 6-2, 5-4, 5-3, or 5-2 (a total of 14 rolls), you will have to leave a blot. In position X-13 the only rolls that force you to leave a blot are 6-1, 5-1, and 4-1.

Thus there are 17 (14 plus the three doubles) blot-leaving rolls in position X-12 and only 9 (6 plus the three doubles) in position X-13.

Diagram X-14

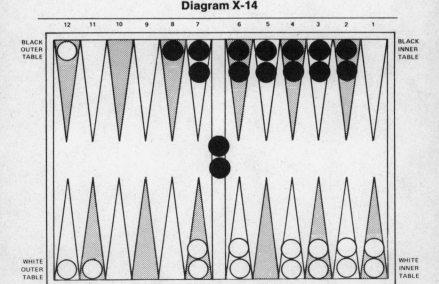

Guarding against a Doublet Rolled by Your Opponent

In the position of Diagram X-14 you roll 4-3. You can move your man on the black twelve point to your ten point and the man on your twelve point to your eight point as your strongest attacking play. This play will leave you with direct shots of 6, 5, 3, and 2, bearing on that open five point. It will also leave you with a headache and a lost game if Black rolls double 5 since with that roll he can bring both men in from the bar and hit your blot on your ten point. Hence, no matter how you finally decide to play that 4-3 don't move a man to your ten point!

Conclusion

When you have an overwhelming position always consider playing for a gammon. When a gammon appears unlikely then play as safe as possible.

Lesson XI

BACK GAMES AND
SPECIAL PROBLEMS

The position in Diagram XI-1 developed after just four plays. You started with 6-4 and ran with a back man. Black's reply was 5-2. He hit your blot with the 2 and moved a man to his eight point with the 5. You rolled 6-5 and used it to bring in your man on the bar and hit his blot on the black eleven point. He rolled 5-1; brought the man on the bar to your five point with the 5 and exposed a blot on his own five point with the 1.

You rolled 5-4, hit the blot on his five point with the 4 and used the 5 to move the man on his eleven point to your nine point. He rolled 4-2, brought the man on the bar in with the 2 and hit the man on your nine point with the 4.

You rolled another 5-4. You made his five point with the 5 and hit his blot with the 4. His fourth roll, 3-2, allowed him to make your two point with the 2 and to move a man from your twelve point to his ten point with the 3.

You should be able to see the reason for all these first plays. He could have used the 3-2 to make your three point; just to bring the man from the bar to your five point; or, instead of exposing a blot with the 3, to move a man from his six point to his three point.

Why did he make the play he did? Because he sees he is well behind and hopes to develop a back game. He has a good start

Diagram XI-1

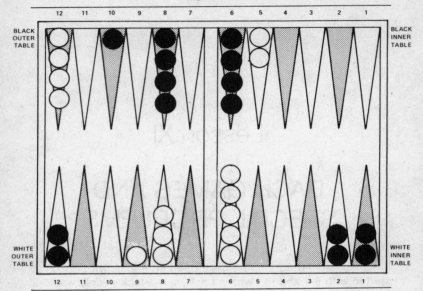

on a back game, but he does not yet have the timing for it. He wants to delay his movement and he offers that blot on your nine point in the hope that you will hit it.

This principle applies in the development of most back games. The man who is behind is not far enough behind to hold a back game. He tries to delay himself by getting you to hit blots. You should do your best not to cooperate. Thus, in this position the last thing you want to do with a 5 is to hit that blot.

If you refuse to delay him in this position Black's best chance is to abandon the back game in favor of a defensive position. To do this he will abandon your one and two points and try to make your four, five, or bar point. He will have the worst of the game but it will be a long time before you become strong enough to double him.

In Diagrams XI-2 and XI-3 you are in the same position against different black back games.

In position XI-2 Black has a really fine back game. He is going to be able to hold points in your inner table for a long time and

Diagram XI-2

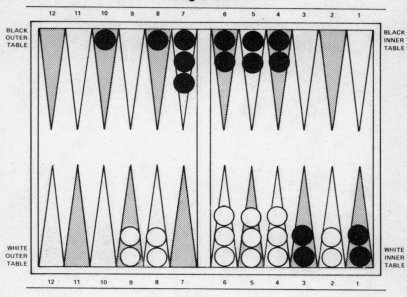

Diagram XI-3

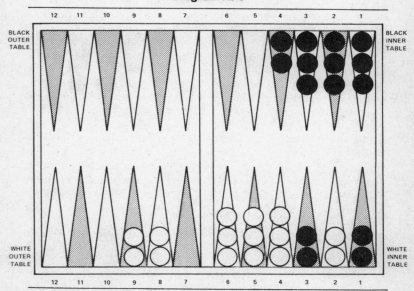

Diagram XI-4

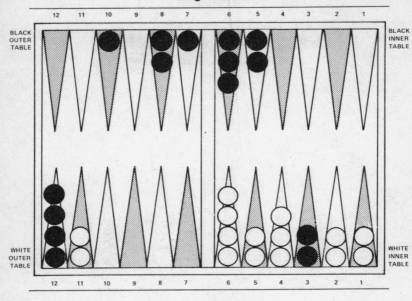

Diagram XI-5

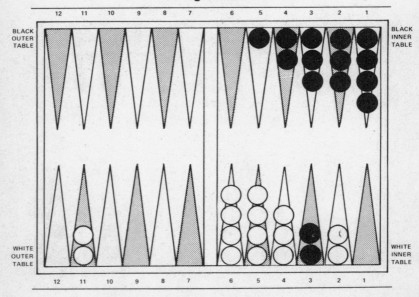

should win the game if he ever hits a blot. On the other hand, if he never hits a blot he will almost surely be gammoned. That is the trouble with back games. If they win, they win; if they lose, they lose double or even triple.

In position XI-3 Black's back game has already collapsed. He has what we like to call a nothing game. Even if you expose a blot and he hits it, you are still a favorite to win.

Therefore, don't go out of your way to develop back games. At best they are a poor gamble.

To Block or Not to Block

In the positions shown in Diagrams XI-4 and XI-5 you have just rolled double 1. You can move the two on your eleven point to your nine point to block a 6 move by either of Black's men on your three point. In position XI-4 that is the last thing you want to do. Black is not going to move those men until he has to. He is far behind in the running game. His one hope is to hit a blot and those are the only men that can do it. If you block his 6's you are also blocking yours. Unless you are lucky enough to roll 5-4, 5-3, 4-3, double 5, 4, 3, 2, or 1, you are going to have to expose a blot to a direct shot.

Leave them where they are or move them forward to your ten point. You still expect to leave a blot but when you do it will be against an indirect shot, not a direct one.

In Diagram XI-5 the reverse holds true. Black wants to move those men if he can. Block off their escape with a 6. You may hold them in chancery until your running game has improved. Furthermore, if one does escape you will be able to hit the other one with any 6, 3, 2, or 1. You may be able to point on him but, even if you can't, hit him!!

Hitting Two Men

Any time you can put two of your opponent's men on the bar he is in trouble. He may get out of it by bringing both men right in but, if you hold just two points in your inner table, he has only sixteen rolls out of thirty-six that will do this for him.

Look at Diagram XI-6. You roll 4-1. You have the better of the game and can play conservatively by moving a man from the black twelve point to your eight point. The trouble with this play is that it does nothing for you. If Black rolls a 4, or double 2, he will make your five point and have an equal game. Other good rolls will allow him to make his bar point or his four point.

Diagram XI-6

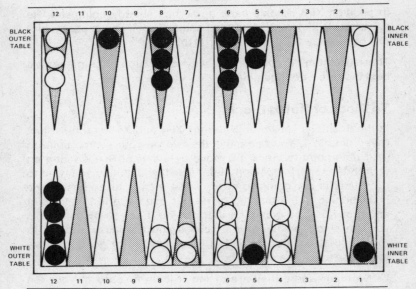

Suppose you hit both his blots with a man from your six point. You might get an unexpected dividend. Black could roll 6-4, double 6, or double 4 and lose his whole turn. If he rolls a 1 his game has improved, but you still have an equal game. If he doesn't roll a 1, or a favorable doublet, you really have done yourself a lot of good.

Attack! Hit the two blots!

In Diagram XI-7 you have a good game and are trying for a gammon. Undoubtedly Black took a bad double some time back and his position has worsened. You roll 6-3. The 6 is forced—you must hit his blot on your one point with it. You can use the 3 to move another man from your bar point to your four point, but this isn't the way to play for a gammon.

Black can roll a 3, or a 2-1, make the three point in your inner table, and practically kill any chance you may have had for a gammon. Or, if he rolls an ace he will hit your blot on your one point and have a good chance to escape from gammon country.

The play for a gammon is to use your 3 to hit his other blot on your three point. This exposes two blots in your inner table but, unless Black rolls 3-1, double 3, or double 1, you should win your gammon.

Hitting a Man to Slow Up Your Opponent

In the position of Diagram XI-8 you roll 4-3. You have to use the 3 to bring your man in from the bar. How do you play the 4?

The safe way is to move the man on your ten point to your six point. This leaves you safe, but probably sorry. If Black rolls any 6, 5, or 3, he can, and almost surely will, hit your man on his three point. Many combinations will allow him to make that point. Other good rolls are so numerous that, if Black were to double you, your only smart course would be to give up.

Suppose you use the 4 to hit his blot on your one point. Your game won't be anything to cause you to burst into cheers, but it will be playable. The chances are that Black won't double; if he does, you can afford to take it.

Diagram XI-7

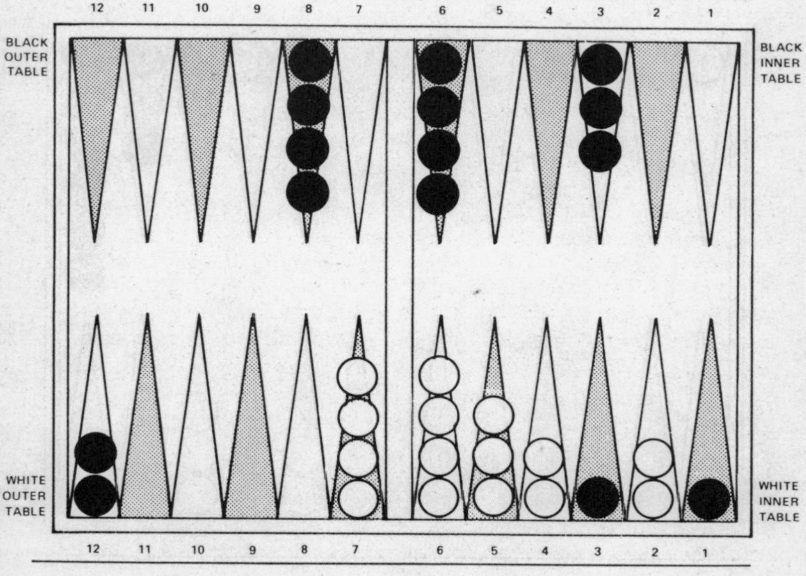

Diagram XI-8

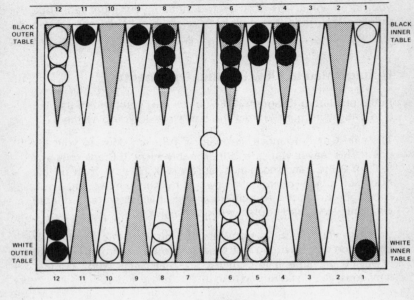

Diagram XI-9

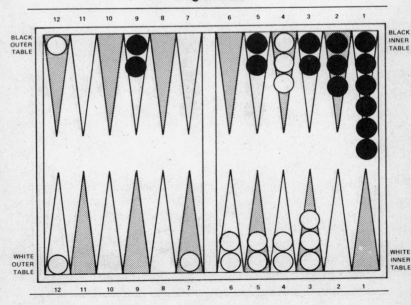

Gambits

In the position of Diagram XI-9 you have some chance to win in a running game. Say one in a thousand. That doesn't mean that your game is hopeless. You have an excellent chance to get a shot and, if you hit, you figure to win easily.

Now you roll 5-2. You use the 5 to make your bar point and your first thought is to use the 2 to bring your man around the corner from the black twelve point.

First thoughts aren't always best and your correct play is to move one of your men on the black four point to the black six point. This play may look silly, but it isn't anything of the kind.

Black can hit that blot effectively with double 3, 5-3, 4-3, and 3-1. In the case of double 3 you are in bad shape regardless of what you have done; in the case of the other rolls he hits you and brings his man to safety. You can hit his blot on the nine point with 6-5, 6-3, or 5-4, but you are unhappy about your gambit.

Now let us look at some of the good things that can happen if you offer up this sacrifice. Suppose Black rolls 6-5, 6-2, 6-1, 5-4, 5-2, or 5-1. That is twelve of his possible thirty-six rolls. He will leave a blot exposed to two direct shots. You will be the favorite to win the game.

Suppose he rolls 6-3. He will hit your blot and be forced to leave that man on his six point exposed to any 6 or to 4-2. How about 3-2? He will probably just give up his five point and hope for a miracle at his next turn.

The other rolls, except for doublets and 6-4, which are good against any play you make, will also be trouble rolls for him. Expose your blot. He won't be happy.

In Diagram XI-10 Black doubled some time back. You took the double because you hoped to get a shot at him but that shot has not materialized. You have just rolled 6-4 and it seems that you will have to give him a shot.

You can move both men forward from the black eight point and only be exposed to any 1 or you can move one man all the way forward to your bar point and leave your blot on the black eight point exposed to 4-1, 3-2, or any 5.

The second play is correct because you don't expect to win this game unless you can send one of his men to the bar. If he hits your blot it is just frosting on the cake for him since all it will do is increase his winning margin.

Diagram XI-10

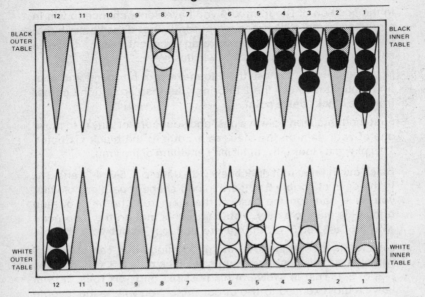

With your man on the black twelve point, if he doesn't hit you with a 1 he goes right by you and wins the running game. With your man on the black eight point if he rolls 6-4, 6-3, 6-2, or 6-1, he has to give you an immediate shot. If he rolls any small number and plays safe by moving forward two of his men in his inner table, you will simply leave your man on his eight point and hope that his next roll will lead to trouble for him.

Diagram XI-11 shows a final gambit. Black was well on his way to gammon you when he had to expose a blot. You hit his blot and this position developed a few moves later. You roll 6-5!

Your correct play is to bear off two men and leave that blot on the six point. If you play safe and he comes right in you have a lost game. If you leave the blot and he hits it you have a chance to hit his man as he continues around the board.

Of course, if he fails to roll a 6 you have an extra man off and, while you aren't the favorite as yet, your position is very good.

Diagram XI-11

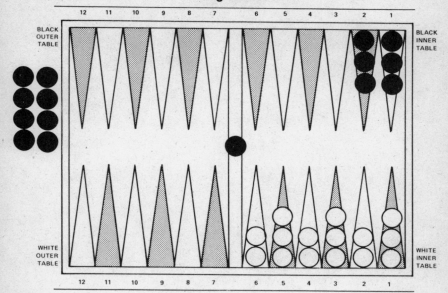

Lesson XII

CHOUETTES AND SETTLEMENTS

When more than two people want to play backgammon, they play what is known as a chouette. In a chouette one man is "in the box," or, more simply, **is** "the box," and plays against all the others.

The man who plays for all the others is known as the captain. He consults with his partners but in the event of argument makes all the decisions except that, when the box doubles, each player has the right to accept or to refuse for himself.

There is a great paradox in a chouette. The box is obviously at a disadvantage. Even the best players in the world make some mistakes and overlook some plays. Several players in consultation are much less likely to do this. In addition, if money is involved (as there usually is), the box is playing for several times the stake of each opponent.

He may hold back on a double he should give. He may refuse a double he should take. He may take the worst of a settlement of one or all of the games he is playing and, in general, has all the worst of it.

Nevertheless the backgammon player's rationale is such that everyone wants to get into the box. The winner wants to win a lot more, the loser wants to get everything back to get even, and the man who is about even wants the action.

The best chouettes consist of from three to five players. When there are more than five, you have to wait too long after losing to roll the dice again and the money pressure on the man in the box becomes too great.

Now let us look at the mechanics of a four-handed game. The box is playing against a captain and players 1 and 2. If the box wins, player 1 becomes captain, player 2 moves up to number 1, and the ex-captain becomes player number 2.

If the box loses, the captain takes the box, the players move up, and the box becomes player number 2.

If the box doubles, any player who refuses the double loses the pre-double stake and has no further interest in the game. In particular, he is not allowed to give advice about plays or re-doubles. In case the captain is one of those refusing the double the senior player accepting takes over the captain's position for the rest of that game.

If the box loses the new captain takes the box. The other players advance in turn with the ex-captain taking the next to last position in the line and the box taking the last place.

New players entering a chouette start at the bottom of the line in the first game in which they participate.

The captain of a chouette is not obliged to consult with his partners about anything and should not do so on unimportant plays. As an example, suppose he gets first play with a 6 against his opponent's 2. There are three ways to play this first roll. We favor moving a man to your own five point but, if we were playing in a chouette and the captain wanted either to run a man to the black nine point or move one man to the black bar point and another to the white eleven point we wouldn't say a word. The difference between the three plays is not enough to warrant slowing up the game with an argument.

In addition, it is important to remember that there may be times when you have a very strong opinion about a play. If you advise all the time your partners may ignore you; if you just advise occasionally you will be listened to.

When the captain has a real problem with his play, he can ask his partners for advice before moving a man or he can make a tentative move and leave the dice on the table until his partners have a chance to discuss the play with him.

Diagram XII-1 shows such a position. You have doubled the man in the box and he has accepted. You then roll double 4.

Diagram XII-1

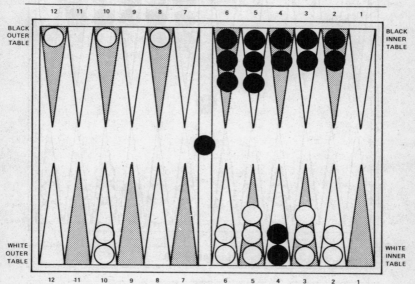

This is a good roll and there are any number of ways to play it. Diagrams XII-2, XII3, and XII4 show the best three of these ways.

XII-2 was produced by moving the man on the black twelve point to your one point and making that point by joining him with one of the men on your five point. This play leaves only one point for Black to enter his man on the bar but, if Black does get that man in quickly, you are likely to have a lot of trouble getting the two men on your ten into your home board without having to leave a direct shot with a 6.

XII-3 results if you use three of your 4's to make your nine point and the fourth one to move the man on the black ten point to your eleven point. It looks good but you are almost surely going to have to give Black a direct 6 or 5 shot later on and may have to leave two direct shots.

XII-4 gets your two men on the ten point into your inner table, makes the black twelve point, and leaves a blot on your eleven point. It has the advantage that you will probably be able to get

Diagram XII-2

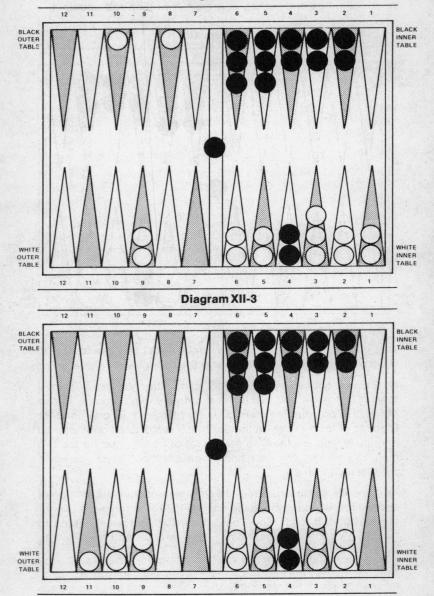

Diagram XII-3

Diagram XII-4

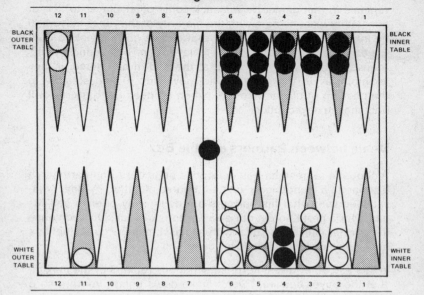

all of your men into your home board without giving any direct shots. It has the weakness that, if you bring in your man from the eleven point and then roll 6-3, you will be forced to use the 6 to move one of your men on the black twelve point to your bar point where it will be exposed to a direct 3. At the same time, your other man back on the black twelve point will be exposed to a 5-4, 6-3, and double 3. The 6-3 and double 3 will hit both of your blots, but the second hit is just another nail in your coffin. The 5-4, however, means that the number of rolls which will cost you the game has risen from eleven to thirteen.

When this situation arose in actual play there were vociferous arguments in favor of each play. The captain finally settled it by moving to position XII-2. Three plays later he had to leave a man exposed on his ten point. Black hit the blot and went on to win the game.

Black might have won the game if White had played either of the other two ways, but no one has been able to convince the other members of the team that the captain had not made a losing decision.

If a player leaves the table during the progress of a game he remains in that game. He may ask some other player to act for him. Otherwise, he acts with the majority of the other players. If he intends to stay away for several games he may ask to continue in the chouette. The other players are not bound by this request and may drop him out at the end of any game. If they let him stay in the chouette he moves up in line steadily to the position of player 1 so that, when he does get back, he will become the next captain.

Deals between Partners and the Box

A chouette represents free enterprise at its best. The partners in a chouette may not agree on their course of action. A player dissatisfied with what his partners are doing may offer to sell his game for a profit, to get out even, or to take a loss. In such case the partner making the deal with him assumes the game that has been given up in addition to his own.

In this and other free enterprise situations remember the maxim, "Let the buyer beware." Don't make deals unless you are sure you know what you are doing.

The box has the right to preempt any deal between partners. Thus suppose the doubling cube is set at 4. The captain offers to give his partners 2 points each for their games and they accept. The box can preempt; pay them the 2 points each and continue just one game.

The box may also initiate and make deals on his own. In this same situation the box may offer 2 points to any man who will take it. Some player may say, "I'll take 3." At this point another player may say, "I'll give you 3." The player accepts his partner's offer whereupon the box may preempt if he wishes.

Of course, the box doesn't always pay. Sometimes he collects. As an example, suppose the box doubles the game from 1 to 2. He rather hopes that some player will give up, but everyone accepts. Now the box is unhappy. He offers to take one-half a point from anyone who will give it to him. Maybe one player accepts, maybe no one accepts, but one man offers to get out even and the box agrees.

When the box offers a deal all of his opponents may accept unless the box makes his offer in some such form as, "I'll take a point from any one player" or some similar offer that precludes settlement by all his opponents.

When the captain settles his game, player 1 takes over. If the captain has settled for a profit he gets to take the box irrespective of who wins the game that is played out. If the captain has settled by paying something he loses all rights and the actual winner becomes the box.

Regular Settlements

A word to the wise here: settlements are for experts. If you get into the habit of settling games you are likely to get all the worst of it unless you know exactly what you are doing.

As an example, look at the position in Diagram XII-5. It is your roll and the cube is at 16. Your chance of winning the game is exactly one-sixth. Your opponent now says, "Your chance is one-sixth. I'll let you out for three-quarters, or 12 points." The offer looks generous but actually is unfair. Let's see what the fair settlement is.

Suppose you reach this position six times. You expect to lose five times and win once for a net loss of four games or 64 points.

Diagram XII-5

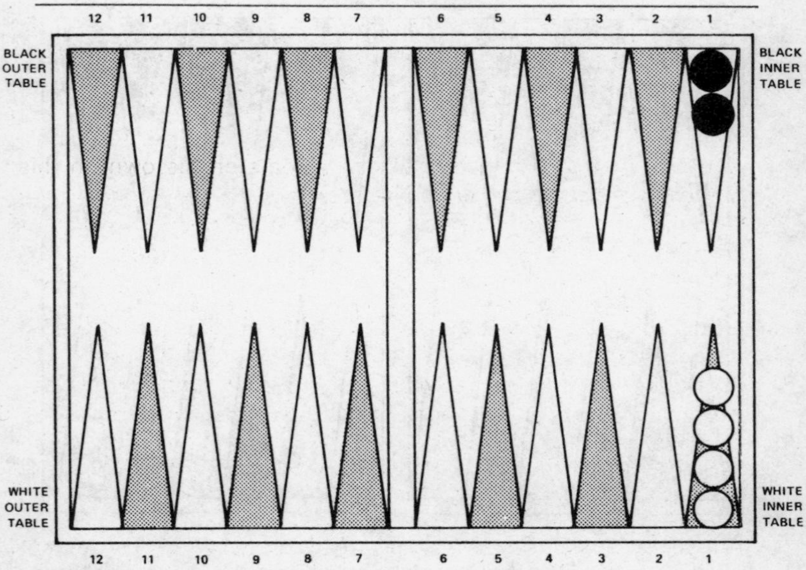

Dividing 64 by 6 gives 10⅔, which is the correct settlement. An offer of 10 would have been generous. The offer of 12 was highway robbery.

Your opponent, however, might have had the best of motives. Most people think that the correct settlement is much larger than it really is and he might have thought that he was being very liberal.

Let's go back to position IX-8. You have just doubled to 4 and your opponent has accepted. Now he offers to pay you one point. How fair is that offer?

In thirty-six games you expect to win 23 and to lose 13 for a net gain of ten games. Your total profit will be 40 units. Divide 40 by 36 and the answer is 1-1/9. He has slightly the best of his offer but it is certainly very close to being correct.

Make your position a trifle better by moving your man from the four point to the three point. Now you have twenty-five winning rolls and expect to show a net profit of $14 \times 4 = 56$ units in 36 games. Your profit expectation per game has risen to 1-5/9

Diagram XII-6

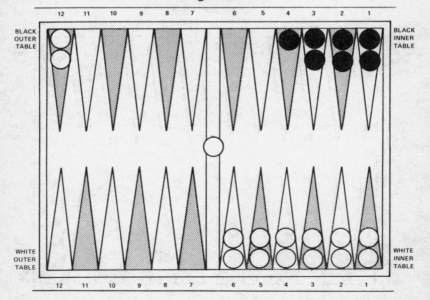

and an offer of 1½ points would be very close to correct. An offer of 2 points would be far too much and 1 point would be far too little.

In the position of Diagram XII-6 it is your roll. If you hit Black's blot as you bring your man in from the bar, you have about an even chance to win the game. If you miss his blot, but come in, the odds are that you will be gammoned. If you miss, but stay on the bar, your opponent will have to leave another blot unless he rolls an ace or double 2. If you miss that next blot, you are almost sure to be gammoned; if you hit it, you still will be unlikely to win the game.

The cube is at 8. What is a fair settlement?

You could work it out by playing a thousand games; otherwise, the best guess is that a fair settlement is that you pay a trifle more than the cube, say 9 or 10 points.

A better way to settle (if all players are in accord) is to play the game (from the present position) four times at 2 points each or twice at 4 points.

You can still win all games and win 8 points or be gammoned every time and lose 16 points. It is likely that you will win one game, lose one game, and be gammoned twice for a net loss of 8.

In making settlements there is no reason why anyone should take the worst of it but, in most of our games, we have a tacit agreement that the man collecting will give his opponent some advantage. Thus, if you are entitled to just over a point and a half, you should be willing to take a point and a half.

Appendix A

PIP COUNT

All else being equal, or nearly equal, the advantage in a running game lies with the player who will require the fewer pips to get his men to his inner table and then bear them off.

Remember that a pip is one of those spots on the dice. When you roll a 6 you advance a man six pips; when you roll an ace you can only advance a man one pip.

Pips don't tell the whole story. At the end of the game, when all of your men are clustered on the one point, a 2-1 roll will be just as good as a 6-5 roll and the mere four pips represented by double 1 can bear off four men for you. However, in the earlier stages of the running game your chance of winning varies directly with the total number of pips it would take you to bring all of your men home and then bear them off.

Experience can give you a rough idea of how you stand but, just as radar is better than a seaman's eye, so an accurate pip count is better than a backgammon player's judgment.

It is very little trouble to learn to count pips. It will slow the game a trifle, but you don't need to make a pip count at every turn to play. Thus, in the early game you have a rough idea as to who has the better of any potential running game. If you have been rolling higher dice and none of your blots have been hit, you will clearly be in front; if the reverse is true, you will be behind.

When behind you try to complicate the position; when ahead

you try to simplify it so as to get into a running game as soon as possible.

Now let's get around to an actual pip count. The count for men in your inner table is easy. It is 6 for a man on the six point; 5 for a man on the five point; and so on. It is just about as easy for men in your outer table. A man on the bar point has a count of 7; a man on the twelve point, a count of 12; other men, counts of 8 to 11 according to the point which they occupy. It is harder to make a count on your opponent's side of the table. For one reason, the numbers are larger; for another, you just can't use the number of the point they are on.

There are all sorts of mathematical formulae for counting these pips but we don't use any of them. Instead we know that the pip count for a man on the enemy twelve point is 13. For any other man in his outer table we count 13 plus the number of pips necessary to bring him to that twelve point. Thus, a man on the black bar point counts $13 + 5 = 18$.

For men in the black inner table we know that a man on the five point counts 20. Men on lower-number points count 20 plus the distance to the five point. In the rare event we have a man on the black six point we note that it is one less pip than a man on the five point, or 19.

At the start of the game your position is even. Let's see what your pip count is. The two men on the black one point count 24 each (total 48). The five men on the black twelve point count 13 each (total 65). The three on your eight point count 8 each (total 24) and the five on your six point count 6 each (total 30). Thus your count is $48 + 65 + 24 + 30 = 167$.

Let us now look again at Diagram II-3, reproduced as Diagram A-1. You will recall that we used this position to illustrate the use of the simplified method of counting combined with the backgammon player's eye. Your exact count is 39 (for the three men on the black twelve point) + 32 (for the four men on your own eight point) + 30 (for the eight men in your inner table) = 101. Black's exact count is 36 (for the two men he has on your bar point) + 22 (for the two men he has on his own eleven point) + 52 (for the eleven men he has in his inner table) = 110.

Note the increased accuracy of this method of determining your position relative to that of your opponent. The simplified count showed that he had the best of it. The simplified count combined

Diagram A-1

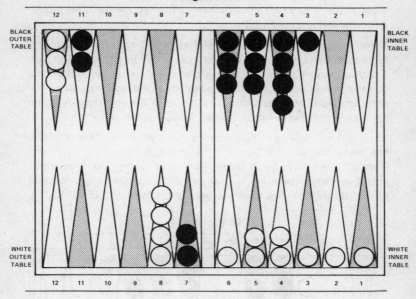

Diagram A-2

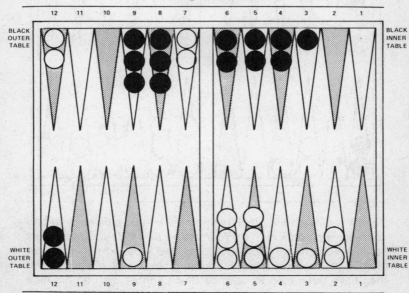

with the backgammon player's eye showed that you had a possible edge. The exact count showed that you were nine pips— over one roll—ahead!!

If you just want to know your relative standing it is always possible to just count the net differences. In the position in Diagram A-2 you haven't bothered with a pip count because neither you nor Black has been considering the idea of doubling since your men on the black bar point and his men on your twelve point are likely to have a lot of trouble passing one another.

Then you roll double 3. You want to move your men forward from the black bar point if you will be in good running shape; you want to keep them back there if you will be behind. You move tentatively to the position in Diagram A-3 and make a quick count of the net differences between your pip count and Black's.

Diagram A-3

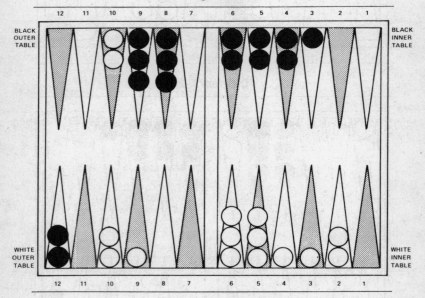

Your two men on the black ten point need two pips each to balance the two black men on your twelve point. You are four pips behind. You charge yourself another two pips to bring your two men on your ten point forward to your nine point where you will then have three men to balance Black's three men on his nine point. You are now six pips behind but you gain 24 to go 18 ahead when you count Black's three men on his eight point against him.

Thus you are 18 pips ahead before starting to count the men in the inner table. You lose 6 for your extra man on the six point and 5 more for your extra man on your five point to cut your lead down to 7 pips. His extra man on his four point exactly balances the two men you have on your own two point.

Since you will be 7 pips ahead after you play, you change your tentative move to an actual one by picking up the dice.

If you want to keep a running score of the net difference as play continues, you can do so. Thus Black rolls 6-1. He was 7 behind; he is now even. You roll 6-3 to go 9 ahead; he rolls 5-2. You are still 2 pips ahead and it is your roll. Not enough to consider doubling.

If you feel that making a pip count is too much trouble, and that you can't add very well anyway, remember you really don't need complete accuracy. If you miss by a pip or two it isn't going to have any great effect on your decisions about running, doubling, et cetera. You still will be doing better than if you just look the position over and try to guess how you stand.

Diagram A-4

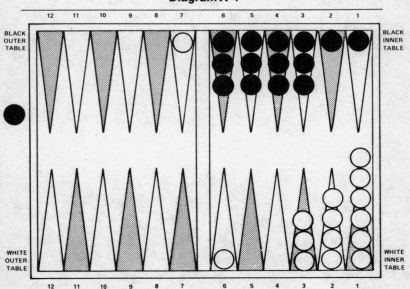

On the other hand, if you learn to make completely accurate pip counts, don't get too fond of your nice toy. Study your position for effectiveness. In general, if several of your men are clustered on one or two points while your opponent's (with the same pip count) are spread around, you have the worst of the position; if your men are spread more than his, you have the better of it.

The position in Diagram A-4 developed because Black had two of your men caught on his one point by a prime. While he was bringing his remaining men around the board you were forced to keep moving men forward in your inner table. Eventually he broke his prime and you immediately rolled double 6 to bring one man to the black bar point and one man to your own six point. He rolled 5-1, bore off a man from his five point with the 5, and moved a man from his two point to his one point with the 1.

It is your roll. Your pip count is 47. Black's pip count is 57. Your lead is 10 pips and the doubling number (see page 91) is less than 5. From a pip count alone your position is so good that you should redouble and he should refuse. From the standpoint of practical backgammon this pip count means nothing. It will probably take you two rolls to get your man on the black bar point around to your inner table. It may even take more. Meanwhile, he will have borne off several men. You may win the game, but right now he is still the decided favorite.

Appendix B

THE OFFICIAL LAWS OF BACKGAMMON

In 1931 Wheaton Vaughan, the Chairman of the Card and Back-gammon Committee of the Racquet and Tennis Club of New York, invited representatives of other clubs to join with the Racquet Club in producing a Code of Laws for Backgammon. The code was prepared and accepted. Oswald Jacoby is the only member of the original committee still alive.

The laws to be presented here, which conform closely to the old ones, were prepared by Jacoby and John Crawford, in conjunction with the Inter-Club League of New York and the International Backgammon Association, and, as far as we know, appear in all modern books on the game.

The laws should never be used to gain an advantage over your opponent. They are designed to prevent arguments, not to cause them.

The Game

1. The game of backgammon is played by two persons.
2. Thirty men, fifteen of one color and fifteen of another, are set up as shown in Diagram B-1 on a standard board of four quarters or tables having six points each.

   In Diagram B-1 the players' home boards (or inner tables) are

Diagram B-1

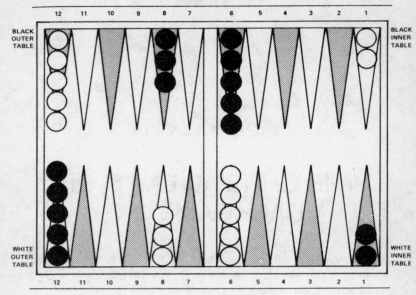

shown at the right. This means that White's home board is opposite his right hand, and Black's home board opposite his left hand. In actual play it is customary to have the home boards nearer the light.

3. For entering and bearing off, the points in both inner tables are considered as numbered from one to six, beginning with the point nearest the edge of the board.

4. Direction of play is from the adversary's inner table to the adversary's outer table, to player's outer table, and then to player's inner (home) table.

5. Play of the men is governed by two dice, thrown (cast) from a cup in which the dice are shaken before casting.

6. (a) For the first game either player may ask to roll for choice of seats, men, or dice. Otherwise they just sit down, set the men up, and play.

   (b) At the start of any later game either player may ask to mix the dice. In this case he shakes the four dice together in one cup and rolls them out. The opponent selects a die

—then the roller—then the opponent—with the roller then taking the last one.

The Throws

7. For the opening throw, each player throws a single die. Each tie requires another opening throw. Whoever throws the higher number wins, and for his first move plays the numbers upon both dice. After that each player in turn throws two dice.

8. The dice must be shaken thoroughly, rolled together, and come to rest flat (not "cocked") upon the table at the player's right, otherwise they must be thrown again.

9. There must be a rethrow if a throw is made before an adversary's play is completed.

10. A play is deemed completed when a player moves his men and starts to pick up his dice. If he starts to pick them up before playing all numbers he legally can, his opponent has the right to compel him to complete or not to complete his play. A roll by the opponent is an acceptance of the play as made (see Law 19).

The Play

11. The play of the men consists of:
    (a) Moving a man (or men) the exact number of points indicated by the number on each of the two dice thrown. One man may be moved the total of the two dice thrown, or one man may be moved the number shown on one die, and an entirely different man the number shown on the other die.
    (b) Entering a man, in the adversary's inner table, on a point corresponding to the number on a die thrown.
    (c) Bearing off a man in the player's inner table, when no man is left outside that table or on the bar, in accordance with Law 17.

12. Doublets require four plays of the number on the dice.

13. Plays must be made for both dice if possible. Either number

may be played first. If either number may be played, but not both, then the higher number thrown must be played.

14. No play may be made which lands, or touches down, on a point held by two or more of the adversary's men.

15. When a play lands on a point occupied by a single man (blot) of the adversary's, such a man is "hit" and must be lifted from the board by the hitter and placed on the bar in the center of the playing board, to await entry in accordance with Law 11(b).

16. A player having a man on the bar may not play any other man until that man has been entered.

17. When in position to bear off, you may bear off a man from a point corresponding to the number on a die thrown, or from the highest occupied point which is lower than the number indicated by a die. If the number is thrown for an unoccupied point, no man below can be borne off, using such number, while any man remains on a higher point. You are not required to bear off a man if you are able to move forward on the board. Law 13 applies here as in all other situations.

For example, in Diagram B-2 you roll 6-1. You may use the 1 to move from your six point to your five point, and then use the 6 to bear a man from the five point; thus, you don't leave a man exposed to a hit by Black's men on your one point. In other words, Law 13, stating that *as long as you play both numbers you may play either one first,* applies in bearing off as well as at all other times.

Errors

18. If an error has been made in the set-up, it must be corrected if either player notices it before the second play of a game has been completed.

19. If an error in play has been made, either player may require its correction before a subsequent throw, but not thereafter. The man played in error must be correctly played if possible.

Scoring

20. A game is won by the player who first bears off all of his men. A gammon (double game) is won if the adversary has not borne off a single man. This doubles the count.

Diagram B-2

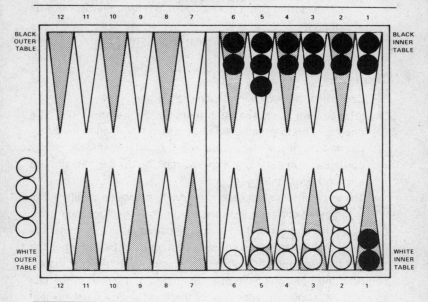

A backgammon (triple game) is won if the adversary has not borne off a single man and has one or more men in the winner's inner table or upon the bar. This triples the count.

21. Doubling game. The count is raised:

    (a) *Automatically:* Each tie in the opening throw doubles the previous count. Automatic doubles are not played unless the players have agreed to use them and an understanding has been reached as to the method and limitations of such doubles.

    (b) *Voluntarily:* Either player may offer the first optional double of the previous count. After that the right to double the previous count alternates, being always with the player who accepted the last double.

    A double or redouble may be offered only when it is the player's turn to play and before he has thrown the dice. He shall be deemed to have thrown the dice even if he rolls cocked dice.

    A double may be accepted or declined. The refusal of a

double terminates the game, and the player refusing loses whatever the count may amount to before the double was offered.

22. Gammons double or triple the last count.

Chouette*

23. Chouette is played by three or more members.

24. In beginning the game each member shall throw a die. The one throwing the highest number is then the "man in the box," the next highest is the "captain." The other members, in accordance with each one's throw, rank below the captain and succeed him in that order.

25. The initial throw shall determine each member's position, but in the event of a tie only those tying throw again for their position. The highest or higher number always has precedence.

26. Any applicant to a chouette may be accepted. He becomes the last ranking member in the first game in which he participates.

27. After the positions have been determined, the man in the box and the captain proceed as in the two-handed game except that all the remaining members are partners of the captain.

28. The man in the box plays alone and scores separately against each one of his adversaries. He retains his position until defeated. In such event, he retires as a player and takes his place as the last ranking member (unless there be an added member). The previous captain then becomes the man in the box.

29. The captain may consult with any or all of the partners on any question that may arise in the course of the game. He is, however, the final arbiter, except as hereafter provided. Should he be defeated, he loses his position and takes his place as last ranking member (unless there be an added member). The highest ranking partner then becomes captain.

30. All partners are bound by the action of the captain except in

*In a chouette too much discussion and contention slows up the game. The captain should ask for advice only when he is really in doubt as to the play, and partners should give advice only when they think the captain is overlooking a play entirely or when they want to suggest that he double.

the case of a double by the man in the box. In this case any player has the right to refuse or accept the double, irrespective of the action by the captain.

31. Should the captain decline to accept a double offered by the man in the box, he loses his position and forfeits to the man in the box his count previous to the proposed double.

32. When a double has been declined by the captain, any or all of the other members may accept it. The highest ranking of those accepting becomes captain until the termination of that game.

33. Accepting or declining a double does not change the rank of any member when the new captain loses; if the new captain wins, he takes the box.

34. Those players who refuse to accept the double are out of the game and may not consult from then on.

Postscripts to the Laws

Learn the Laws of Backgammon and follow them. Making your own laws leads to anarchy and can ruin an otherwise fine game. Still there are some modifications that you may want to play. We will start with something for chouettes.

Modification for Chouettes

In some chouettes the captain may arbitrarily insist on doubling a game even though his partners don't want to. According to the Laws the captain's decision holds, but most players prefer:

(a) When the captain insists on doubling and *a majority of his part-ners object,* they may demand that the captain pay them off at the current game stake. In this case the man in the box has the right to preempt and pay them off.

(b) When the captain insists on doubling and *half or less than half of his partners* object, the objectors may withdraw from the game entirely. In this case the man in the box has the right to demand that the captain take over their games.

This rule has one very salutary effect. It keeps the captain from making silly doubles and redoubles.

Modification Pertaining to Undoubled Games

This is sometimes called the Jacoby Rule because Oswald Jacoby was the first person to have suggested it. It provides that, unless a double has been made and accepted, either player can concede a single game at any time.

Sometimes a player gains an overwhelming advantage right at the start. He may decide to play on for gammon, rather than double and end the game immediately. This leads to a long, boring game.

The Jacoby Rule should not be played in tournaments, or matches, but it is fair to all players and makes regular backgammon more fun.

Optional Rerolls

Some people go double crazy. They like to see the cube at 32, 64, or even higher. In order to get there they allow several automatic doubles at the start of the game. Some of these come from optional doubles. You roll 2 and your opponent 1. You refuse this roll, turn the cube to 2, and roll two dice. If your reroll happens to be a doublet you turn the cube to 4 and play the doublet.

Now your opponent makes his first play. If he doesn't like his roll he turns the cube up a notch and rolls again. If he gets a doublet either time, that also moves the cube up.

Initial Double Dice

Double dice lead to even more automatic doubles. In this game each player rolls both dice initially. High man plays first (doublets count as plain total only; double 3 is just six).

If the high man does not like his roll he has the option of turning the cube and rolling again. The second player also may reroll if he wishes to do so.

A doublet turns the cube; if each player rolls the same total the cube is turned. If they roll identical rolls it results in two turns of the cube. Suppose each player starts by rolling double 4. This turns the cube right to 16. Two doubles for identical rolls and one double for each doublet.

When you play this type of game for any stakes at all you should put some limitations on the cube. One way is to determine an upper and a lower limit. The best ones are 4 and 8 (or 8 and 16). Then remember if you start all games at 4 or 8 you are playing for a stake which is, at the least, four times the agreed amount. A dollar a point becomes at least a four-dollar game.

As for playing without limitations, just refuse to. If you play for just a nickel a point and let the cube start at 1024 you are playing for over fifty dollars a point, which is a far cry from a nickel.

Technique of Double Dice Play

The only technique of double dice play is to remember you don't have to reroll. If you start with 3-1 or 6-1, take your roll. On the other hand, if your opponent starts with double 1, which puts the cube at 4, don't reroll to get it to 8. Take your beating at 4.

GLOSSARY

Around the corner. When you move a man from the opponent's side of the board to your own side you are said to be moving him around the corner.

Automatic doubles. A modification of the normal rules, automatically doubling the stakes at the beginning of a game if both players roll the same number in tossing for first play.

Back game. Defensive strategy employed by a player when his position is such that he sees no chance to win a running game.

Backgammon. If, when you bear off your last man and thus win the game, your opponent not only has not borne off a single man but has one or more men in your inner table or on the bar, you have won a backgammon, and the stake, if any, is tripled.

Back men. Men in your opponent's inner table. You start the game with two back men on your opponent's one point.

Bar. The strip in the middle of the board which separates the inner and outer tables, usually raised.

Bar point. Each player's seven point.

Bearing off. Removing your men from the board, in accordance with the Laws, after you have moved all fifteen of your men into your inner table.

Block. *See* Making a point.

Blocking game.   A defensive game where you try to impede your opponent's progress by placing blocks, or made points, in his way.

Blot.   An "exposed man," *i.e.* a single man on a point.

Board.   Either the entire backgammon table or one of its four parts—synonymous with "table."

Box.   The "man in the box" in a chouette. He plays against all other players in the game.

Break a prime.   *See* Prime.

Builder.   A blot which is in good position to help make a point or a third man on a point.

Captain.   In a chouette, the leader of those playing against the box.

Chouette.   A form of backgammon for more than two players.

Closed board.   When you have made all six points in your inner table you are said to have a closed board.

Cocked dice.   Dice which do not come to rest flat upon the board.

Combination shot.   *See* Indirect shot.

Come in or on.   To bring a man from the bar into your opponent's inner table. Also called "entering," "reentering," or "entering from the bar."

Contact.   Positions where all of one player's men have not yet passed all of the opponent's men; positions where theoretically it is still possible for one player to hit the other's blot.

Counters.   *See* Men.

Count the position.   *See* Pip count.

Cover a blot.   Move a second man to the point occupied by your blot and thus make that point.

Cube.   *See* Doubling cube.

Cup (or dice cup).   The cup in which the dice are shaken before being cast.

Dice, die.   Plural and singular for the cubes used in casting. They are normal dice with each of the six sides being marked with one to six dots, or pips.

Direct shot. A position where the blot is 6 or less points away from the opponent's threatening man; one where the blot can be hit if the proper number appears upon either die. *See* Indirect shot.

Double. To offer to increase the game stake by doubling it. If the opponent declines the double the game is over.

Double game. Same as a gammon.

Doubles or doublets. The same number is thrown on both dice. When you roll a doublet you must play that number four times.

Doubling cube. Sometimes merely called the cube. An over-sized die with the six faces marked with the numbers 2, 4, 8, 16, 32, and 64. It is used to keep track of the number of units for which the players are playing at any stage in the game. When a double is offered and accepted the cube is turned to the next higher number.

Early game. As the name implies, the first part of the game.

End game. The last stages of play. The tactics employed by the players toward the end of the game.

Enter. *See* Come in.

Exposed man. *See* Blot.

Gammon. If, when you bear off your last man and thus win the game, your opponent has not borne off a single man you have won a gammon and the stake, if any, is doubled.

Hit. Moving one of your own men to a point occupied by one of the opponent's blots. You are said to have hit that blot. The blot, after being hit, is picked up and placed upon the bar.

Home board. *See* Inner table.

Indirect shot. A position where the blot is 7 or more points away from the opponent's threatening man; one where it takes a combination of both numbers on the dice for the blot to be hit.

In the box. In chouette the box (or man in the box).

Inner table. The quarter of the board comprising the first six points. Men are entered or borne off this table. Same as inner board, home table, or home board.

Lead. The difference in the pip count of the two players.

Lover's leap. The move of one of your back men from the opponent's one point to the opponent's twelve point when you have thrown a 6-5.

Making a point. You are said to have made any point which you occupy with two or more of your men; your opponent's men cannot touch down or land on such a point.

Man in the box. *See* Box.

Men. The counters, discs, or checkers, which you move around the board during the course of play. A player has fifteen men of the same color. His opponent has fifteen men of a different color.

Off the board. When a blot is hit it is sent off the board.

Outer table. The quarter of the board comprising points seven to twelve. Same as outer board.

Pip. One of the spots on the dice.

Pip count. The number of pips needed to bear off all of your men (assuming no waste motion). Same as counting your position.

Point. Each of the twenty-four narrow triangles on the board, twelve on each player's side.

Point on a blot. To hit a blot at the same time that you make the point it had occupied.

Position. The location of your men and your opponent's men at any given time in the game.

Prime. Six consecutive made points anywhere on the board. Your opponent cannot move a man past your prime. When you remove all (or all but one) of your men from one of the points forming the prime you are said to break your prime.

Rail. Same as bar.

Redouble. Offering to double the game stake after a double has been previously made. It can only be offered by the player who accepted the last double. It can, of course, be refused or accepted. If refused the game is over.

Re-enter. *See* Come in.

Running game. The position in which all of each player's men have either passed or are nearly certain of passing all of his opponent's men.

Safe, or safety.   Moving a second man to a point occupied by your blot. Same as cover a blot.

Semi-back game.   A player who is behind holds his opponent's four or five point and tries to impede his progress while at the same time running with his other men.

Set up.   The original arrangement of the men on the board. See Diagram B-1 in Appendix B on the Laws.

Staying back.   Keeping some men in your opponent's inner table as part of a back game or a semi-back game.

Table.   Same as board. Usually used, however, in connection with the qualifying terms "inner" and "outer."

Taking off.   Same as bearing off.

Triple game.   Same as backgammon.

Quality Nonfiction for Every Interest—from PLUME Books

☐ **P. E. T. PARENT EFFECTIVENESS TRAINING: The Tested New Way to Raise Responsible Children by Dr. Thomas Gordon.** With a new Introduction by the author. The "no-lose" method for raising happier, more responsible, more cooperative children that has become "a national movement."—*The New York Times.* This book and its program have been endorsed by churches, schools, youth organizations, and other agencies serving parents and children.
(#Z5168—$5.95)

☐ **THE SAND ART BOOK: A Complete Course in Creating Sand Art by Suzie and Frank Green.** Written by two pioneering masters of sand art in America, this profusely illustrated book provides a complete home course that tells you everything you need to know to achieve a galaxy of your own gorgeous constructions in containers or planters.
(#Z5129—$4.95)

☐ **COUNTRY FURNITURE written and illustrated by Aldren A. Watson.** "A handsome, readable study of the early American woodcrafter and his work . . . valuable to a woodworker and entertaining for the most casual reader."—*The New York Times.* With over 300 beautiful pencil sketches.
(#Z5130—$4.95)

☐ **MAGIC: The Great Illusions Revealed and Explained by David H. Charney.** For everyone who has ever been held spellbound by an illusionist, and for anyone who wishes to be one, here is the book that will explain at last how the most astounding triumphs in the art of illusion are accomplished. With over 100 vintage illustrations. (#Z5131—$3.95)

☐ **HOW TO BE YOUR OWN BOSS: The Complete Handbook for Starting and Running a Small Business edited by Walter Szykitka.** Here is the most comprehensive and practical book available on the subject—and the first step to take in realizing your dream. Included here is every ingredient the small-time businessman needs to know to make it in today's market. (#Z5172—$4.95)

In Canada, please add $1.00 to the price of each book.

To order these titles, please use coupon on page 179.

More Quality Paperbacks from PLUME

☐ **MOVIE MAGIC: The Story of Special Effects in the Cinema by John Brosnan.** From the earliest days of the silents to the spectacular disaster movies of today, the role of the special effects men has been one of the most important yet least publicized aspects of moviemaking. Enhanced by diagrams, photos, and memory-stirring movie stills, this rich, nostalgic book traces the development through cinema history of this very special artistry. (#Z5123—$3.95)*

☐ **MOMMA: The Sourcebook for Single Mothers edited by Karol Hope and Nancy Young.** Here are the actual voices of the mothers of MOMMA—a nonprofit organization dedicated to improving the single-mother experience. Included are probing interviews with and statements from single mothers all over the country, and helpful, practical information crucial to the survival of the single mother. (#Z5121—$3.95)

☐ **THE SUPERMARKET HANDBOOK: Access to Whole Foods by Nikki and David Goldbeck.** This book will prove invaluable to any shopper concerned with the quality and nutritive value of the foods available in today's supermarkets. "An enormously useful and heartening work!"—*The New York Times* (#Z5151—$4.95)

☐ **EVERYMAN'S DICTIONARY OF MUSIC by Eric Blom. Revised by Sir Jack Westrup, Professor of Music, University of Oxford.** Here, arranged for easy reference, is the entire spectrum of musical knowledge—everything that anyone would want to know about the music he hears, plays, or loves, whether it comes from the most distant past or the constantly evolving musical present. (#Z5193—$5.95)*

☐ **THE APARTMENT GARDENER by Stan and Floss Dworkin.** Easy-to-follow instructions for raising plants. Everything you need to know about potting, feeding, pruning and how to go about analyzing the first symptoms of disease—everything you'll need to know about apartment plants from America's well-known hosts of radio and television. (#Z5203—$4.95)

*Not available in Canada.
In Canada, please add $1.00 to the price of each book.

To order these titles, please use coupon on page 179.

The Best Fiction from PLUME Books

☐ **THE THIRD POLICEMAN by Flann O'Brien.**
(#Z5134—$3.95)*

☐ **THE GRASS IS SINGING by Doris Lessing.**
(#Z5119—$2.95)*

☐ **THE HABIT OF LOVING by Doris Lessing.**
(#Z5120—$2.95)*

☐ **LANDLOCKED by Doris Lessing.** (#Z5138—$3.95)*

☐ **MARTHA QUEST by Doris Lessing.** (#Z5095—$3.95)*

☐ **A RIPPLE FROM THE STORM by Doris Lessing.**
(#Z5137—$3.95)*

☐ **A PROPER MARRIAGE by Doris Lessing.** (#Z5093—$3.95)*

☐ **THE FOUR-GATED CITY by Doris Lessing.**
(#Z5135—$5.95)*

☐ **THE LITTLE DISTURBANCES OF MAN by Grace Paley.**
(#Z5073—$2.95)

☐ **THE DANGLING MAN by Saul Bellow.** (#Z5090—$2.95)

☐ **THE VICTIM by Saul Bellow.** (#Z5154—$3.95)

☐ **THE ECSTASY OF OWEN MUIR by Ring Lardner, Jr.**
(#Z5067—$1.95)

☐ **THE UNIVERSAL BASEBALL ASSOCIATION, INC., J. HENRY WAUGH, PROP. by Robert Coover.** (#Z5127—$3.95)

☐ **PRICKSONGS AND DESCANTS by Robert Coover.**
(#Z5208—$3.95)

☐ **A HERO ON A DONKEY by Miodrag Bulatovic.**
(#Z5025—$2.75)*

☐ **GOING PLACES by Leonard Michaels.** (#Z5074—$2.95)

☐ **AUGUST IS A WICKED MONTH by Edna O'Brien**
(#Z5100—$2.95)*

* Not available in Canada
In Canada, please add $1.00 to the price of each book.
To order these titles, please use coupon on page 179.

The MERIDIAN Quality Paperback Collection

Ø

Game Books from SIGNET

Having *your* Baby

Having *your* Baby

Gill Thorn

FISHER
BOOKS™

For my husband, Dennis

Commissioning Editor: Sian Facer

Art Director: Jacqui Small

Executive Art Editor: Keith Martin

Designers: Emma Jones
and Nina Pickup

Editors: Mary Lambert
and Jane McIntosh

North American Editors: Margaret Martin
and Sarah Trotta

Managing Editor: Sarah Trotta

Special Photography: Daniel Pangbourne

Jacket Photography: Sandra Lousada

Stylist: Sheila Birkenshaw

Hair and Makeup: Leslie Sayles

Illustrations: Melanie Northover

Picture Research: Wendy Gay

Production Controller: Victoria Merrington

Cover Design: FifthStreet*design*

Library of Congress Cataloging-in-Publication Data

Thorn, Gill.
  Having your baby : the complete illustrated guide / Gill Thorn.
    p. cm.
  Includes bibliographical references and index.
  ISBN 1-55561-133-8
  1. Pregnancy. 2. Childbirth. I. Title.
RG525.T54 1997
618.2--DC21   97-3675
                                       CIP

Published by:
Fisher Books
4239 W. Ina Road, Suite 101
Tucson, AZ 85741
(520) 744-6110

ISBN 1-66651-133-8

The moral right of the author has been asserted.

First published in Great Britain in 1995 under the title of *Pregnancy & Birth* by Hamlyn, an imprint of Reed Consumer Books, part of Reed International Books Limited, Michelin House, 81 Fulham Road, London SW3 6RB and Auckland, Melbourne, Singapore and Toronto

Produced by Mandarin Offset
Printed in Hong Kong
Printing 5 4 3 2 1

Notice: The information in this book is true and complete to the best of our knowledge. This book is intended only as an informative guide for those wishing to know more about pregnancy. In no way is this book intended to replace, countermand or conflict with the advice given to you by your own physician. The ultimate decision concerning care should be made between you and your doctor. We strongly recommend you follow his or her advice. The information in this book is general and is offered with no guarantees on the part of the author or Fisher Books. The author and publisher disclaim all liability in connection with the use of this book.

Contents

Introduction   7

Chapter 1. Planning Pregnancy   9

Chapter 2. Conception   21

Chapter 3. Early Pregnancy   35

Chapter 4. Prenatal Care   49

Chapter 5. Mid-Pregnancy   65

Chapter 6. Plans and Choices   83

Chapter 7. Late Pregnancy   95

Chapter 8. Preparing for the Birth   109

Chapter 9. Labor and Birth   127

Chapter 10. Help during and after the Birth   145

Chapter 11. Special Situations   159

Chapter 12. The Early Days   173

Chapter 13. Getting Back to Normal   187

Appendix   202

Index   204

Acknowledgements   208

Introduction

Babies bring joy to their families and also to the wider community. It's exciting to be expecting a baby and there are many things to think about and learn. This book tells you what you want to know about pregnancy, birth and the early weeks with your new baby. It can help you enjoy this special time in your life by offering up-to-date information, reassurance and practical tips from other parents.

Most parents these days want to think about the options and share the decisions that affect them. This includes the type of prenatal care they receive and where their baby is born. And whether labor is allowed to progress naturally or is actively managed using the latest technology. The book offers a comprehensive guide to the options available and can help you to make intelligent choices among them. Everyone's experience is different, so it doesn't tell you what you ought to do. The decisions are up to you.

I have learned how varied the individual experience of having a baby can be from thousands of parents who have shared their joys, hopes and fears with me in more than 20 years of teaching. I'd like to acknowledge my debt to them, and to the friends who read the manuscript and made helpful comments: Sue Copello and Val Gardner, psychologist and doctor respectively and both new mothers; Helen Gill, editor of *Practical Parenting*, whose sound judgment I have valued from my first contribution to the magazine soon after its launch; and my daughters, Joanna and Annabel Thorn, who prevented me from taking anything for granted! I also want to thank Margaret Martin for her careful editing of this North American edition.

G. C. T.

1

Planning Pregnancy

❝Parenthood is a privilege, not a right. Thinking about why I wanted a child—the responsibilities as well as the joys—made me feel confident and ready to commit myself: I plan to enjoy pregnancy and give my baby a good start in life. ❞

WHY PLAN YOUR PREGNANCY?

It may seem strange to plan something as natural as having a baby, but thinking ahead can help you start pregnancy in good health and a positive frame of mind. It can enhance your chances of conceiving, reduce the likelihood of problems during pregnancy and spare you a certain amount of worry. Pregnancy today has actually never been safer but it can be an anxious time, not the least because of all the information available and the tests to make sure you and the baby are all right. Thinking carefully about it in advance helps you put everything in perspective.

Sharing the preparations for a new and exciting phase of your lives can bring you and your partner closer together. There are ups and downs and anxieties with any aspect of life. While advance planning for pregnancy cannot get rid of them all, it can make your journey smoother and help you get the most out of a very special experience.

How you may feel about parenthood

For most women, deciding to have a baby is exciting and brings a new sense of purpose to life. You can re-enter the world of childhood in a new role, think about the little garments and nursery items to buy, and remember forgotten childhood pleasures. There is the challenge of rearing a child your way, using some of your parents' tried-and-tested methods and reinventing others. You may suddenly feel closer to friends and relatives with children and look forward to continuing family traditions and forming new ones.

You will probably also experience some less positive feelings. You may worry about giving up your freedom, losing out in your career, becoming dependent on your partner or just facing the responsibilities of parenthood. If you have had a miscarriage, you may fear that it will happen again. You may worry about the physical demands of pregnancy, any illness that might affect your baby, or having a child with a disability. You may be concerned about being a good mother, coping with day-to-day childcare and about how much your partner will really help you.

Any major change in life involves losses as well as gains, and a few mixed feelings will stop you from viewing motherhood through rose-colored glasses. You will have to work through some of your doubts, but others will disappear once you are pregnant.

Your partner's feelings

Many men take great delight in young children, are proud to think of becoming a father and are enthusiastic and eager to share the preparations. Others are pleased but reserved about it. Like you, your partner will have moments of doubt. He may worry about being a good father, about taking on the financial responsibility for you and the baby and about your safety during pregnancy and birth. He may also be concerned about changes in your social life, your sex life and your relationship with each other.

Worries about the future can outweigh optimism when it comes to fatherhood. If your partner's reactions are lukewarm, try to find out why. He may have unhappy memories of his own childhood, be afraid of the changes a baby will bring, or not feel ready for the responsibilities of parenthood. Some men may feel concerned because they have no interest in babies, although they like older children. Others simply may not appreciate children at all.

"The hardest thing about having a baby was taking the plunge. We kept putting it off, first until I'd had a promotion, then until the house was straight or we'd had a vacation. There was always a good reason, but really I think we were scared of making the commitment. It seemed like such a grown-up step to take." DEANA

All relationships are different. You may be happy to accept most of the parenting responsibility yourself. Only you can decide if you would resent this as time goes on. On the other hand, some men who insist that they do not want children change their minds as soon as a baby arrives!

PREPARING FOR PREGNANCY

It's never too late to improve your state of health, but if you and your partner have the chance to do so before you become pregnant, take it! Healthy parents tend to have healthy babies and fit mothers tend to experience fewer problems during pregnancy and birth.

A child will be dependent on you for many years, even if you return to work, so your life will and should change; pregnancy starts the process of adaptation. It can be frustrating to find that your body slows down and you can't concentrate on much beyond your own and the baby's needs as pregnancy advances. But the less-rushed, new rhythm is more suited to the needs of a baby. Many women are glad to have a reason to find a slower but more satisfying pace of life. Most preparation for pregnancy is simply common sense and ideally should involve both partners. For example:

- Look at ways of reducing the stress in your life. Reduce unnecessary work commitments. Reorganize your social life.
- Go to your healthcare provider for a checkup so you start pregnancy with a clean bill of health. Your provider can prescribe folic-acid supplements and may recommend you take them for at least a month before becoming pregnant.
- Look at the balance between work and play, activity and relaxation, your own needs and those of others in your life. If one aspect dominates another, try to modify it.
- Concentrate on exercising more and improving your diet.
- Change habits you know are bad for you. Quit smoking and stop drinking alcohol.

Getting healthy

The special needs of pregnancy often become obvious to women too late, when they realize how much harder everything is if they are not healthy! If you increase your flexibility, strength and stamina before becoming pregnant you'll be able to carry a baby more easily, reduce the risk of backache and other discomforts, and find you get less tired. It's not wise to start a rigorous exercise program during pregnancy. Treat with caution any activity you are not used to doing. Swimming and brisk walking are safe for most women, but ask your doctor for advice.

Women have been discouraged from taking part in activities such as skiing and horseback riding during pregnancy, but there is little evidence for a complete ban. It depends on individual circumstances. If your pregnancy is normal and you are fit and skilled at an activity you'll probably find you can continue it in a modified form. Always consult your doctor first. Marathon runner Ingrid Kristiansen competed at the international level when she was seven months pregnant, but most women are content with more modest goals!

Eating healthfully

Good nutrition is the foundation for good health. It protects the body against infection by building a strong immune system and helps rid the system of toxins. It improves the feeling of well-being and increases the chances of conceiving and having a successful pregnancy.

Research suggests that drinking more than three cups of coffee (or the equivalent) per day can delay the chance of conception. Caffeine is addictive and you may want to cut down for other reasons, such as its interference with sleep patterns and the fact that it is a diuretic.

It may seem incredible that your body can provide everything needed to grow a healthy baby using the simplest essentials: water, oxygen and good food. Try to eat some foods like these every day to help insure that you and your baby get the best nourishment possible.

WHOLESOME FOODS

- *Take salad items such as carrot and celery sticks to work in a plastic container, to eat with a whole-wheat roll.*
- *Choose fruit or lowfat yogurt for dessert. Eat snacks of sunflower seeds, dried apricots or raisins instead of potato chips and cookies.*
- *To make the transition from white rice or flour to brown easier, mix them in equal quantities at first.*
- *Vegetables from large supermarket chains are usually very fresh. Stir-fry or steam them to retain vitamins and minerals.*
- *Buy a natural-foods cookbook and try out a new recipe every week.*
- *See page 40 for foods to avoid when you're pregnant.*

A wholesome diet should include fresh vegetables and fruit, unrefined carbohydrates such as whole-wheat bread and brown rice, and protein such as meat, fish, milk, eggs, nuts and legumes. While these foods should provide all the vitamins, minerals and other nutrients you need, it is important to take prenatal vitamins. If your diet consists mainly of processed or fat-laden foods, try to improve it for your own and your baby's sake.

Stopping contraception

If you are taking the Pill or using an intrauterine device (IUD) consider using another form of contraception for about three months before attempting to get pregnant. This will allow your body to return to normal, because both forms of contraception can alter the body's balance of nutrients such as zinc, copper and certain vitamins. Good nutrition, plus a short break from the Pill or an IUD, will help put you in a healthy condition for pregnancy. Allowing your periods time to settle down to a regular pattern also makes dating your pregnancy much more accurate.

RISKS IN PREGNANCY

Being pregnant today may appear to be risky because bad news always gets more attention than good news. However, the risks are actually less than they used to be because women in general are better nourished, better housed, have fewer children and are able to plan when to have them more easily. These factors are very important in making pregnancy safer than it was for previous generations.

If you make yourself aware of the avoidable risks and take steps to reduce them, you can put the others in proportion and relax, knowing that you have done your best.

Older motherhood

Physically, the best time to have a baby is in your early 20s. However, many of the risk factors associated with giving birth when you're older could affect any woman, whatever her age; being overweight, having had several babies or suffered infertility problems. These factors just happen to be more common in older women.

The risk of chromosomal abnormalities does increase with age (see page 55) but most problems, including heart defects, spina bifida, cleft palate and club foot are no more common in older mothers. Some problems, for example, congenital dislocation of the hip (clicky hips), are actually less common. Keep an eye on your weight and exercise regularly to improve your fitness before becoming pregnant. There is sound evidence that older women who are fit and of average weight for their height (see chart) suffer fewer problems in pregnancy and birth. They also cope just as well physically as younger women.

If you're over 35 and smoke, you are five times as likely to have a baby who suffers poor growth (see page 103) and who could have problems in early life. The risk of minor malformations in the baby is significantly increased. So it is even more important for older women to stop smoking (see page 41).

In general, the older you are, the better you know yourself and the more motivated you may be to help yourself by planning ahead. You may also be more financially secure and able to get the most out of the emotional and spiritual side of pregnancy.

The right weight for your height

If you eat a balanced diet, are physically active and have plenty of energy most of the time, your weight is probably about right for you. For a more precise guide, look at the chart on the next page and convert your height into meters and your weight into kilograms. Now divide your weight by your height squared.

For example, if you weigh 151 pounds (68.5kg) and are 5ft. 7in. (1.7m) tall:

$$\frac{\text{wt in kg}}{(\text{ht in m}) \times (\text{ht in m})} \quad = \quad \frac{68.5}{1.7 \times 1.7} \quad = \quad 23.7$$

A score of around 20 to 25 is the best range for pregnancy, although a little more is fine. If you are generally healthy and fall within this range you will not benefit from gaining or losing weight, so concentrate on the quality of the food you eat.

Underweight women can be perfectly healthy but may find it harder to conceive. If you score under 20, you may want to eat more, or more often, to gain some weight. If you score over 30 you are at greater risk of problems such as gestational diabetes (see page 53) during pregnancy, so you might want to lose a few pounds before trying to become pregnant. Talk to your healthcare provider if you are concerned.

Weight conversion chart: 1lb = 0.454kg

lb.	kg	lb.	kg	lb.	kg
98	44.5	126	57.2	154	69.9
99	44.9	127	57.6	155	70.3
100	45.4	128	58.1	156	70.8
101	45.8	129	58.5	157	71.2
102	46.3	130	59.0	158	71.7
103	46.7	131	59.4	159	72.1
104	47.2	132	59.9	160	72.6
105	47.6	133	60.3	161	73.0
106	48.1	134	60.8	162	73.5
107	48.5	135	61.2	163	73.9
108	49.0	136	61.7	164	74.4
109	49.4	137	62.1	165	74.8
110	49.9	138	62.6	166	75.3
111	50.4	139	63.1	167	75.8
112	50.8	140	63.5	168	76.2
113	51.3	141	64.0	169	76.7
114	51.7	142	64.4	170	77.1
115	52.2	143	64.9	171	77.6
116	52.6	144	65.3	172	78.1
117	53.1	145	65.8	173	78.5
118	53.5	146	66.2	174	79.0
119	54.0	147	66.7	175	79.5
120	54.4	148	67.1		
121	54.9	149	67.6	182	82.6
122	55.3	150	68.0		
123	55.8	151	68.5	189	85.8
124	56.3	152	69.0		
125	56.7	153	69.4	194	89.0

Height conversion chart: ft/in to meters   1in = 2.54cm   1ft = 0.305m

ft	in	m	ft	in	m	ft	in	m
4	8	1.42	5	2	1.57	5	8	1.72
	9	1.45		3	1.60		9	1.75
	10	1.47		4	1.62		10	1.77
	11	1.50		5	1.65		11	1.80
5	0	1.52		6	1.67	6	0	1.83
	1	1.55		7	1.70		1	1.86

" *It's a good idea to plan your pregnancy if you can. I gave up smoking before I was expecting my son, and cut out chips and burgers for salads and greens.*

There are risks in everything, even crossing the street, and you have to get them into perspective. Of course I worried when I was pregnant. It's part of caring for the baby. Basically I just follow sensible advice and use common sense. If you become paranoid you spoil that lovely special feeling you get when you're expecting a baby. **"** JANICE

Smoking

Smoking is one of the main culprits in a range of pregnancy problems from miscarriage to pre-term delivery. The major cause of infant illness and death is being born too small (see page 103). About one-third of low-birth-weight babies are like this because their mothers smoked during pregnancy. The risks continue as the child grows up; babies of mothers who smoked during pregnancy are less healthy, more likely to be hyperactive and more at risk from sudden infant death syndrome (SIDS).

If you continue to smoke during pregnancy you'll either choose to believe that your baby will escape harm, or you'll suffer agonizing guilt and self-reproach. It's best to tackle the problem before you conceive. There are some ideas to help you stop smoking in Chapter 3.

Passive smoking also affects the developing baby, so ask your partner to give up smoking, or to smoke outside or in another room. Try to avoid smokers in your workplace if you possibly can.

Alcohol

Considerable research shows that drinking alcohol can be harmful to your unborn child. Your baby is at greatest risk from heavy or binge drinking. No one can say what is "safe" for an individual, so doctors advise women not to drink at all when pregnant. If you're at all worried about your current drinking habits, call the National Center for Nutrition and Dietetics' Consumer-Nutrition Hotline, toll-free, at 1-800-366-1655, to speak directly with a nutritionist. The American College of Obstetricians and Gynecologists (see Appendix) can also provide you with accurate information about alcohol and pregnancy.

Drugs

All illegal and addictive drugs potentially cause harm to the developing baby. We know as little about the use of marijuana and cocaine in pregnancy as was known about cigarette smoking 20 years ago, so more problems will probably be discovered. Cocaine crosses the placenta and may damage it, leading to poor fetal growth (see page 103) and some serious complications of pregnancy, including stillbirth. Long-term effects on the baby include irritability, excessive crying and abnormal brain-wave patterns. Marijuana can interfere with conception and has been linked with severe pregnancy sickness and complications such as abnormally long or rapid labors. It affects placental efficiency and can lead to low-birth-weight babies.

Medicines

Most women know not to take any pills or medicines, such as multivitamins, common cold remedies and painkillers including aspirin, without advice from a doctor or pharmacist during pregnancy. Some prescription drugs have withstood the test of time and are perfectly safe. Others, including common drugs such as tranquilizers, may carry risks to the baby. In certain cases, the risk may be outweighed by the benefits of taking the drug.

If you need to take regular medication, before attempting to become pregnant, check with your doctor, who will have access to the latest information. There may be other forms of treatment or lower-risk medication you could try. You could discuss taking smaller doses for a shorter time or using an alternative therapy, if appropriate. Your doctor will probably prescribe prenatal vitamins.

MEDICAL AND PHYSICAL CONDITIONS

If you suffer from a condition such as chronic backache or have a pre-existing infection, it makes sense to have it treated before you conceive. Once you are pregnant it may be harder to clear up, either because of the effects of hormones or because the appropriate medication is unsafe in pregnancy.

It's useful to find out about how pregnancy could affect any chronic medical condition you may have. Knowing what to expect can be reassuring and it's easier to look after yourself well. For example, people with asthma whose condition is well controlled usually have normal pregnancies. About two-thirds find their condition stays the same or improves, although the most severe sufferers may find that it worsens, especially after the fourth month. Diabetics who keep the disease under control have as good a chance as anyone else of having an uncomplicated pregnancy these days, provided they always follow medical advice.

Women with a physical disability often feel isolated when they are pregnant. Access to buildings, facilities and information can be restricted. Some disabled women have said that they were not allowed to make any decisions about their pregnancy and decisions were made for them, or they had the impression they were an interesting medical condition rather than a person! You will probably have to find information for yourself (see Appendix) but planning can minimize problems and enable you to enjoy pregnancy as much as anyone else.

Genetic problems

Most people probably have a few less-than-perfect genes without knowing it. For the majority of serious genetic conditions, a baby has to inherit a faulty gene from each parent before being affected.

Be sure to get advice if you know you're in a higher-risk group for a particular defect. This includes regional or ethnic groups in which a condition is more prevalent, such as people of Eastern European Jewish origin for Tay-Sach's disease, and couples where one partner suffers from a congenital problem. Couples who know about an inherited disorder in either family, or who are closely related, should also get genetic counseling.

There are about 5,000 rare single-gene defects known at present, so testing everyone randomly for them would be like looking for a needle in a haystack. Where a defect is known or suspected, a genetic counselor can give you the odds of your child being affected, help you decide whether to take the risk, and tell you if there is a test that could find out if a baby is affected.

QUESTIONS AND ANSWERS

Q: We have a small farm and keep a few sheep, goats and chickens as well as having a sheepdog and two cats as pets. Are there any risks from looking after the animals during my pregnancy?

A: The main risk from household pets is *toxoplasmosis*, an infection that can damage the fetus in the early weeks of pregnancy or be passed directly to the baby in the later months, although only about one in 10,000 babies is born with it. If your pets have an active infection they could pass it to you; or you could acquire it by drinking unpasteurized milk. On the other hand, you may already be immune to the disease.

Ask your doctor to test for antibodies before you become pregnant. If you are immune, this will give you peace of mind; if not, you could be tested again if you develop a slight fever and swollen glands followed by a rash. Any toxoplasmosis antibodies discovered would be the result of a recent infection.

You should be careful about hygiene when caring for farm animals. In particular, an infection that causes sheep to miscarry (*Chlamydia psittaci*) poses a similar threat to women. When you are pregnant, ask someone else to milk your ewes and help with lambing. Call your healthcare provider if you experience flulike symptoms after you have been in contact with sheep.

Q: My lifestyle is busy and my work involves a great deal of traveling. I don't always eat very well. Should I take vitamin and mineral supplements before becoming pregnant?

A: Talk with your doctor before taking pills of any sort. As you are aware, a poor diet may not supply all the nutrients you need, so you could start pregnancy with a deficit. Your doctor will probably prescribe prenatal vitamins, which include vitamins and minerals in the amounts recommended for pregnancy. They also contain extra iron and folate (for folic acid). It is important to take these prenatal vitamins regularly throughout your pregnancy. If you are anemic, your doctor may prescribe additional iron tablets.

Nutrients ought to come from a healthful diet because that's how the body uses them most effectively. A poor diet plus a vitamin and mineral supplement or a special drink fortified with vitamins does not equal a good diet!

Even the best pill cannot supply nutrients that haven't been isolated in food yet—and there may be many of these. It's better to improve your eating habits before conceiving.

Q: I work in a nursery where we have a child who was damaged by rubella. Is there any way I can find out if I'm immune to this illness, and if not, can I be immunized before pregnancy?

A: About 85% of women are immune to rubella (German measles), having already had it or been vaccinated against it. It's no longer a common disease in the community, so even if you have no immunity you are unlikely to contract it.

For peace of mind, your blood could be tested for antibodies before conception. Or, your healthcare provider may suggest vaccinating you just in case and advise you to delay pregnancy for three months afterwards as a precaution. Even if you were vaccinated and later discovered that you were pregnant, your baby will probably be fine. Damage caused by the live virus has not been reported after vaccination.

Q: I am 38, single and would dearly love to have a baby. A close friend has offered to be the father provided he has no further contact with the child. As time is running out I can see the advantages to this, but what are the pitfalls?

A: Your friend might find it hard to relinquish responsibility for his child. Although a man who donates sperm to a licensed clinic may remain anonymous, private arrangements do not. At the very least you could be under considerable pressure to name your friend. A schoolteacher in Indiana was recently ordered to pay a large sum towards his child's support even though the mother had signed a contract saying she would never make any claims. Our legal systems protect a child's right to support from both parents until he or she becomes an adult.

How would you react if the baby inherited a defect, or if your friend had second thoughts and came back to claim his parental rights, for instance? Further, your child would one day want to know about, and possibly search for, his father.

The issues are very complex and personal and you need to think them through carefully. Before proceeding, it would be wise to seek the advice of an attorney who specializes in issues of family law.

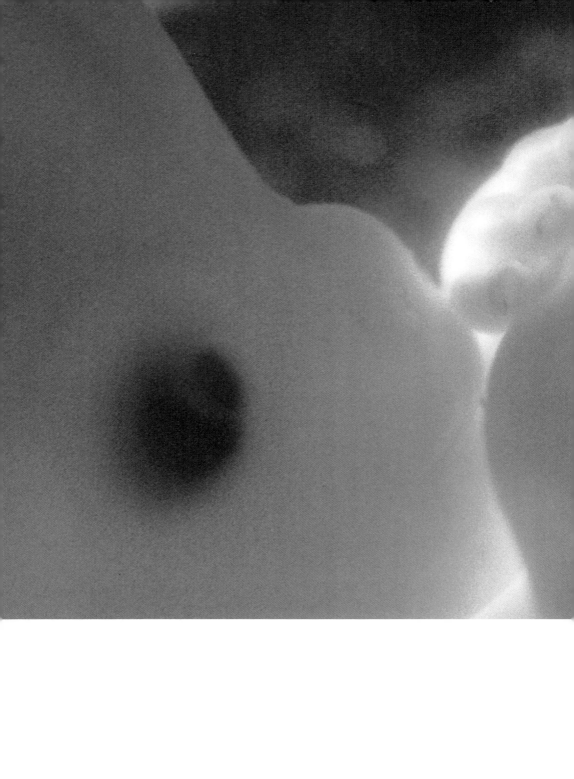

2

Conception

"I couldn't make up my mind about having a baby for ages, but when it happened I was really pleased! Becoming pregnant is the best thing I've ever done and I can't stop smiling."

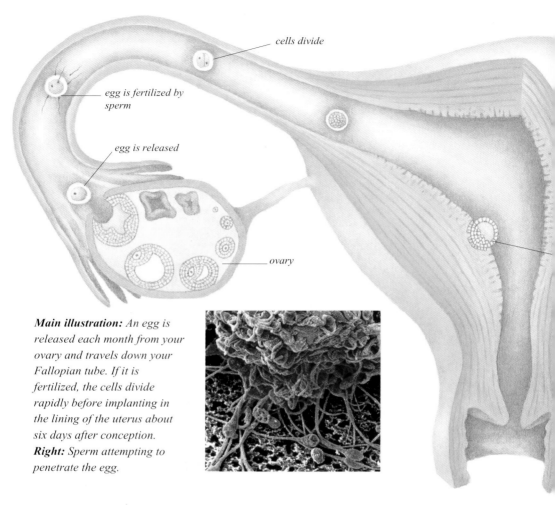

cells divide

egg is fertilized by
sperm

egg is released

ovary

Main illustration: An egg is
released each month from your
ovary and travels down your
Fallopian tube. If it is
fertilized, the cells divide
rapidly before implanting in
the lining of the uterus about
six days after conception.
Right: Sperm attempting to
penetrate the egg.

HOW CONCEPTION OCCURS

About halfway through each menstrual cycle an egg is released from your
ovary and drawn into the opening of your Fallopian tube. There are about
400-million sperm in each male ejaculation and they can survive for up to
five days in your body. Unless the egg is fertilized within about 24 hours, your
body reabsorbs it. You are fertile for about six days each month.

During this period the mucus in your cervix changes to a fern-like structure
through which the sperm can swim toward the egg. Many sperm take a wrong
turn or get lost in the folds of the Fallopian tube, but even so, thousands
reach and surround the egg. When one of them penetrates its outer coating,
the membrane changes instantly to prevent others from following.

The victorious sperm burrows inward until its nucleus fuses with the nucleus
of the egg. Fertilization results in a single cell, smaller than the period following this sentence. From this tiny, dynamic beginning a new life is formed.

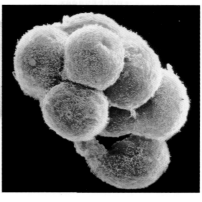

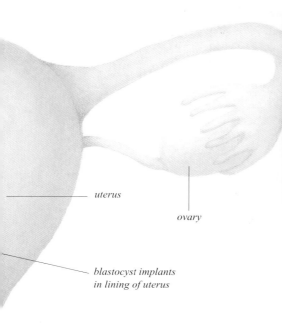

uterus

ovary

blastocyst implants
in lining of uterus

Above: *The fertilized egg divides to form a blackberry-like cluster of cells called a* morula. *The inner cells of the morula will form the embryo and the outer cells will become the placenta and amniotic sac.*

Twins

If two eggs are released and fertilized by separate sperm, the result is non-identical (fraternal) twins. If a fertilized egg splits to form two embryos, you get identical twins who will always be the same sex.

Non-identical twins (or triplets) have separate placentas and can be different sexes, like brothers and sisters who happen to share the same uterus. They are more common in families with a history of non-identical twins, women over 35 and people of African origin. The increase in multiple births, which has increased from about 1% to almost 2% over a generation, is largely due to the use of fertility drugs.

Identical twins share a placenta and have the same genes, because they come from the same egg and sperm. About a third of sets of twins are identical and they are spread equally throughout the population.

Genes and chromosomes

Most living cells contain *deoxyribonucleic acid*, better known as DNA, a substance that includes the chemical formula to make the cell individual. It resembles two strands that spiral around each other. This famous double helix is packed into each of the thousands of genes that in turn are threaded like beads into the 23 pairs of chromosomes that form the nucleus of a human cell.

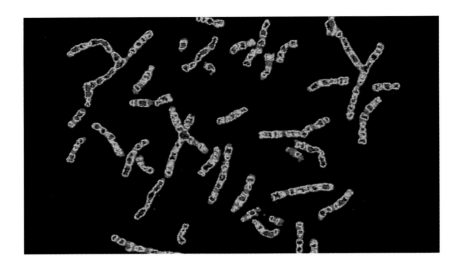

Your egg and your partner's sperm each contribute 23 chromosomes to your baby. Most chromosomes look *Chromosomes are composed of the genetic material DNA.*

like a little "x" under the microscope, but the chromosome that determines gender in the sperm can be an "x" or a "y". Fertilization by an "x" sperm results in a girl, while a "y" sperm results in a boy.

DNA, genes and chromosomes are the master plan for your baby's individual characteristics, determining everything from his temperament to the color of his eyes. Half of the thousands of bits of information come from your partner's side of the family and half from yours. Environment and life experiences will alter certain aspects of your child's physiology or personality, but her essential being is determined at the moment of conception.

CHANGES IN YOUR BODY

During pregnancy your blood supply increases, your heart works harder, your lungs expand to provide more oxygen and up to 12 pints (7 liters) of extra fluid circulates around your body.

Hormones are released to stop your periods, although your cycle can also be temporarily upset by other things such as medication, sudden weight changes, fear of pregnancy, stress, travel or exhaustion.

"It was kind of a shock, getting pregnant so soon. I came off the Pill and never had a period. The first I knew about it was that my breasts felt firmer, and blue veins showed up on them. Then I started to fall asleep as soon as I got home from work." MARILYN

Pregnancy hormones enable you to carry on with daily life while your baby grows and your body changes, but they also produce mood swings and some of the less welcome symptoms of early pregnancy. For example, estrogen and progesterone relax the smooth muscles of your internal organs so your body can adapt as your uterus grows. They also contribute to heartburn, constipation and varicose veins. Relaxin helps make your ligaments flexible in preparation for the birth, but this increases the likelihood of over-straining yourself by lifting or poor posture. However, many of the discomforts caused by pregnancy hormones can be avoided (see page 72).

"Every time we saw my husband's family, someone asked me when we were going to have a son. When I found out I was pregnant, all I could think about at first was I'd let them down if the baby was a girl. I was so worried about it that I made myself sick.

My husband said to ignore them, because it was our baby and we would welcome either a girl or a boy. He told his family that we wanted a daughter and he made me realize that you can't live to please other people all the time. I'm enjoying my pregnancy now, but I've discovered a strange craving for pickle with everything!" SHEENA

HOW YOU MAY FEEL

When you first suspect you are pregnant, you may be delirious with excitement. If you have been actively trying to conceive, your success will be a cause for great celebration and will help you handle any minor discomforts without being concerned.

However, many women feel neutral or negative about pregnancy at first. Even if it was half-expected or planned, discovering that it has actually happened may be a shock. Some women take a while to realize how much they really want the baby.

If pregnancy is unwelcome, you may feel guilty, anxious about telling your partner or your family, or not sure about what to do. You may not want to think about pregnancy, and this is not a bad instinct for a week or two. Once the turmoil settles down you will be able to think more clearly. Many children in loving families were conceived at the wrong time or in the wrong circumstances. Far from being the disaster they seemed at first, unwelcome pregnancies often turn into much-loved babies.

RELATIONSHIP WITH YOUR PARTNER

Some men are fascinated by the development of a baby and the progress of pregnancy. Others regard the whole process in the way that women often feel about cars: as long as it keeps going they don't want to know what goes on under the hood. Although it can be disappointing if your partner feels like this, it's no more a reflection on his ability to be a good father than tuning a car proves you are a good driver!

Changes usually have more impact on those who are experiencing them than on spectators. However interested your partner may be, he can experience pregnancy only through you. Even if he is less than enthusiastic about the personal details of having a baby, he will probably want to share decisions about prenatal care, tests and the place where your baby will be born.

Along with the joy of expecting a baby, every expectant mother has moments when she wonders what she has let herself in for. Ideally your flashes of worry will coincide with your partner's moments of confidence and you'll help each other through them. But life isn't always like this! You may hit doubts together, and feel as though you are rowing a boat in opposite directions. It's scary to feel that your relationship is under strain when you need it to be strongest, but many people take time to adjust to a new future, however welcome the change.

PREGNANCY TESTS

Your doctor or family planning clinic can provide a pregnancy test, although some charge for this. You can also buy a home test. Laboratory tests are slightly more accurate, but home tests have the advantage of speed and privacy.

Pregnancy tests differ slightly, but they work by detecting the presence of HCG (human chorionic gonadotrophin), a hormone that is secreted into your blood and passed in urine a few days after conception. If you take the test as soon as your period is overdue, a positive result is likely to be accurate. A false negative could occur because insufficient HCG is being secreted, so some kits include a second test to confirm a negative result a few days later. If your test is positive, or you still "feel" pregnant after two negative results, visit your healthcare provider.

Announcing the news

Finding out that you are pregnant can be one of the most exciting moments of your life, comparable only to holding your baby in your arms for the first time. Like any highly charged emotional event, it makes you see the world in a different light. Although it can be tempting to shout the news of your pregnancy from the rooftops, many women wait until after the first 12 weeks, when there is less likelihood of miscarriage, before telling the world. Others delay announcing the news until tests for fetal abnormalities (see page 55) are completed, and some decide not to tell their employer or friends at work, at least for a while.

"I was hysterically excited when my test was positive. We went out to dinner to celebrate, and I drank orange juice virtuously all evening while my partner drank enough wine for both of us and told complete strangers he was going to be a dad!

We'd been trying to conceive for so long that we decided not to tell anyone else except our parents, but somehow the secret got out. In no time, everyone at work was coming up to congratulate me. " SHARON

◆ *Remember that your body is built for pregnancy and knows exactly what to do.*

◆ *Extra rest will help you cope with the changes of early pregnancy, making it easier to handle personal relationships.*

◆ *Share your feelings about pregnancy and parenthood with your partner. Some worries disappear when brought into the open; others can be handled better by two people.*

◆ *Get a book or video to discover together how a baby grows from a seed as small as a grain of sand into a little person.*

◆ *Uncertainty is part of life, so put it in perspective and take pleasure together in celebrating this special time.*

◆ *Give yourself a few weeks to adjust. Women who are pregnant for the first time often feel disoriented and unsure of themselves.*

MATERNITY CARE

As soon as you know you're pregnant it's time to think about prenatal care. Your own doctor can care for you, or you can seek care from a midwife, a family physician or an obstetrician. If you prefer not to use an obstetrician or a family physician, get in touch with midwives practicing in your area directly. Contact the nearest birthing center for referral or the National Association of Childbearing Centers (NACC), American College of Nurse-Midwives (ACNM), Midwives Alliance of North America (MANA), or Informed Home Birth (see Appendix). Local childbirth educators may also provide referral to qualified practicing midwives.

You might think that labor is a long way off, but maternity care is usually linked to the type of birth you choose (see page 84). If you have your baby in a hospital, your entire care may take place there, and you may see different nurses in the prenatal clinic, the labor room and the recovery wards.

Most women prefer to see familiar faces, so some areas offer "team care," where a group of doctors or midwives provide all your maternity care, including the delivery, which could be in a hospital, a birthing center or at home. If you choose to give birth in a birthing center or at home, most of your care will be provided by an individual or team midwife at a local clinic.

It's the duty of your doctor or midwife to arrange prenatal care that is acceptable to you. You are not obliged to accept a form of care you dislike, or treatment from someone who upsets you.

CALCULATING YOUR EXPECTED DELIVERY DATE

The average length of a pregnancy is 266 days, or 280 days from the start of your last menstrual period (LMP), because you conceive about 14 days later. Your expected date of delivery (EDD) is calculated as nine calendar months plus one week from this date. For example, if your LMP started September 17, plus nine months = June 17, plus seven days = baby due June 24. To use the EDD chart, find the month and day your last menstrual period started on the top line (bold type). The month and day your baby is due is on the line below.

Your EDD is really a guide for measuring your baby's progress. It is imprecise for several reasons. Some months are longer than others; you may have a longer or shorter cycle than the "average" of 28 days; you may bleed a little while pregnant or miss a period before conception without realizing it, and so on. If you don't know the date of your LMP, or if other signs such as the size of your uterus don't agree with this date, your doctor may suggest an ultrasound scan (see page 56). This is the most accurate way of dating a pregnancy.

January
1 2 3 4 5 6 7 8 9 10 11 12 13 14 15 16 17 18 19 20 21 22 23 24 25 26 27 28 29 30 31
October
8 9 10 11 12 13 14 15 16 17 18 19 20 21 22 23 24 25 26 27 28 29 30 31 1 2 3 4 5 6 7

February
1 2 3 4 5 6 7 8 9 10 11 12 13 14 15 16 17 18 19 20 21 22 23 24 25 26 27 28
November
8 9 10 11 12 13 14 15 16 17 18 19 20 21 22 23 24 25 26 27 28 29 30 1 2 3 4 5

March
1 2 3 4 5 6 7 8 9 10 11 12 13 14 15 16 17 18 19 20 21 22 23 24 25 26 27 28 29 30 31
December
6 7 8 9 10 11 12 13 14 15 16 17 18 19 20 21 22 23 24 25 26 27 28 29 30 31 1 2 3 4 5

April
1 2 3 4 5 6 7 8 9 10 11 12 13 14 15 16 17 18 19 20 21 22 23 24 25 26 27 28 29 30
January
6 7 8 9 10 11 12 13 14 15 16 17 18 19 20 21 22 23 24 25 26 27 28 29 30 31 1 2 3 4

May
1 2 3 4 5 6 7 8 9 10 11 12 13 14 15 16 17 18 19 20 21 22 23 24 25 26 27 28 29 30 31
February
5 6 7 8 9 10 11 12 13 14 15 16 17 18 19 20 21 22 23 24 25 26 27 28 1 2 3 4 5 6 7

June
1 2 3 4 5 6 7 8 9 10 11 12 13 14 15 16 17 18 19 20 21 22 23 24 25 26 27 28 29 30
March
8 9 10 11 12 13 14 15 16 17 18 19 20 21 22 23 24 25 26 27 28 29 30 31 1 2 3 4 5 6

July
1 2 3 4 5 6 7 8 9 10 11 12 13 14 15 16 17 18 19 20 21 22 23 24 25 26 27 28 29 30 31
April
7 8 9 10 11 12 13 14 15 16 17 18 19 20 21 22 23 24 25 26 27 28 29 30 1 2 3 4 5 6 7

August
1 2 3 4 5 6 7 8 9 10 11 12 13 14 15 16 17 18 19 20 21 22 23 24 25 26 27 28 29 30 31
May
8 9 10 11 12 13 14 15 16 17 18 19 20 21 22 23 24 25 26 27 28 29 30 31 1 2 3 4 5 6 7

September
1 2 3 4 5 6 7 8 9 10 11 12 13 14 15 16 17 18 19 20 21 22 23 24 25 26 27 28 29 30
June
8 9 10 11 12 13 14 15 16 17 18 19 20 21 22 23 24 25 26 27 28 29 30 1 2 3 4 5 6

October
1 2 3 4 5 6 7 8 9 10 11 12 13 14 15 16 17 18 19 20 21 22 23 24 25 26 27 28 29 30 31
July
8 9 10 11 12 13 14 15 16 17 18 19 20 21 22 23 24 25 26 27 28 29 30 31 1 2 3 4 5 6 7

November
1 2 3 4 5 6 7 8 9 10 11 12 13 14 15 16 17 18 19 20 21 22 23 24 25 26 27 28 29 30
August
8 9 10 11 12 13 14 15 16 17 18 19 20 21 22 23 24 25 26 27 28 29 30 31 1 2 3 4 5 6

December
1 2 3 4 5 6 7 8 9 10 11 12 13 14 15 16 17 18 19 20 21 22 23 24 25 26 27 28 29 30 31
September
7 8 9 10 11 12 13 14 15 16 17 18 19 20 21 22 23 24 25 26 27 28 29 30 1 2 3 4 5 6 7

INFERTILITY

One couple in eight takes more than a year to conceive a baby. About half achieve a pregnancy without help and 20% of the rest succeed after treatment. About 35% of problems can be traced to the man, 35% to the woman. The rest are shared by both partners.

Infertility can be caused by problems such as blocked tubes, hormone imbalances, infections and general ill health, or by factors such as fear of pregnancy or sexual difficulties. Overheating, stress or coming off the Pill can cause temporary problems. Finding that you can't conceive a baby when you want to, and when other couples seem to manage it so easily, causes a lot of anguish. However, although the problem seems to be growing, so does research into potential solutions, including assistance such as in-vitro fertilization (IVF). Planned Parenthood (see Appendix) has information about achieving a successful pregnancy.

ECTOPIC PREGNANCY

About one in 350 embryos implants outside the uterus, usually in a Fallopian tube. If the pregnancy were allowed to continue, the tube would rupture, which might lead to infertility.

The first symptom of an ectopic pregnancy is usually pain low down on one side of the abdomen, often between the sixth and twelfth week. It may be worse when you cough or move and there may be spotting or dark-brown bleeding. If you have pain, tenderness or bleeding, contact your doctor.

If a pregnancy test is positive but an ultrasound scan (see page 56) shows no signs of pregnancy in the uterus, a laparoscopy may be performed. A fine instrument is inserted through the abdomen to look directly at the tubes. Early diagnosis and treatment can save the tube in 80% of cases, so that you have a good chance of conceiving again.

TO INCREASE YOUR CHANCES OF CONCEIVING:

- *You and your partner should make changes to your lifestyle to reduce stress caused by overwork and exhaustion.*
- *You and your partner should stop smoking and check your diet (see pages 12-13 and 39-41).*
- *Check if any chemicals you or your partner work with are linked to infertility.*
- *Your partner could try to avoid overheating from hot baths or tight underwear and jeans. If you are not pregnant after a year (six months if you are over 35) ask your healthcare provider to refer you to a specialist.*

MISCARRIAGE

Up to 40% of pregnancies are thought to miscarry very early, before they are confirmed. Your reaction to a miscarriage depends on how you felt about your pregnancy, but it causes grief and considerable loss of confidence to many women. However, the chances are strongly in your favor when a pregnancy has been confirmed, because at least 85% of them continue successfully.

An abnormal embryo is the most likely cause of miscarriage in the first 10 weeks. Investigations to find a cause are usually considered only after three successive early miscarriages. This seems hard, but it's an expression of confidence that there is probably not a problem and you have just been unlucky.

Miscarriages between 12 and 20 weeks occur in 1% to 2% of pregnancies, but are rare where everything is otherwise normal. A fifth to a quarter of all late miscarriages may be caused by the cervix opening too soon, possibly because of damage from surgical treatment or a previous birth. If you have suffered such a tragedy in the past, your cervix may be closed with a stitch at 12 to 16 weeks to help support it.

Most women experience aches, cramps or light spotting at some stage during pregnancy without any problem. Emotional upsets, minor falls, sex and things like lifting toddlers or shopping do not usually cause miscarriages. But if you have a history of them your healthcare provider may suggest you avoid such activities.

Vaginal bleeding could indicate a threatened miscarriage. Some doctors advise extra rest, but there is no evidence that it makes any difference. If nothing else happens, the chances of your pregnancy continuing are high, with no extra risk of abnormality in the baby.

If you have a history of miscarriage, if bleeding or pain is severe, or if you pass clots or other material, seek immediate treatment from a doctor or the nearest hospital. Otherwise, contact your healthcare provider if you are worried or have any of these symptoms:
- Cramps accompanied by bleeding.
- Pain that is severe or lasts more than 24 hours without bleeding.
- Bleeding that is as heavy as a normal period.
- Light spotting or staining continuing for more than three days.

After a miscarriage

Miscarriage happens to lots of women and most go on to have babies successfully. After an early miscarriage you may be offered a D&C: the neck of the uterus is gently dilated and the lining scraped or aspirated to make sure nothing remains to cause infection. Some doctors suggest waiting three to six months before trying to conceive again (although lovemaking can resume before this) to give yourself time to recover physically and emotionally. The Pregnancy & Infant Loss Center and Perinatal Loss (see Appendix) can offer advice and support.

QUESTIONS AND ANSWERS

Q: I was shocked to discover that I was pregnant, because I didn't feel ready for a baby. My partner blamed me for missing my Pill and we had some spectacular fights before coming to our senses. Now we are looking forward to becoming parents, but I'm overwhelmed with guilt and fear. Could our baby have been affected by the stress we were under at first?

A: Unexpected pregnancies are not always welcome and it can be hard to relate to a baby and imagine yourselves as parents at first. Couples often think and say things they regret later. Emotional stresses do affect the fetus but unless they are severe and prolonged they are unlikely to make more than a temporary impression. A baby learns only when he reaches the right stage of maturity for a particular experience. In the early months he is both emotionally and physically immature.

Although many studies have been made, no sound, direct evidence suggests that emotional stress affects a baby adversely before birth. Indirect evidence suggests that the fetus is exposed to the sort of stress levels that he will have to learn to handle in everyday life, but is protected from excess stress. Most women will have some negative thoughts or a few arguments during pregnancy. The positive feelings you now have about your pregnancy are probably more significant.

Q: We want to have a daughter. Is there any way to boost our chances, and could we find out our baby's gender before birth?

A: Investigations such as ultrasound scans and amniocentesis (see page 57) can usually determine whether you are carrying a boy or a girl, but they are not always correct and would not be used for choosing the gender of your baby.

There is a new technique where "y" (male) and "x" (female) sperm are separated in the laboratory and artificial insemination is carried out to increase the chances of conceiving the desired gender. Ask your doctor about it.

Other suggestions for increasing your chances of having a girl or a boy are less expensive but require more dedication. In 1979, doctors in a Paris maternity hospital claimed an 80% success rate with a special diet. To conceive a girl, the mother ate food that included starch and milk products, raw or frozen vegetables, unsalted butter and fruit, with the exception of pineapple, peaches and prunes. For a boy, the diet had to be rich in salty foods, meat and fruit, and include dried vegetables and salted butter.

Another theory holds that timing intercourse is important because female sperm swim slowly but live longer than male sperm. Couples who want a girl should have intercourse two days before ovulation, so that most of the "y" sperm will have died before the egg arrives. For a boy, you should have intercourse on the day an egg is released, so that faster-swimming male sperm are more likely to fertilize it. Of course it is not always easy to know when an egg will be released. You can buy a special thermometer at the pharmacy to pinpoint ovulation, but you would need to keep a record of your temperature for several months beforehand for it to have any degree of accuracy.

It can be fun to try to influence the sex of your baby, but don't pin your hopes on methods that can never be foolproof! Most parents are happy to welcome a boy or a girl into their family.

Q: My doctor says that I have a retroverted or "tipped" uterus. Will this make it harder to conceive, and does it affect pregnancy?

A: The uterus usually bends forward towards your pubic bone with its upper segment above your bladder. The position of a retroverted or "tipped" uterus is more upright, aligned with your spine. About 17% to 20% lie in this position naturally. Very occasionally the uterus becomes retroverted as a result of disease or pelvic infection; these could cause infertility rather than the position of the uterus.

For most women with a retroverted uterus, conception is no less likely and miscarriage no more likely than for anyone else. The uterus usually moves forward spontaneously somewhere between the ninth and twelfth week and the pregnancy is just like any other.

Q: Our baby was conceived shortly before our vacation in Greece. Not knowing, I happily ate the local seafood and drank more than a little wine. I haven't had problems but I feel guilty now, because my baby's organs were forming. Is it likely that they were harmed?

A: It's possible. But many actions increase a risk without turning it into a certainty. Drinking alcohol and eating seafood are *potential*, not inevitable, causes of harm. An embryo that is damaged during the early stages of development is often miscarried, so your healthy pregnancy suggests that your baby may be unaffected by anything you did on vacation.

It's hard to avoid all hazards, even after you have become pregnant. Your protective feelings about your baby are designed to be a positive influence on what you do from now on, not to make you feel guilty about risks you took before you knew you were pregnant.

Q: A friend says it is dangerous to have a high temperature in early pregnancy because the baby can be affected. How can I avoid it and what should I do if I get a fever?

A: An increase in body temperature to over 104F (40C) for a day, or over 102F (38.5C) for two days or more, *may* cause birth defects, particularly between the third and seventh weeks of pregnancy.

You cannot isolate yourself from everyday life in case you catch something! Thousands of women who had flu or some other illness before realizing they were pregnant have gone on to have healthy babies. A strong immune system built on a good diet and a sensible lifestyle will help to protect you from infections.

If you have a high temperature, say over 101F (38C), don't take any home remedies. Contact your healthcare provider, who may suggest bringing it down by sponging yourself with tepid water or having a cool bath (but stop if you start to shiver). Other treatment would depend on how high your temperature was and your doctor's advice.

Q: I've read that VDTs (visual display terminals) can cause miscarriages and birth defects, and I work in an open-plan office full of them. Is it true, and if so can anything be done about it?

A: No pregnancy-related problems have been reported among women who use VDTs for 20 hours a week or less. Even if you work full time some experts say that modem equipment emits such low levels of radiation that they could not possibly harm a fetus, and that stress in the working situation may be more significant. But talk to your company's doctor if there is one. Some employers have agreements that allow women who have worked with the business for a certain length of time to move to other work during pregnancy.

More radiation is emitted from the back of a VDT than from the screen, so if your desk is near someone else's VDT you could ask to be moved. Don't strain to see the screen and have a break away from your desk for a few minutes every hour. Perhaps you could alternate VDT work with other work during the day.

3

Early
Pregnancy

(MONTHS 1 to 3)

"When I was first pregnant I felt so proud, as though I'd grown up and proved myself. But then came the fears. Did I want to give up my freedom, would I be a good mother, could I stand the sleepless nights or the pain of the birth? The first three months crept by, with sickness and self-doubt, and indescribable joy at the new life I was secretly nurturing."

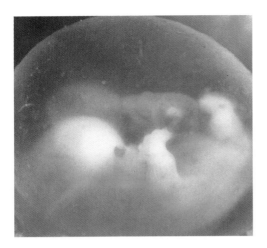

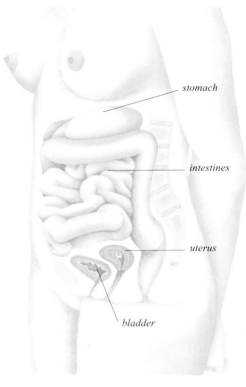

stomach

intestines

uterus

bladder

ONE MONTH

Above: *An embryo at seven weeks, protected in the fluid-filled amniotic sac. All the organs of a future adult are beginning to function.*
Right: *First month: Your internal organs are in the same position as before conception.*
Second month: Hormones soften your ligaments so that your organs can adapt as your uterus grows.
Third month: Your pregnancy may barely show but your uterus has already doubled in size.

HOW YOUR BABY DEVELOPS

After conception, the cells of your fertilized egg divide rapidly and roll down the Fallopian tube, increasing in size like a snowball. Seven days later (week three of pregnancy), dozens of cells of different shapes and sizes form a cluster. The outer layer of cells becomes the placenta and amniotic sac and the inner layer becomes the baby.

The cluster of cells *(blastocyst)* attaches to the lining of the uterus *(endometrium)* with tiny projections *(villi)*, like ivy clinging to a wall. As the cells multiply an embryo forms, about the size of the period at the end of this sentence. By the fifth week the embryo is a three-layered disc as big as a lentil. The inner layer will become the baby's lungs, intestines, bladder and digestive system. The middle layer will form her heart, genitals, kidneys, bones and muscles, and the outer layer will form her brain, nervous system, external features and skin.

The embryo's head and brain develop first, followed by her body and then

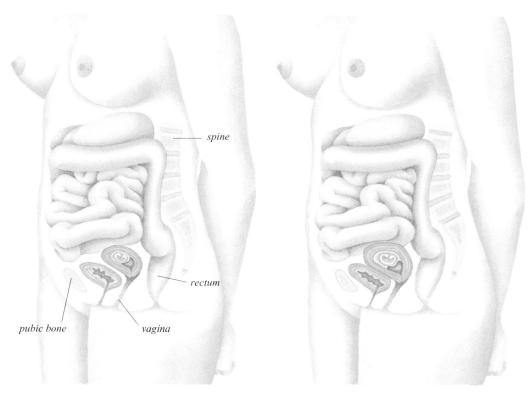

spine

rectum

pubic bone   vagina

TWO MONTHS   THREE MONTHS

her limbs. By six weeks she's roughly the size of a grain of rice and her heart has started to beat. By eight weeks she's the size of a peanut. Tiny limbs and muscles develop. A week later eyes and ears have formed and her fingers and toes are almost separated. When you are 10 weeks pregnant, the embryo is about as long as the top joint of your little finger, and all her main body parts, including the bones, are formed. Finishing touches, such as eyelids and finger-nails, are added. Twelve weeks after conception (week 14 of pregnancy) everything is beginning to function. Even egg (or sperm) cells are present.

HOW YOU MAY FEEL

If you are thrilled to be pregnant and your hormones cause little discomfort you may feel fitter and happier than ever before, and have glowing skin and shining hair. But many women experience mixed feelings in the early weeks. Although there is little to show and the outside world may be unaware of your pregnancy, enormous physical and emotional changes are taking place.

Periods of change can be stressful and unsettling. It takes time to adjust to having a baby, especially if it is unexpected or unwelcome. The demands that pregnancy makes on your body can sap your energy and make you feel exhausted. Hormone activity may cause symptoms that are distressing for you but are not considered important by anyone else because they don't harm the baby. Your feelings may swing from joy and excitement to self-doubt or despair. Common symptoms of early pregnancy include:

- A bloated, irrational feeling like pre-menstrual tension; tender breasts or painful nipples in cold weather.
- Flushes of heat or dizziness in stuffy rooms.
- A taste for strong flavors, such as orange juice or pickles.
- Nausea, vomiting or distaste for certain smells or foods.
- A need to urinate more frequently, caused by the growing uterus pressing on your bladder.
- Digestive upsets such as constipation or flatulence.
- Excessive saliva or a metallic taste in the mouth.
- Breakthrough bleeding when your period would have been due.
- Lifeless hair and greasy skin, or spots.
- Pulling pains at the sides of the abdomen, caused by the round ligaments stretching as the uterus moves into the abdomen.

RELATIONSHIP WITH YOUR PARTNER

Once a baby is on the way, the relationship between you and your partner is bound to alter as you adjust to new roles. Many couples worry about this, but change is not necessarily negative.

Pregnancy may bring you and your partner closer together as you share new and exciting hopes for the future. Many fathers-to-be are both practically and emotionally supportive. If your partner seems confused or doesn't want to be involved, talk to him about it. He may not understand your needs or why you feel the way you do. He may find it hard to adjust to your pregnancy. You become the focus of everyone's attention and he is expected to support you, but he may have his own worries. Some men feel proud of the pregnancy but not sure about becoming a father. Life will change and your partner may be anxious about the commitment required, new responsibilities and the loss of freedom. About 10% of men suffer from symptoms of mild anxiety, such as toothache, that are severe enough to make them seek help.

Accepting and talking about each other's feelings really does help. Try setting aside half an hour a week, with five minutes each to express your feelings without interruption and 20 minutes to discuss anything else that comes up. You'll learn more about each other, and you'll build a framework that makes it easier to deal with sensitive issues before they become damaging resentments that may threaten your relationship.

Relationship with your family

Babies bring great joy to the wider family. They provide a chance for other women to recall the special time when their own children were tiny, and men to take an interest they may have missed out on a generation ago. If you and your partner have children from previous liaisons, your new baby will be a brother or sister to all of them, which can build positive bridges and help bring families together.

It will give other family members great pleasure if you share your pregnancy as far as possible. Phone them with news if they live far away; send them photocopies if you have a clear picture from an ultrasound scan; find patterns you like if an auntie wants to knit booties! If you are overwhelmed with offers to buy equipment, explain that you prefer to wait until you have decided what you need. Meanwhile, it costs nothing to smile and say "thank you."

You may find yourself sensitive to unwanted advice and comments, but try to take them all in your stride. It's good to listen to other people's views, but deciding what is right for your baby is *your* responsibility, however well-meaning and experienced other family members may be. Family ties change, especially when you are expecting your first child, but with give and take new and rewarding relationships can be built.

YOUR LIFESTYLE

A healthful lifestyle means you're more likely to have a trouble-free pregnancy and a healthy baby. It's worth taking a look at your daily routine. Small changes can have a really positive effect on both you and the baby.

What to eat

If your diet is good, you are more likely to have healthy blood, supple skin and muscles that function efficiently. The old saying "you are what you eat" applies equally to you and your baby. The early months of pregnancy, when the baby's organs are developing, are especially important. Mothers who eat a good or excellent diet are much less likely to have sickly, premature or low birth-weight babies.

It's not really possible to give detailed instructions about what you should eat because nutritional needs differ with age, build, metabolic rate and so on. As a rough guide, you might aim to eat three to five portions of protein foods, plus five portions of bread and cereals and five of fruit and vegetables daily. Leafy green vegetables are especially valuable because they contain folic acid, which is important for cell reproduction.

You gain more nutrients from fresh, whole foods than from processed foods. Try to eat some raw vegetables, something containing iron, such as meat, nuts or dried fruit, and about four servings of calcium-rich foods such as milk or milk products every day. Your body needs some fat, but fat is hidden in many foods and is high in calories, so two servings of butter, margarine or oil per day is adequate. If you don't eat well one day, try to make up for it the next day.

FOOD PRECAUTIONS

◆ *Avoid soft and blue-veined cheeses, unpasteurized milk or cheese, shellfish, uncooked egg, pâté and undercooked meat to reduce the risk of infection caused by listeria or salmonella bacteria. Avoid liver because its high concentration of vitamin A could harm the baby. Eating peanuts during pregnancy is thought to be linked to nut allergies in babies.*

◆ *Avoid foods and drinks with artificial sweetners.*

◆ *Cook home-prepared foods thoroughly (especially reheated foods). Check that the temperature of your refrigerator is below 39°F (4°C).*

◆ *Store raw meat separately from other foods. Wash your hands and all utensils and surfaces that have touched raw meat with hot, soapy water.*

◆ *Wash all fruits and vegetables before eating.*

Chances are you think your diet is already reasonably good, but look at the labels when you're shopping. Some foods are more efficient sources of nutrients than others. For example, a pint of 1% or nonfat milk gives you the same amount of protein but fewer calories and more calcium than whole milk.

Alcohol

Considerable research shows that drinking alcohol can be harmful to your unborn child. Your baby is at greatest risk from heavy or binge drinking. No one can say what is "safe" for an individual, so doctors advise women not to drink at all when pregnant. If you're at all worried about your current drinking habits, call the National Center for Nutrition and Dietetics' Consumer-Nutrition Hotline, toll-free, at 1-800-366-1655, to speak directly with a nutritionist. The American College of Obstetricians and Gynecologists (see Appendix) can also provide you with accurate information about alcohol and pregnancy.

Smoking

Smoking is a habit as well as an addiction. Don't despair if you find it hard to give up, but keep trying. Ask your healthcare provider to refer you to a "Stop Smoking" group, or contact the American Cancer Society or the American Lung Association (see Appendix) for information, referral and support.

*❝Nobody can see that you're pregnant in the early weeks. I was so proud I wanted to shout it from the rooftops, and when I found out it was twins I grinned from ear to ear all the way home! I felt so special, and people were excited in a way they usually aren't when it's not your first baby. Of course there were moments of panic and my husband was a little worried about how we'd cope. But I was so determined to enjoy this pregnancy. ❞*PAULINE

AVOIDING RISKS

One of the down sides to any pregnancy is worry. The world can seem a dangerous place when you become aware of the growing list of what pregnant women should avoid! However, most babies are born healthy even when their mothers have been exposed to risks. Worrying about things you have no control over, or that happened in the past, is pointless. Just be sensible and avoid unnecessary risks:

- Avoid chemicals such as waterproofing sprays for jackets and tents, paint fumes, hair dyes, pesticides and other garden sprays. Cleaning fluids are often toxic. Avoid substances with any toxic warnings on the can. If you live in a farming area, ask to be notified before crops are sprayed.
- Cats or dogs may carry active toxoplasmosis (see page 18). Pet lovers often develop immunity to this disease, but use rubber gloves to empty litter trays, or ask someone else to do it.
- Wear gloves for gardening and wash all home-grown fruit and vegetables as carefully as you would store-bought produce.
- Avoid excess heat from very hot baths, saunas, electric blankets, heating pads or over-enthusiastic workouts.
- Have appliances such as your refrigerator (for safety of food storage) and microwave checked to make sure they are all working properly. With your microwave, avoid standing in front of it when it's working.
- Tell the dentist or X-ray technician if you are or could be pregnant. Ask for a shield over your abdomen. If possible, avoid X-rays because they can harm your baby.

REDUCE THE SMOKING RISK

- *Link your decision to stop smoking with an emotional incident. Many women use the joyful discovery that they're pregnant.*
- *Change your normal routine. Go for a brisk walk in the fresh air, or complete a task when you would normally smoke a cigarette. Have a mint instead of a cigarette after a meal.*
- *Cut down by smoking only half a cigarette and deliberately stubbing it out.*
- *Avoid smoke-filled rooms and smoking areas in public places and restaurants. Ask your partner to go outside if he wants to smoke.*
- *Pay attention to what you eat, because an excellent diet gives some protection against the ill effects of passive smoking. Contact Human Resources at work if other people's smoking is a problem.*

HOW TO RELAX

- ◆ *Watch your posture (see page 44) to prevent causing unnecessary tension in your muscles.*
- ◆ *To relax your shoulders, pull them down and let go. They'll settle into a relaxed position. Check them every time you wait for a pot to boil or place a phone call.*
- ◆ *Loosen your fingers. Tension from clenched hands travels up your arms and into your shoulders. Your face will reflect tension in your body. Relax the muscles around your eyes. Part your lips slightly and gently close them to relax your jaw and mouth.*
- ◆ *Buy a relaxation tape and spend some time each day learning the art of relaxing at will.*

Learn to relax

At this point, being pregnant may seem so full of pitfalls that it seems impossible to relax even for a minute! But life is full of risks and most people manage to come through unscathed. Certain environmental risks are unproved while others account for only a tiny proportion of birth defects or pregnancy complications. It's far more important to eat a good diet, have regular prenatal checkups and avoid smoking or taking nonprescription drugs. Try to put risks into proportion instead of feeling anxious and guilty over every little misstep. Do your best and then relax.

Many women feel exhausted around the second and third months of pregnancy. Even after a good night's sleep they doze at their desk at work or fall asleep over dinner. It may not be easy to relax physically when you're working or looking after a lively toddler, but try to pace yourself during the day. Make allowances for the unseen changes of pregnancy and don't push yourself, especially if you're feeling under the weather. It's better to decline an invitation or make a meal from the freezer than to end up feeling frazzled. Many women feel guilty if they sit down without having a good excuse, but growing a baby is the best possible reason to rest!

"*When I became pregnant, my life changed overnight. I didn't resent the changes, but I felt ill, emotional and mixed up and had no idea how to help myself or where to go for advice. I assumed if you had morning sickness you'd wake up, be sick and it would be over, whereas mine lasted all day. I lost weight and felt totally different inside. My partner was very supportive but he didn't understand why I cried all the time.*

I couldn't relate to a baby—it all seemed too remote. Everyone was delighted, but I had little enthusiasm because I felt so awful. I thought there must be something wrong with me. I didn't realize that other women also felt emotionally drained or found life very difficult in the early weeks. **"** FRANCESCA

COPING WITH MORNING SICKNESS

It's little comfort, but the first known record of this complaint is in a papyrus dated 2000 BC, and some form of it is suffered by up to 70% of women. It may be caused by the hormone HCG (human chorionic gonadotrophin), which is produced a few days after conception, reaches a peak at about 10 weeks and usually drops dramatically after 12 to 16 weeks.

Morning sickness ranges from mild nausea in the mornings for a few weeks to severe nausea and vomiting lasting all day; in some cases, throughout the entire pregnancy. It is often trivialized because it does not affect the baby adversely, but if you suffer badly from it you deserve everyone's sympathy and understanding.

Stress makes symptoms worse, but psychological factors such as "unconscious rejection of the baby" are no longer thought to play a major role in the problem; neither is diet, although there may be links to certain minerals and vitamins, especially vitamin B6.

Sickness is often worst at the time when your baby's organs are forming, so never take over-the-counter remedies without professional advice. This includes herbal or homeopathic preparations and vitamin supplements. If you can't keep anything down you should certainly tell your doctor.

Otherwise, some of these suggestions may help:

- Accept the nausea and change your lifestyle temporarily.
- Ask your partner to do the cooking.
- Slow down, get extra rest, get fresh air every day and go to bed early.
- Don't worry about your diet for the time being. Eat little and often, whatever you can keep down. Take snacks like gingersnaps or tiny sandwiches to eat at work.
- Sucking hard candy or crystallized ginger may banish the metallic taste in your mouth. Try fresh ginger in cooking.
- Ice pops, plain water, carbonated drinks or herb teas may help.
- Find somebody to listen to your worries and give practical help when you feel awful. There may be no remedy for your misery except time, but you need support to live through it.

ACHES AND PAINS

In early pregnancy the action of hormones softens all your ligaments so that as your baby grows your uterus can move out of your pelvic basin into your abdominal cavity. Ligaments that would normally stabilize your joints are softened too, and can be strained by poor posture when standing, sitting or lifting. Tense shoulder muscles, weak abdominal or buttock muscles, and wearing high heels that tilt your pelvis can cause backache. To avoid strains, watch your posture carefully, sleep on a supportive mattress, and roll onto your side before getting up.

Taking care of your back

Pregnancy is an excellent time to review how you use your body. If you have picked up bad postural habits over the years it will take thought at first. However, good posture quickly becomes automatic, avoiding aches and pains.

Standing: Keep your back upright, with your shoulders relaxed, pelvis balanced and feet apart. Don't rest with your weight on one hip or stick out your stomach.

Lifting: Bend your knees and keep your back straight. Try not to lift and twist at the same time—move your feet instead. Keep the weight close to your body unless it's as light as this empty bucket.

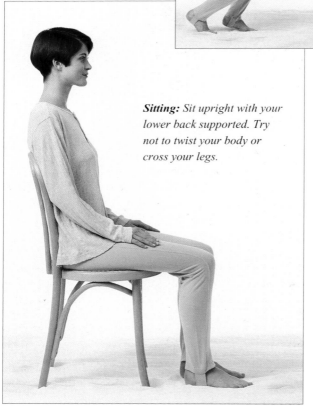

Sitting: Sit upright with your lower back supported. Try not to twist your body or cross your legs.

YOUR PELVIC FLOOR

If there is one part of the body that all women should know about, it's the pelvic floor, the muscles between your legs that form the base of the pelvic basin. To locate them, look at the illustration below. Cough into your hand and you'll feel the muscles bulge a little.

They are important because they support your bladder, vagina and bowel, and control their *sphincters* or exits. They carry the growing weight of your uterus and baby and withstand the extra pressure when your baby's head engages (see page 52) before labor. When your baby is born, the muscles guide her head to align it with your pubic arch and stretch to let her emerge. They need to be strong but flexible.

During pregnancy your pelvic floor sags a little with the extra weight, but muscles with good tone (the normal firmness of healthy tissue) return to their normal horizontal state after the birth. Over a long period, lax muscles allow your pelvic organs to change position, making it harder for the supporting muscles to function properly. This could lead to problems such as stress incontinence.

How to tone your pelvic floor

Breathing normally, slowly draw up the muscles, hold them momentarily, and release them gently. Repeat this six times, several times every day without using your abdominal and buttock muscles. Concentrate on becoming more aware of the sensations you feel. Some women find it easiest to lean forward with their knees apart and their buttocks resting on the edge of a chair seat.

Imagine that your pelvic floor is an elevator in a department store. Tighten it upwards, pausing at each floor before moving to the next. You may reach the second floor or the seventh, depending on how much control you have. Try to stop at each floor on the way down again!

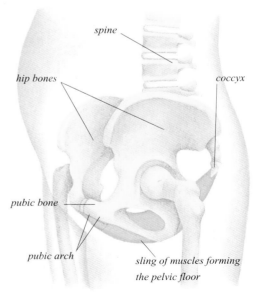

spine

hip bones

coccyx

pubic bone

pubic arch

sling of muscles forming the pelvic floor

Your pelvic floor muscles are more complex, but this shows their hammock-like structure, which support your internal organs. From front to back there are three openings: the urethra, leading from the bladder; the vagina, from the uterus; and the anus, from the bowel.

RIGHTS AND BENEFITS

If you work during pregnancy, you have legal rights that protect your health and job. Some apply to all pregnant women in paid employment. Others, such as rights to move from a job involving heavy lifting to a suitable alternative if one is available, and to return to your original job after your baby is born, may depend on qualifying employment periods.

If you are on a low income you may be eligible for free prenatal care and maternity services through Medicaid (in the United States). You may also be able to claim free food coupons in the United States through the W.I.C. Program (Women, Infants, and Children Supplemental Feeding Program). Contact your state or local public health department for information and referral. In Canada, contact your provincial or territorial Ministry of Health for information about prenatal and birth services (See Appendix).

Some employers offer better maternity benefits than required by law, so find out the terms that apply to you.

YOUR PREGNANCY PLANNER - MONTHS 1 TO 3

◆ *Prenatal checkups: Appointments are usually once a month after the first eight weeks of pregnancy. Ask about special tests for fetal abnormality (see page 55).*

◆ *Stop smoking, cut out alcohol and make improvements to your diet now— it's important for you and your baby. If you need help, you'll find useful addresses in the Appendix.*

◆ *If you are uncertain about your rights at work, contact the Women's Bureau in the United States for a summary of state laws on family leave (see Appendix). In Canada, contact your provincial or territorial Ministry of Health (see Appendix).*

◆ *Start thinking about various birth options and getting information about different hospitals, birthing centers (see page 85) and prenatal classes (see page 79). Refer to the Appendix for organizations that can provide up-to-date childbirth information to help you make choices.*

QUESTIONS AND ANSWERS

Q: My back has always been one of my weak spots, and I don't want to suffer during pregnancy. In addition to watching my posture, what can I do to help myself avoid backache problems?

A: You could strengthen your back muscles with gentle pelvic rocking. Stand with your feet apart and your knees bent. Tighten your buttocks and tilt your pelvis forward, then release them and tilt it backwards, rocking it slowly and rhythmically. This movement also helps relieve existing backache.

If you get a backache under your shoulder blades, circle your shoulders to release stiffness. Try wearing a larger bra or let the hooks out, and make sure that you sit with your back straight and supported. For pain that is lower and to one side of your spine (probably a strained sacroiliac ligament), ask your partner to massage the area firmly and apply some gentle heat.

Q: I have been a vegetarian for 10 years but am now a vegan. Is this diet adequate for pregnancy, or should I take supplements?

A: Vegetarians who are healthy and eat a good, varied diet do not usually need supplements, because their blood mineral levels fall within normal ranges. Most doctors will prescribe prenatal vitamin and mineral supplements. You will also need to make sure that you get enough protein, between 80 and 100 grams per day.

Vegetarians and vegans have the same needs as other pregnant women and any diet is only as good as you make it. Contact the National Center for Nutrition and Dietetics' Consumer-Nutrition Hotline (1-800-366-1655) for more information. In the United States, if you are on a low income, your local W.I.C. Program (Women, Infants, and Children Supplemental Feeding Program) can provide good nutritional information and support. For the W.I.C. Program nearest you, call your state or local department of public health. In Canada, contact your provincial or territorial Ministry of Health (see Appendix) for prenatal nutrition information and support.

Q: I'm delighted to be pregnant but I'm having nightmares about the birth. We were shown a film in school and although it was years ago, the memory is still vivid. How can I overcome my fear?

A: The feelings and emotions that are part of giving birth and can make it a special experience rarely come across in films. In real life, giving birth is not like being in a movie and it's your baby, which makes a world of difference.

When negative thoughts float into your mind, try not to dwell on them—replace them with positive ones. For example, remind yourself that women are designed to give birth; that you won't be entering a competition or giving a performance, just doing your best. Concentrate on enjoying your pregnancy and looking forward to seeing your baby. The birth is simply the bridge between the two.

It's not too soon to look for prenatal classes (see page 79) to attend later on, because good ones are often booked early. Part of the job of a childbirth education teacher is to explain about birth more fully and teach you ways of coping. After you have been to classes and as the birth gets closer you'll probably wonder why you ever felt so afraid.

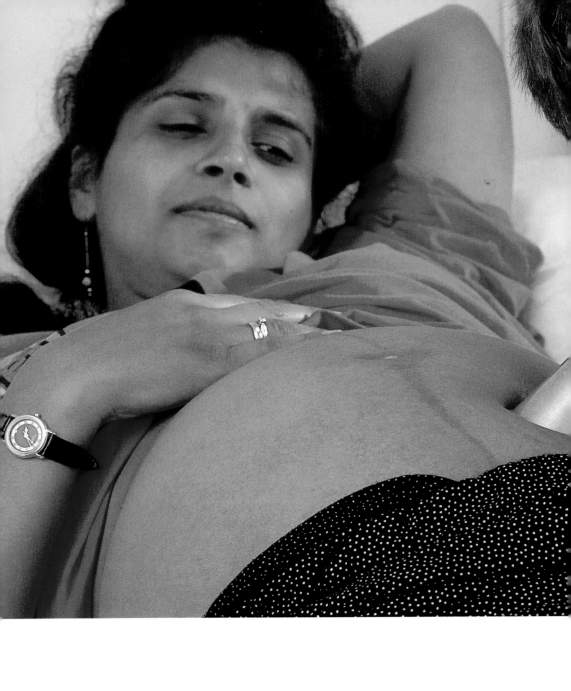

4

Prenatal Care

"Getting to know my way around the system was like learning the ropes in my first semester in high school. I hardly knew what I was doing but I was swept along in a friendly way while I asked questions and learned new names for familiar things. "

WHAT IS A "NORMAL" PREGNANCY?

Your pregnancy is normal if it progresses like the majority of pregnancies, and if any unusual symptoms you get are not generally thought to be harmful to mothers or babies. What is considered normal depends to some extent on the experience of the people concerned and on current scientific understanding.

Routine prenatal checks distinguish harmless symptoms from potentially dangerous ones, so that you and your baby stay healthy and any problems are picked up early. They also give you a chance to ask questions and find out enough information to help you make informed decisions.

Pregnancy is a state of health with just an occasional problem, although doctors sometimes forget this! If you are never singled out for special attention, rest assured everything is going well. Even if closer attention is paid to a particular symptom, it doesn't always mean there is a problem. Women are so individual that something could be abnormal for some women but be normal for you.

PRENATAL VISITS

Prenatal checkups are usually carried out by a healthcare provider each month until the 32nd week of pregnancy, then every two weeks until the 36th week and then weekly until your baby is born. You may have more checkups if your pregnancy is unusual. Women with normal pregnancies often have fewer checkups. But contact your doctor or midwife between visits if you have any worries.

Your partner can attend your checkups; the first is usually longer than later ones. The provider takes your history, recording details such as your job, your lifestyle, your past and present health plus that of your partner and both families if possible. The aim is to find out your individual circumstances and anything that could affect your pregnancy. Previous pregnancies, terminations or adoptions will be noted, but say if you don't want something written down.

Your height and weight will be checked. The weigh-in gives a baseline for later visits. Failure to put on weight could mean your baby isn't growing properly, and a sudden weight gain could indicate fluid retention. But not all gains or losses are important. For instance, you might be wearing lighter or heavier clothes because the weather has changed, or be adding fat on your bottom or thighs, which is normally used up while breastfeeding.

"I had prenatal care at my family doctor's prenatal clinic and got to know Jane, my midwife, so well that she became a friend. Thinking about tests is the worst part of pregnancy, but she discussed it until I felt ready to make a decision. She listens to the baby's heart and the first time she heard it she let me hear it too. I don't know which of us was more excited.

Going for checkups made me feel special because of Jane's attitude. I could ask anything without feeling silly. I don't have anyone to share the excitement of pregnancy with; luckily, Jane seemed as interested in every little detail as I was. " ALISON

◆ *Take your partner, a friend or a book to your first prenatal visit—you may have to wait between examinations.*

◆ *Be open about any symptoms you have and ask questions about suggested tests or treatments.*

◆ *If your blood pressure is high because of anxiety or stress, ask if it can be taken again in half an hour and use the time to consciously relax. This often brings it down to normal.*

A doctor will give you a physical examination to check your current state of health. Blood samples (see below) will be taken and you may be asked to provide a midstream urine sample (pass urine for a short time, then catch the sample in a supplied container) to check for infection. An ultrasound scan or other special tests (see page 56) may be offered.

At each prenatal visit your urine will be tested for sugar and protein, possible signs of gestational diabetes (see page 53) and pre-eclampsia (see page 102). Your blood pressure when your heart is pumping and at rest will be taken using an inflated cuff around your upper arm. The healthcare provider will also feel your stomach to check the height of your uterus and later, your baby's position. From about 20 weeks, or earlier with sophisticated equipment, she will listen to your baby's heartbeat and feel your ankles to test for any swelling (see page 102).

Prenatal care should be considered a partnership between you and your healthcare provider. It's part of her job to give you unbiased information and help you make informed decisions about what tests to have, where to have your baby and so on. No examination or test is compulsory. The decisions are up to you. At each visit you can ask for advice and discuss anything that worries or interests you.

Routine blood tests

Blood samples are taken at your first visit and later in pregnancy. The analysis varies but includes checking for blood type, count, and the rhesus factor (see page 53) in case you need an emergency transfusion, plus tests for glucose, syphilis, rubella and hepatitis B. If you have no rubella antibodies you will be offered immunization after the birth. The other diseases could harm your baby if left untreated. You may receive a full glucose-tolerance test on a separate occasion (see gestational diabetes, page 53). HIV tests are not routine or compulsory but may be carried out anonymously to monitor levels in the population. You would not be told your results.

Your hemoglobin level will be checked. Hemoglobin is the substance in red blood cells that carries oxygen around your body. The average blood count in

What your notes mean

If there is anything you don't understand it's better to ask than to go home and worry! Here are some common phrases and abbreviations:

Your notes:

Para 0/1/2+1	You have had 0, 1 or 2 previous births. +1 means a miscarriage or termination before 28 weeks.
LB or SB	Live birth or stillbirth.
TCA 3/7 (4/52)	To come again in 3 days (or 4 weeks).
Brim	The inlet or upper rim of your pelvis.
Fundus	The top of your uterus, which rises in your abdomen as your baby grows and descends a little when the baby's head engages (see below).
BP	Blood pressure.
PET	Pre-eclampsia (pre-eclamptic toxemia) (see page 102).
US or USS	Ultrasound scan.

Urine:

NAD	Nothing abnormal discovered.
Alb/Tr Prot+ (or ++)	Albumin/trace of protein. The plus signs indicate the amount of protein found. This could signify the start of pre-eclampsia.
0 Gluc	No glucose found in the urine. 2% or more glucose would be considered high.

Blood:

Bloods	Blood tests done.
Hb	Hemoglobin or blood count.
Fe	Iron tablets. The prescription may be recorded.
WR	Syphilis test VDRL/TPHA or FTA-Abs are alternatives.

The baby's health:

FMF or FMNF	Fetal movements felt, or not felt.
FH	Fetal heart. H or NH means "heard" or "not heard." The heart rate (usually between 120 and 160 beats per minute) may be recorded.

The baby's position:

LOA/ROA	Left (or right) occiput anterior or LOP/ROP posterior (see page 105).
PP	Presenting part, or the part of your baby nearest to the cervix and likely to emerge first.
Vx or Ceph	Vertex or cephalic, meaning "head down."
Br/Tr	Breech (bottom down), or transverse (lying across the uterus).
Eng or E	Engaged (Dropped). This refers to how far down your baby's head is in your pelvis. When recorded in fifths it means the proportion of your baby's head above the brim of your pelvis. So 1/5 means the head is almost fully dropped, ready for the birth, while 4/5 means it has started to drop.
NEng or NE	Not engaged.

pregnancy is about 12g. When you are anemic (that is, your hemoglobin level is too low) your heart has to work harder to supply your baby with oxygen, so you may be given iron tablets and folic-acid supplements if your blood count is under about 10g.

Individual tests may be performed if you are at risk from a disease that needs special care in pregnancy, such as sickle cell anemia, thalassemia, toxoplasmosis (see page 18) or diabetes.

The RH factor: If a mother is RH negative and her partner, like 80% of the population, is RH positive, a problem may arise in future pregnancies if the baby inherits the father's blood group. The baby's blood will contain a D antigen and the mother's does not. If the baby's blood passes into the mother, as can happen during birth, miscarriage or termination, the mother's blood will form antibodies against the D antigen. These may attack the red blood cells of any future RH-positive baby the mother carries.

If you are RH negative, you will have extra blood tests to monitor your antibody status. Within three days of the birth you will be given an anti-D injection to destroy any cells from the baby's blood before antibodies are formed. About 2% of women need treatment during pregnancy because the baby's blood cells have leaked across the placenta.

Blood pressure: Normal blood pressure is about 110/70. In pregnancy it varies, usually somewhere between 95/60 and 135/85. The systolic (upper) figure (measuring your heart when pumping) can be affected by stress, including anxiety or rushing to your appointment. The diastolic (lower) figure records your heart at rest. If it rises by 20 points above your normal baseline, it could indicate pre-eclampsia (see page 102). The usual cutoff point for concern is 140/90, although in the absence of other symptoms there may be nothing to worry about.

High blood pressure can make you feel energetic just when you ought to be resting to help bring it down, while low blood pressure may make you feel faint or excessively tired. Although blood pressure outside the normal range is a potential problem during pregnancy, it isn't your fault!

Gestational diabetes

Insulin regulates the glucose in your blood and eliminates any excess. To meet the needs of the baby, anti-insulin hormones in pregnancy enable extra glucose to circulate. If there is too much for the mother's and the baby's needs, the excess is excreted. About 50% of pregnant women show traces of sugar in the urine at some stage, and more insulin is usually produced to compensate.

Women with gestational diabetes have high levels of sugar in their blood and urine because the anti-insulin hormones work so well that the women cannot produce enough insulin, or cannot use the insulin they produce efficiently. This is rarely linked to "ordinary" diabetes (inability to produce enough insulin when you aren't pregnant), although treatments for the two conditions are similar, including a good diet and extra monitoring to keep your blood sugar at normal levels. With good care the risks to mother or baby from gestational diabetes is much reduced. Prenatal care for women with "ordinary" diabetes should begin prior to conception. Early and continuing prenatal care for such women is important to reduce the risk of problems associated with ordinary diabetes.

Do you have any questions?

At the end of your prenatal checkup you'll be asked if you have any questions. When you're pregnant for the first time it can be hard to think of any questions because you feel everything is new. Later on you'll probably think of plenty of things to ask. But at your first visit there are things you might want to know, so that you don't miss out on something or find out about it too late. Take the time to write down a list of questions to take along to your first prenatal appointment.

Ask where you could have your baby, to discover all the possibilities in your area. Some women get the impression that they have to go to a certain hospital, but this is not always true. Much depends upon how you plan to pay for the birth, what your insurance covers (if you *have* insurance coverage) and so forth. Before your visit you might like to look at the pros and cons of the hospital, birthing center and home birth beginning on page 84. You don't have to make up your mind immediately about where to have your baby. You can decide later after you've thought about it.

Ask what sort of prenatal care you can have. This is usually linked to where you have your baby. Look at the possibilities on page 27 and find out what's offered in your area.

Finally, ask what tests are available to check that your baby is healthy. These are discussed on the next page. Some tests are done very early in pregnancy, or you might have to visit a specialist to have them.

WHEN TO CONTACT YOUR DOCTOR

Even normal changes in pregnancy can make you worry when you first experience them. Here are the symptoms you should always report to your healthcare provider:

- *Vaginal bleeding—it may not be a problem, but it's best to check.*
- *Abdominal pain or cramps that get increasingly severe.*
- *High temperature, fever symptoms or excessive vomiting.*
- *Severe headache that doesn't respond to the usual remedies, blurred vision or swelling of your feet so that you can't put your shoes on. These could indicate pre-eclampsia (see page 102).*
- *Any other symptom that worries you.*

WILL MY BABY BE ALL RIGHT?

Anxiety about whether your baby will be perfect is natural. About 4% of live born babies have an abnormality. No one knows what causes most of these, but more than half of them are either mild, such as an extra toe or a birthmark, or moderate, such as a cleft palate or congenital dislocation of the hip. They may need no treatment or an operation (sometimes very minor), and the baby will lead a normal life.

Older mothers often worry that they are at greater risk of having a child with a disability than younger mothers, but only chromosomal abnormalities increase with age. For example, there is a one in 800 chance of having a baby with a major chromosomal abnormality at age 30. At age 35 it's one in 335, at 40 it's one in 100 and at 45 it's one in 25.

Testing for fetal abnormalities is part of prenatal care. If you feel that a termination is preferable to bringing a baby with disabilities into the world, tests may be able to identify potential disabilities. They may also offer reassurance so that you can enjoy the rest of your pregnancy.

But tests have disadvantages: They are not totally accurate and they detect only certain problems. For example, most rare single-gene defects are not detectable at present. They cannot show the degree of disability, which may vary considerably.

If you are not particularly worried, think carefully before having a test just because it's available. Some hospitals offer tests with the expectation that if an abnormality is diagnosed you will want a termination (abortion), but not all women agree with this. It's better to clarify your feelings in advance rather than jump on a train that may be difficult to stop.

Most women will be reassured by their results. Those who are not face difficult choices: to have more tests, to continue pregnancy knowing their baby may have a problem, or to opt for termination. Such decisions are never easy to make.

Special tests

Broadly speaking, invasive tests like amniocentesis, chorionic villus sampling (CVS) and cordocentesis carry small risks but they do diagnose with a good measure of certainty the presence of chromosomal, genetic and metabolic defects. Procedures such as ultrasound scans and blood tests that do not involve penetrating the uterus carry fewer risks to the baby, but give less information.

Policies regarding how and when tests are performed vary. Most women are offered an ultrasound scan, although routine scans do not always check for abnormalities. In some areas women over 35 or with a family history of a disability are usually offered amniocentesis. In others, all women are offered a blood test followed by amniocentesis if the results suggest that the baby might have a disability. If a test is not available locally, you may be referred to a center that provides it. If you are considered low risk, your insurance plan may not cover the cost of some tests.

The more experienced a healthcare provider is at providing tests and interpreting results, the safer the procedure is likely to be. Recently introduced tests may be less reliable and carry more risks. Ask your doctor for up-to-date local information.

Blood tests select pregnancies where the baby may be at higher risk of certain defects so that the mother can be offered further tests. The AFP test analyzes alpha-fetoprotein levels to assess the risk of neural-tube defects such as spina bifida. The triple-marker screen and triple-plus tests combine various markers with your age to give a predicted risk for neural-tube defects and chromosome abnormalities such as Down syndrome.

The triple-plus test is performed from 13 weeks; the others, from about 15 to 22 weeks. Results are available in a week or two. Ten percent of women score below one-in-250 and will be offered amniocentesis.

Blood tests can cause unnecessary anxiety. They are not very reliable— 60% (triple-marker) and about 80% (triple-plus). Only 10% of women with raised AFP levels will be carrying a baby with a defect.

Ultrasound scans: Scans can date a pregnancy fairly accurately at 16 to 18 weeks (see page 62), check your baby's growth, diagnose multiple pregnancies and establish the position of your baby or placenta. They detect abnormalities in the spine and organs such as the heart or kidneys, although before 13 weeks most scans only pick up major defects. They cannot detect genetic, metabolic or chromosomal abnormalities unless there are physical signs associated with them.

The best time for anomaly screening is between 18 and 22 weeks, or 30-plus weeks for minor defects. A scan's effectiveness at detecting defects depends on the quality of the equipment, the skill of the technician, your baby's position and the time taken over the procedure.

"I enjoyed my prenatal care, except for waiting around at my first visit to the hospital. I wanted my baby to be healthy so I took all the advice offered, but of course I had moments of wondering what I'd do if she wasn't.

I decided not to have tests after talking to my partner, my doctor and friends who'd had them. I didn't think the evidence would tell me enough to base a decision on, and felt that I wouldn't be given anything I couldn't cope with. That was more important than numbers on paper saying I was low-risk or whatever. " JOANNE

Before a scan, you drink plenty of water, because a full bladder pushes the uterus forward to give a better picture. Your abdomen is lubricated with gel and a transducer bounces high-frequency waves off your baby to build a picture on a TV screen. It's exciting to see your baby and can help you feel close to her. But although scans appear to be safe, nobody knows if there are long-term risks to future generations. Some people feel they should not be used routinely. If you are

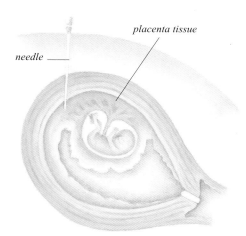

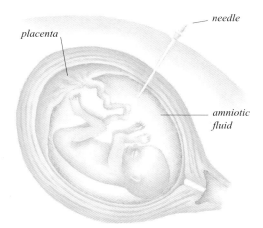

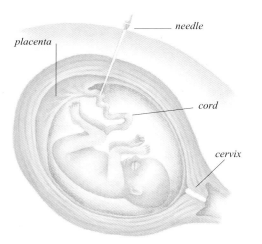

Above: *Chorionic villus sampling (CVS). Cells are taken from the edge of the placenta at 10 to 14 weeks.*

Above right: *Amniocentesis. A sample of amniotic fluid is withdrawn at 16 to 18 weeks.*

Right: *Cordocentesis. A sample of the baby's blood is withdrawn from near the placenta after 18 weeks.*

uncertain, ask the reason for the scan.

Amniocentesis: Amniocentesis is performed at 16 to 18 weeks to detect abnormalities such as Down syndrome, cystic fibrosis and Tay Sach's disease. Guided by a scan, a fine, hollow needle is passed through your abdomen and a sample of amniotic fluid is taken from around your baby. Cells are cultured, so results take three to five weeks to come through. You may wish to ask your baby's sex; if you're told it's a girl there's a slight chance that the female cells cultured could be yours, not your baby's.

Occasionally amniocentesis causes infection. There is a 1% risk of miscarriage and a 1% risk that the test will need to be repeated, with the same risk of miscarriage. Three percent of tested babies have breathing problems after birth, but these are usually temporary and mild.

Chorionic villus sampling (CVS): This detects abnormalities similar to those picked up by amniocentesis. A sample of the chorionic villi (the tissue

"If you decide to have tests, you need to talk it over with your partner so you're both sure what you would do if there was a problem. Our experience ended happily with the birth of a perfect baby, but my pregnancy was stressful.

My triple test suggested a risk of Down syndrome, so I had an amniocentesis. This showed an abnormality and I went to a specialist for cordocentesis. Although we were given the all-clear, my husband and I were still afraid that something was wrong. We didn't admit it to each other until afterwards, but I couldn't look forward to the birth in case something happened." ANNETTE

that will later develop into the placenta) is taken through the vagina or the abdomen at 11 to 12 weeks. Results take a few days. There may be at least 1% risk of miscarriage, up to 2% risk of false-positive results (changes in the cells of the chorionic villi that are not present in your baby), and 1% chance that the test may need to be repeated. The skills of the laboratory technician and the doctor who carries out the test are significant in maximizing reliability and safety. A doctor needs to perform about 75 tests to learn the technique.

Cordocentesis (fetal-blood sampling): Cordocentesis tests for a wide range of defects plus diseases such as rubella and toxoplasmosis. A needle is inserted through the abdomen into the umbilical vein in the cord close to the placenta, and a sample of blood is withdrawn. It is performed after 18 weeks when the baby's blood vessels are big enough.

This test is not widely available and is only done to confirm a diagnosis suspected after other tests. The results are available in about two days, depending on the problem. The miscarriage risk is 2% to 4%, or less if the doctor performs more than 30 tests a year.

Early tests

Specialists can perform early tests, although some are still under evaluation and may carry greater risks. However, reassurance or termination if necessary is available sooner in pregnancy. For many women this is an important advantage.

First-trimester scan: Using high-quality equipment at between 11 and 13 weeks it's possible to measure a dark space behind the baby's neck. If this space is 3mm or more, the risk that the baby has a chromosomal abnormality is at least five times higher than your age alone would predict, and you will be offered CVS or amniocentesis. If it is less than 3mm, the risk is six to seven times less than that of any woman of your age and you might feel sufficiently reassured not to have an invasive test carrying the risk of miscarriage. Women with normal or reduced risks are usually advised to have an anomaly scan at about 20 weeks to exclude defects not linked with chromosomal abnormalities.

Coelocentesis: This involves testing the coelomic fluid around the amniotic sac for chromosomal defects. It can be performed before 10 weeks and may carry less risk of miscarriage than CVS.

Deciding about tests

Fetal testing produces dilemmas that previous generations never had to face. The burden of responsibility may feel impossibly heavy to bear when you realize that the tests themselves carry potential risks as well as benefits, and the decisions are yours to make.

Whether you decide to have testing depends on how you weigh the risks and benefits. For instance, at the age of 40, the risks of amniocentesis causing a miscarriage or detecting a major chromosomal defect are equal: one in a hundred. If you are under 40 years of age, the risk of miscarriage is greater than the likelihood of detecting a problem. If you're over 40 years old, it's the other way around.

You might also want to consider factors such as how easily you conceive, how important *this* baby is to you and how you feel about having an affected child. If you were 38 years old and worried about having a baby with Down syndrome, detecting this might outweigh the risk of a miscarriage. On the other hand, a woman of 42 who had trouble conceiving and has fewer chances of conceiving again might feel the risk of losing a baby through an invasive test is too high.

Many people with a disability are saddened by the fear their condition arouses in others. But fear is not always rational. It depends on your view of the world, your emotional and financial resources, your experience of children with a disability and the effects you feel such a child would have on you and your family.

Some reasons for having tests:

- You simply could not cope with a baby with disabilities. Tests may reassure you or give you the option of termination.
- You already have a child with a disability or a family history of a defect and want to know if this baby is affected.
- You feel that having tests means you have done everything possible to avoid having a child with a disability.
- You feel the potential drawbacks are a small price to pay for the information or reassurance tests could provide.

Some reasons for not having tests:

- You feel that they would not give you accurate enough information on which to base decisions.
- You are not unduly anxious and want to enjoy your pregnancy without the worry tests might cause.
- You prefer to accept what comes and would accept a disability and cope with it if it happened.

The following summary may help you decide, with your family and your doctor, on the test that is right for you.

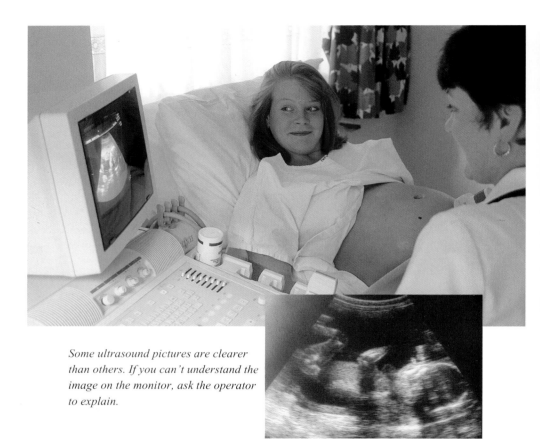

Some ultrasound pictures are clearer than others. If you can't understand the image on the monitor, ask the operator to explain.

Blood test: Blood tests carry no risks but they may increase anxiety. Think twice if you don't want to risk an invasive test. If you are considered high risk but want to avoid amniocentesis, a blood test might reassure you. If you are not offered a blood test through your insurance plan, or if you do not have insurance coverage, you could pay for it yourself. The triple-plus test is more reliable than the triple-marker screen.

Amniocentesis: If you want a definite diagnosis, waiting for blood test results would delay this, so consider choosing amniocentesis.

CVS: An option if you want a definite diagnosis early in pregnancy.

Ultrasound scans: Brief routine scans do not check for all physical defects, but an anomaly scan at 20 weeks might reassure you. A first-trimester scan to measure the dark space behind the baby's neck might help you decide whether to have further tests.

Waiting for results

Waiting for results may be more stressful than you anticipate. Wondering if your baby has a disability brings unexpected and distressing emotions. If further tests are suggested, most women expect the worst, so waiting is especially stressful. You never think you'll face this situation so it's always a shock, and your confidence may be so shaken that you won't feel completely reassured until your baby is born.

Remember that more than half the women who are offered further tests will be told that all is well; and that around half of all abnormalities are mild or moderate defects that can be treated.

Facing an unwanted result: Many women intend to have a termination if there's a problem. But what seemed the obvious choice when there was a strong possibility it would not be necessary can be much harder when your pregnancy is showing and you can feel your baby moving.

You may worry about ending a pregnancy needlessly because the test was wrong, or the baby is only mildly affected. This is something you will never know so it's best to assume the test is correct. Termination is not, of course, the only option. You could continue your pregnancy, even though your baby might not live or might be disabled. Another possibility you could consider is foster care or adoption.

Don't be pressured into making quick judgments; thinking about things for a few days will make little difference. The decision has to be one that you can live with. It isn't easy and you will need support.

Discuss the results with your doctor or a genetic specialist and your family. It may help to talk to parents who have faced similar decisions, or to someone with the same disability. Organizations such as the March of Dimes, listed in the Appendix, can give you information or refer you to support groups, whatever your decision.

Coping with termination: Although it is distressing to think about, knowing what may happen can make termination less discouraging. You will be admitted to the gynecology or maternity ward, and will probably be given a private room. If the pregnancy is less than 14 weeks, the neck of the uterus is usually dilated and the fetus is removed under local or general anesthetic. After 14 weeks, obstetricians have different policies, some favoring dilation and evacuation under general anesthesia and others feeling that induced labor is safer, using prostaglandin suppositories or an I.V. (see page 146). Because the uterus is not ready for labor, it can be longer and more painful, but your partner or a friend can be with you and pain relief will be available. The thought of going through labor may be profoundly upsetting, but some healthcare providers feel this really is safer for you.

Termination inevitably causes great sadness. It's hard to take such a responsibility, but uncertainty is part of life and you can only make a decision with the knowledge you have at the time. If you have done your best, you have to assume your choice was the right one. Discuss how you feel with a good listener. Your healthcare provider or a sympathetic friend may help if your partner feels unable to talk about it because of his own distress.

Give yourself time to come to terms with feelings of grief or guilt. Emotional pain cannot be anesthetized; it has to be faced and lived through. Taking positive steps to come to terms with it will help you move forward more confidently to a new pregnancy.

QUESTIONS AND ANSWERS

Q: Going by my last period, my baby is due on May 17. An ultrasound at 12 weeks said I am due on May 22 but another at 20 weeks gave May 14 as my due date. A midwife said they judge when a baby is due from the scan dates, but which ones?

A: Ultrasound scans date a pregnancy accurately to within a few days at 7 to 12 weeks. From 13 to 20 weeks they are slightly less accurate (within a week), and after 20 weeks they are steadily less reliable. The earlier scan date is probably the one to go by. Your baby is likely to arrive within a week either side of May 22. Having said this, babies sometimes ignore what they are supposed to do and arrive when they feel like it!

Q: When I was scanned at 14 weeks I was told that my placenta is low and I'll need another scan later on to see if it has moved. If not, I may need a Cesarean section. Why is this?

A: Usually the placenta implants in the upper wall, well out of the way of the cervix, or neck of the uterus. If it was low down, it might begin to detach when the cervix opens. Depending on the degree, a Cesarean section might be the safest option. A placenta that lies completely over the cervix (*placenta previa*) would prevent the baby from emerging safely, so a Cesarean birth would certainly be planned.

The placenta doesn't physically change position, but early in pregnancy it's hard to tell if it has implanted in the lower area of the uterus or what will become the upper part. This can be checked by another scan later on, when the uterus is bigger. The majority are found to be absolutely fine.

Q: I'm three months pregnant and my doctor says I've put on half the total weight gain I'm allowed already. Should I go on a diet?

A: In early pregnancy, women who suffer nausea and vomiting sometimes put on no weight. Others gain weight rapidly, adding fat stores on thighs and buttocks that are used up when breastfeeding. Doctors often suggest a total gain of 25 to 45 pounds (11-20kg) is reasonable. A large-framed woman would be towards the upper end and a petite woman at the lower end.

These are guidelines and there are wide variations. Excess weight increases the risk of minor problems such as varicose veins and backache and may contribute to more serious problems.

The quality of the food you eat is probably more important than the quantity. Eat according to your appetite, and no more. But don't diet, except on medical advice, because using up your fat stores would only provide your baby with calories and babies also need a steady supply of nutrients to grow in a healthy way.

Q: My sister prevented stretch marks by rubbing oil into her stomach every day, but a friend who also did so said it made no difference. What should I do?

A: Stretch marks appear on your stomach, thighs or breasts. They look like purplish streaks under the skin and are caused by the lower layers stretching. Women who gain weight rapidly tend to have more of them but it also depends on skin type. Rubbing in oil or special creams doesn't prevent them, although it may make your skin feel more comfortable. If your sister has no stretch marks, you may have inherited skin with good elasticity. About 90% of women develop at least a few, and some women get a lot.

Occasionally a rash develops, but your healthcare provider can prescribe something for it. Stretch marks gradually fade to cream or silvery gray. Look on them as a badge of motherhood!

Q: I have a small frame and my midwife says my baby is a good size. I'm worried about having a difficult birth. Should I eat less so that the baby will be smaller?

A: When your midwife says your baby is a "good size," she may mean exactly right for you, or she may simply be making conversation! It can be remarkably hard to judge a baby's size before birth. Anxiety often makes women give doctors' and midwives' pronouncements unjustified significance.

The sort of birth you have depends on the size of your pelvic cavity (not your overall frame, so don't worry about your height or shoe size), the amount of the hormone relaxin circulating to increase its dimensions, and the position of the baby. A small woman with a good-sized pelvic cavity or plenty of relaxin circulating could give birth to a big baby more easily than a large woman whose baby was in an awkward position.

Eat nutritious food according to your appetite, because a healthy mother is more likely to have a normal birth. If you eat slightly less than your body requires your own health will suffer because your baby is served first; if you eat much less, your baby will fail to grow. This is undesirable and could make the birth more complicated rather than easier.

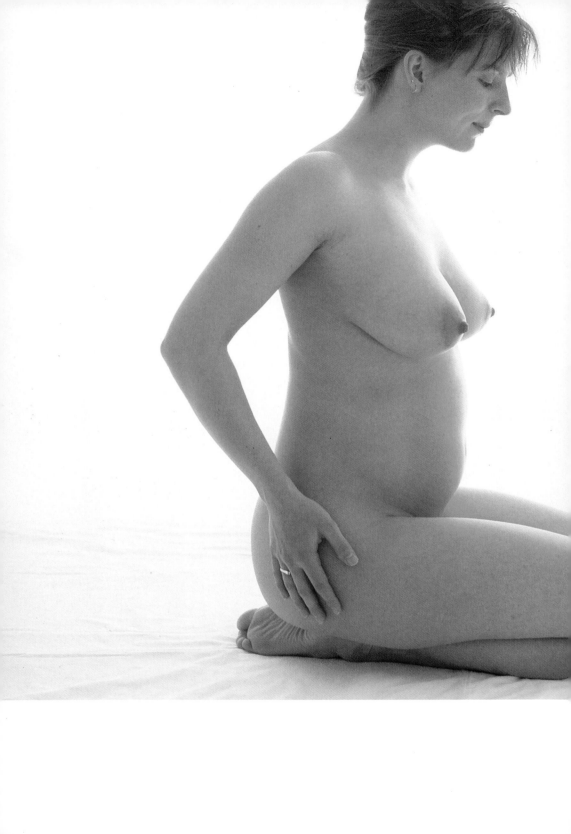

5

Mid-
Pregnancy

(MONTHS 4 to 6)

"I felt my baby flutter today! Suddenly I'm alive and full of energy. Everywhere the world seems filled with pregnant women like me. I never really noticed how many there are around before I got pregnant myself!"

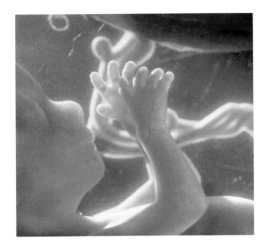

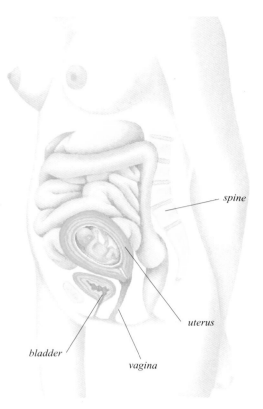

spine

bladder

uterus

vagina

FOUR MONTHS

Above: *This fetus is about four months. You can see the umbilical cord by the hands.*
Right: *Fourth month: Your uterus has expanded into your abdominal cavity and soon you'll feel the baby's movements. Fifth month: There's less room for your intestines and stomach as your uterus takes up the space.*
Sixth month: Your baby still has room to turn somersaults in your uterus.

HOW YOUR BABY DEVELOPS

In the fourth month, your baby and the placenta are each about the length of your first finger. "Placenta" means *cake* in Latin, reflecting both its shape and its nourishing function.

The blood vessels in the umbilical cord carry food and waste products between you and your baby. Their walls are like a chain-link fence, excluding large molecules while allowing small molecules and gases to filter through. So anesthetics and some infections can pass from mother to baby and certain drugs can be used to treat the baby through the mother. Like a water-filled garden hose, the cord rarely becomes knotted because it tends to uncurl if the baby's movements tangle it.

By 16 weeks, your baby is as long as your hand and as heavy as an apple. He floats in about a teacupful of amniotic fluid. His eyes, ears and nose are well formed and his fingernails and genitals can now be identified. At the end of the fifth month he measures about 12 inches (30cm) and weighs 1 pound

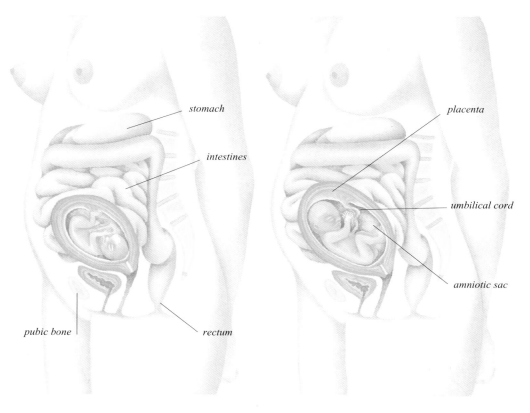

stomach

intestines

placenta

umbilical cord

pubic bone

rectum

amniotic sac

FIVE MONTHS   SIX MONTHS

(450g). Now he has eyelashes and pale-pink nipples and the buds of his permanent teeth are forming. Your baby opens his eyes and looks around. His grip develops and he makes breathing movements with his chest. Although still too immature to function on his own, all his bodily systems are beginning to work.

HOW YOU MAY FEEL

By about 16 weeks the exhaustion, sickness and see-saw emotions you may have been experiencing usually settle down. It's a great morale booster to feel pregnant rather than ill! A first pregnancy often barely shows for five or six months, but with later pregnancies you may lose your waist by the fourth month. Most women enjoy looking pregnant, but some are mildly embarrassed or feel that instead of looking pregnant they simply look fat!

For the next few weeks you may feel relaxed and fulfilled, although you could also experience apprehension about the future, and a feeling that you

- *Hair and skin problems similar to those experienced before a period, caused by increased secretion of oils.*
- *Red, itchy patches or dark pigmentation on your skin, brittle nails or a heightened sense of smell.*
- *An ache at one or both sides of your abdomen, caused by the fibrous ligaments that anchor the uterus in your body stretching as your baby grows.*
- *Increased vaginal secretions and a tendency to overheat more easily because of the extra blood circulating.*
- *Vivid dreams because your sleep is disturbed by your baby's movements and you wake up more frequently.*

cannot quite keep your usual grip on life. Fortunately, these moments of self-doubt often occur between periods when you feel utterly confident and almost euphoric.

Many women feel and look healthy, with thicker hair and a clear skin, but others wonder when the flower of womanhood will start to bloom. As the growing uterus takes up space in your abdomen, moving your intestines and stomach aside to make room, you may begin to experience annoying discomforts. If they are troublesome, talk to your doctor or try a self-help remedy (see page 72). The symptoms listed at the top of this page usually disappear soon after the birth.

RELATIONSHIP WITH YOUR PARTNER

Your partner also has to adjust to parenthood, which will affect him as profoundly as it affects you. As your pregnancy progresses he may become more actively involved, encouraging your efforts to get fit, or helping to gather information and make decisions about the birth. He may rethink his attitude to work or life in general, make changes in his commitments, notice small jobs around the home that have been ignored for months, or enthusiastically decide you should move to another house before the birth.

However, some men react by spending more time away from home where they feel more confident; for example, taking on extra work or spending more time with their friends. If your partner resists taking an active interest, don't pressure him. He may change his mind in time.

Pregnancy is a time of transition for both partners but, while you have your expanding girth to focus attention on you, your partner has no physical signs to single him out in any way. It's easy to overlook his needs, especially if, like many men, he finds it hard to talk about feelings.

About one man in 10 suffers mild anxiety symptoms, such as toothache, stomachache, loss of appetite or sickness. This is called the *couvade* and in some cultures it is expected and ritualized because it refocuses attention on the father and helps him to handle change. Many fathers become less anxious as the pregnancy advances and they begin to adjust to the new role.

Making love

Some couples want to make love more often during pregnancy and others find their libido declines. The most common experience is that sexual desire fluctuates, often increasing in mid-pregnancy and declining nearer the birth. You may be more aware of your sexuality during the fifth and sixth months, when your blood supply and vaginal secretions are increased. Enthusiasm is catching and can lead to a more satisfying sex life than ever. The physical and emotional changes of pregnancy affect desire and pleasure positively and negatively. Body image can be a real issue for some couples. Some women dislike having a rounded body and need reassurance that they are still attractive. Some men find the voluptuous shapes and stronger smells of pregnancy turn them off. Equally, many couples find these factors a novel delight.

Your partner may become anxious about the baby, but intercourse that is comfortable and enjoyable for you is not harmful, although you may need to choose positions that do not cause pressure on your abdomen or deep penetration. If you are having problems with your pregnancy, your doctor might suggest no intercourse. Orgasm may cause colostrum (a creamy substance) to leak from your breasts, or mild, harmless contractions, but it does not normally cause miscarriage or premature labor. Oral sex is safe and can be a substitute for intercourse if you both find it enjoyable.

The quality of a relationship is built not on expertise in bed but on communication, love and understanding. Your sexual needs and your partner's may alter as pregnancy progresses. Be patient and talk about any difficulties. You will find that making these adjustments infinitely strengthens your love life.

FEELING THE BABY MOVE

For most women, feeling the baby move for the first time is a red-letter day. It can happen any time between 16 and 25 weeks. Babies are particularly active between 24 and 28 weeks. Later, they have distinct periods of rest and activity and the kicks feel stronger, a daily reminder that they are fine. If you have not felt movement for a while, try sending a "thought message" to your baby—you may get a reassuring kick in reply. A series of rhythmic knocks means your baby has hiccups!

Typically, women begin to feel movements at about 18 weeks for a first baby and somewhat earlier for subsequent babies, but they describe the sensation of those first kicks differently:

"It felt soft and fluttery, like a butterfly kiss on the cheek. I wasn't sure if I was imagining it at first."

"I thought a fly had landed on my tummy. When I looked there was nothing there, but I felt it again and knew immediately what it was."

"It was like somebody knocking or bumping against my stomach, but from the inside. It became more definite over a week or two."

"The nearest I can describe it is as a rolling or lurching sensation. I thought it was gas at first!"

Getting to know your baby

You may think that bonding is something that only happens after the birth, but for most women the process starts long before this. Thinking about your baby's welfare, worrying that he will be all right, or imagining your future life together is evidence of the bond between you.

Finding out about your baby's likes and dislikes can be great fun. He may respond to certain types of music or to his father's voice. He may stop kicking when you massage your abdomen, sing to him or sway your body; or he may decide that it's playtime as soon as you sit or lie down!

When he's in the mood he may play "games" with you, pushing your hand away when you gently press the bulge of a foot or a hand. The more you get to know your baby before he's born, the more familiar he will feel when you hold him in your arms.

STAYING HEALTHY

Considering the changes your body undergoes in pregnancy, a certain amount of discomfort is to be expected. Doctors rarely treat common symptoms such as cramps and backache unless they are extremely troublesome, because they are caused by the very things that help to maintain a healthy pregnancy—your hormones, extra blood supply and increasing weight. This doesn't mean that you have to suffer silently. Many minor problems can be avoided by common sense or alleviated by self-help remedies.

Remember to take care of your body! Get some fresh air and exercise every day and make sufficient rest a priority. Eat regularly and drink plenty of fluids. These simple things will help you cope with the extra demands of pregnancy and may prevent a range of symptoms, from mild headaches to backache and constipation. If you still have a problem, check with your healthcare provider to make sure it's nothing serious, then try a self-help remedy or alternative therapy.

"Feeling movements makes up for everything else in pregnancy. At first I thought of the baby as a fish-like creature, but now I think of her as a little person. I feel very protective and grateful for each kick, because I know she's all right. She won't kick for my partner, though. As soon as he puts his hand on my tummy, she stays still and quiet!" DEE

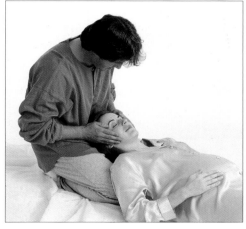

Massage Techniques

Sit or kneel while your partner massages your shoulders. He presses his thumbs on either side of your spine, working in small circles around the line of your shoulder blades.

Alternatively, lie on your back, resting your head in your partner's lap while he sits or kneels. He gently strokes along your jaw, your cheeks and your forehead.

You could also kneel or lie on your side while your partner slowly and firmly strokes his palms down your back, hand over hand. This can be comforting in early labor.

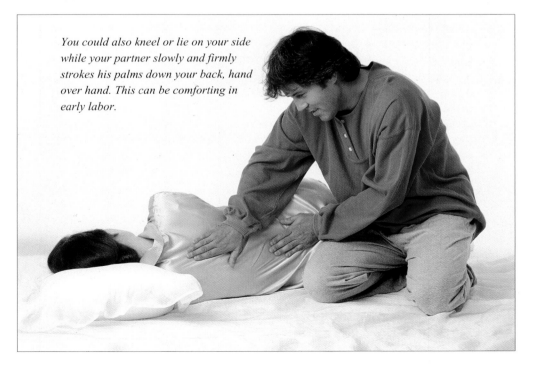

How to help yourself

Try the following self-help remedies for these common pregnancy problems:

Cramp: Painful muscle spasm, often in your leg or foot.

Self-help: Pull your foot upward instead of pointing your toes when you stretch on waking up. To improve your circulation, roll an empty bottle vigorously under your bare foot every night before going to bed. Aromatherapy massage may help. Try increasing your intake of calcium (in milk and cheese, for example) or cut down if you eat a lot of any food, such as dairy products, produce or bananas.

Fainting: Feeling light-headed or dizzy may be caused by lowered blood pressure or low blood-sugar levels.

Self-help: Lie on your side or prop yourself up with pillows (see page 101). Keep a healthful snack handy to maintain your blood-sugar levels. Dress in layers and carry a battery fan, mineral water or a spray to refresh yourself. To prevent dizziness, press down on the balls of your feet. If you feel faint, sit with your head between your knees or lie down.

Varicose veins: Soft, blue knotted veins in the legs, caused by extra blood passing through veins with relaxed walls.

Self-help: Put up your feet whenever possible, but shift your weight from foot to foot if you have to stand. Avoid crossing your legs, sitting on a hard chair edge, wearing tight underwear, elastic knee-highs or hold-up stockings. Keep support hose under your pillow and put them on before getting up. If you forget, raise your legs and hips for 10 minutes to drain blood towards your heart before putting them on.

Constipation: Hormones and your growing uterus slow down the passage of waste from the body.

Self-help: Drink more fluids and eat more fruit, vegetables or fiber-rich foods, such as bran or oats. Prune juice or dried prunes are natural laxatives. If iron tablets make you constipated, ask your healthcare provider to prescribe a different brand. Always go to the toilet when you need to—raise your feet on a footstool or upturned bucket and relax your pelvic floor (see page 45).

Hemorrhoids: Swollen veins in the rectum or around the anus that may bleed or be itchy and painful.

Self-help: Avoid straining on the toilet. Drink plenty of fluids and do pelvic-floor exercises (see page 45) to improve your blood circulation. Avoid hot baths, which make blood vessels dilate; warm baths may be soothing. Ice packs, a prescribed cream or a pad soaked in witch-hazel lotion from the pharmacist may give temporary relief. Increasing your intake of vitamins C, E and B6 may help.

Stress incontinence: When you cough or laugh you "leak" urine, or you need to go to the toilet when your bladder is empty.

Self-help: Do pelvic-floor exercises (see page 45). Never try to hold on if you know your bladder is full. If you feel the urge when you know your bladder is empty, gently tighten your pelvic floor and fix your mind on something else until the sensation subsides—in a few days things should improve.

Heartburn: A burning pain in your chest or a sour taste in your mouth. Pressure on the relaxed stomach valve allows acid from partly digested food to "burn" your esophagus.

Self-help: Eat little and often, drink separately so that your stomach is not too full, and avoid spicy and fatty foods. At the first sign of heartburn, take something alkaline, such as a sip of milk, to neutralize the acid in your esophagus and prevent a sore spot from developing. Don't exercise or bend before a meal has had time to be digested. Raise your head and shoulders on pillows in bed. Ask your healthcare provider or pharmacist for an antacid preparation.

Itchiness: Dry, stretched skin may itch late in pregnancy if you are over-tired or too hot.

Self-help: Drink plenty of water to help flush out your system. Calamine lotion or half a cupful of bicarbonate of soda in a warm bath may soothe itching. Use aqueous cream or emulsifying ointment (from the pharmacist) instead of soap, which can be drying.

Alternative therapies

These can be helpful to treat pregnancy discomforts and make you feel good. Some of them can be harmful during pregnancy, so it's very important that you only go to a qualified practitioner. Mention your pregnancy from the start, even if you think it's obvious! Here are some therapies:

Acupuncture: Fine sterile needles are inserted at certain points to balance the flow of energy in the body. This can stimulate your body to produce *endorphins* (pain-relieving substances) and help relieve problems such as nausea or fluid retention.

Aromatherapy: Essential oils or plant extracts are massaged into the body. Treatment may seem to be a pleasantly scented massage that gives a feeling of well-being, but it can affect your nervous system and hormones. To be safe, only consult someone who is fully qualified.

Homeopathy: Based on the principle "like treats like," minute amounts of substances that produce the symptom are given to stimulate the body's own defenses. It can alleviate nausea and digestive problems, for example, and also prepare your body for the birth and help speed recovery.

Medical herbalism: This ancient healing art uses the entire leaf, bark or root of a plant instead of extracting an active ingredient from it. It's gentle, but treatments can be just as powerful as conventional drugs and need similar caution. Morning sickness and anemia often respond well.

Osteopathy and chiropractic: These are widely accepted therapies that treat skeletal and muscle problems using leverage and manipulation. Many complaints of pregnancy, especially those that involve strain to the back, pelvis, and neck, respond well to manipulation.

Exercise in pregnancy

Good circulation and suppleness will make pregnancy more comfortable. Any form of exercise that helps develop stamina and suppleness is beneficial. For example, you could swim regularly, or combine exercise, fresh air and recreation by taking a brisk walk for half an hour two or three times a week.

These stretching exercises make you more aware of your body and reduce stiffness. Hormone-softened ligaments can be overstrained easily, so warm up gently first and stretch slowly, holding a pose for a few seconds up to a few minutes. Repeat each exercise about six times, and do not overdo things.

Some exercises can be adapted; for example, if you get uncomfortable or light-headed lying on the floor, do the exercise on page 77 standing against a wall: with your knees bent, tighten your abdominal muscles and pull your back firmly against the wall, holding it for a few seconds.

Above: Inner Thighs

Sit for a few minutes each day with your back straight and the soles of your feet together. Rest your forearms on your knees and let them relax downwards without forcing or bouncing them.

Left: Back and Thighs

Sit with your back straight and legs apart. Lean gently forward, pushing your heels away. Feel your back, thighs and calves stretch. Relax and rotate your ankles to improve your circulation.

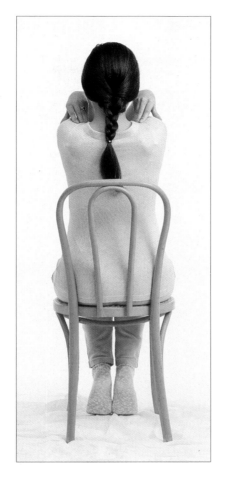

Right and below: Neck and Upper Back
Sit up straight, with your hands on your shoulders. Sweep your elbows in wide circles. Feel the stretch loosening any stiffness.

It's worth doing upper body exercises such as these if you use a wheelchair. You may be able to adapt other exercises from a book, or ask a physiotherapist for advice.

EXERCISE IN PREGNANCY

◆ *If you have any doubts about suitable exercise, ask your healthcare provider's advice.*

◆ *Join a pregnancy exercise class where you'll meet other mothers-to-be and may form friendships to enjoy after your baby is born. Ask at your local health club, recreation center, swimming pool, hospital or health clinic.*

◆ *If you have a disability, talk to the class teacher first to make sure that the location is suitable and she can provide appropriate exercises.*

◆ *If you join a general exercise class, make sure the instructor knows that you are pregnant and can advise you.*

◆ *Be wary of taking up a new sport in pregnancy, and of any competitive sports or activities that could prevent you from listening to your own body.*

◆ *Stop any exercise that feels "wrong," hurts or leaves you exhausted rather than refreshed.*

Pelvic Rock
Right: *Stand with your feet apart and your knees slightly bent. Tighten your buttock muscles and tuck your "tail" under.*
Far right: *Release your buttocks and swing your pelvis gently back with your body upright and your knees in the same position throughout.*

  Rock your pelvis back and forth to loosen it and help prevent backache. When you feel comfortable with this, move your pelvis from side to side like a belly dancer (not illustrated).

Abdominal Exercise *(see page 74)*
1. Lie on the floor with your arms a little way from your body and your knees hip-width apart and bent.

2. Flatten your back to the floor. Notice the difference between pictures 1 and 2.

3. Very slowly slide your feet along the floor while keeping your back pressed down firmly. As soon as it begins to arch, bend your knees and try again.

PREGNANCY AND WORK

In mid-pregnancy you usually have more energy, so working is easier; but it's still tiring, so don't expect too much of yourself. Most women stop work when maternity pay and leave become available. Depending on certain regulations, your health and the demands of your job, you may want to stop sooner than just before delivery. If you want to work up to delivery, your employer may require a letter from your doctor saying that it's OK.

You may count the days until you can stop work, or you may dread leaving. Either way, most women have mixed feelings when they stop working. While you are adjusting to this change, take time to make friends in your neighborhood. It can be harder to make the effort after the birth.

A good balance between work, recreation and rest will help you enjoy your pregnancy. Try these tips:

- Conserve energy whenever you can and use every spare moment to consciously relax. Don't rush around during your lunch hour. Instead, try resting at your desk or in the car, or put your feet up in your company's restroom.
- Put your social life on "slow" for a while and plan for regular early nights.
- Rearrange your work hours to avoid travel during rush hour. Ask politely for a seat on public transportation.
- Don't leave things like decorating the nursery too late. You may not feel energetic by the time you get maternity leave.

MATERNITY CLOTHES

The golden rule for maternity wear is comfort, so avoid tight waistbands, skirts that ride up or very high heels that throw your pelvis out of balance and cause backache.

If you are too large for your regular clothes but feel awkward wearing maternity clothes, raid your partner's wardrobe for bigger shirts and sweaters, or buy clothes a size or two larger than usual that you can wear later on. You will not be your normal size for several weeks after the birth, but most women do not want to continue wearing maternity clothes.

In the past, there has been a lack of stylish, affordable business clothes but this problem has been tackled by a number of companies. Look for addresses in the small advertisements of parenting magazines, in your telephone book or your local paper.

"I'm used to being active and it's frustrating not being able to do as much as usual. I run out of steam in the afternoon, so at lunch time I lie down in the company lounge.

My husband and I have our main meal in the cafeteria so we don't have to cook in the evening. We have salad or put a pizza in the oven for supper and I eat with my feet up in front of the TV. It gives me a real boost of energy."
SALLY

USEFUL MATERNITY WEAR

- *For work, buy a good-quality maternity skirt that will not lose its shape. Wear it with a variety of loose tops.*
- *For leisure, wear comfortable pants with jersey tops and large T-shirts.*
- *Extra weight and swollen feet can ruin shoes. Buy one or two pairs to wear throughout pregnancy and discard them afterwards.*
- *If you intend to breastfeed, buy loose, front-opening nightwear or use a big T-shirt. Your bust will be larger at the end of pregnancy and in the early weeks of breastfeeding.*
- *A serape, cape or poncho makes a comfortable outer garment in winter, or borrow a coat from a friend.*
- *For special occasions, check your local paper and yellow pages for clothing-rental firms that include maternity wear. When choosing an outfit for a wedding, remember that the size and fit of your dress is more important than the style. A specialist bridal shop can offer you good advice.*

PRENATAL CLASSES

Nothing guarantees an easy birth but if you go to prenatal classes you'll know what may happen and you'll be able to talk about pregnancy without feeling that your friends and family are stifling yawns! Classes vary in size, formality and the range of topics covered. You usually attend them later in pregnancy but good ones tend to fill up early, so plan ahead.

Hospital-based classes may be run by a nurse or other staff members. They can be excellent, although some hospitals give them low priority and a lot depends on the staff involved. A maternity-facilities tour may be included but you don't need to attend the classes to join it. Private classes usually go into more detail about birth. They are held at the teacher's home or a local hall for a fee. Groups are small, the approach is informal, and the teachers are usually knowledgeable and supportive.

Ask your doctor, midwife and your friends to recommend a class or check the bulletin board at the hospital or clinic.

"I was so sick for the first four months of pregnancy that I couldn't exercise and ended up feeling very sorry for myself. As soon as I was better, I joined a pregnancy exercise class and met some neat people on my wavelength.

We talk about anything, from how we're all secretly nervous about the birth to getting stranded in those incredible sex positions they show you in the books! I've learned that you don't have to be virtuous all the time. Sometimes we all meet for a healthy swim and end up in a coffee shop eating doughnuts instead!"
GINA

◆ *Attend monthly prenatal checkups. Write down questions to ask your healthcare provider in case you forget.*

◆ *Improve your fitness—go for brisk walks, swim or join a pregnancy exercise class.*

◆ *Sign up for prenatal classes now, and start to think about the sort of birth you hope to have (see page 84).*

◆ *Plan a vacation at home or away before you become too large to enjoy it, and before you face restrictions on air travel (see next page).*

◆ *Give your employer sufficient written notice before leaving work, to retain your rights.*

◆ *Check out baby equipment now—you may feel too tired to visit the baby stores in late pregnancy.*

◆ *Find out about alternative therapies (see page 73) for pregnancy discomforts and to help you feel good.*

The organizations listed in the Appendix will also be able to provide you with referrals to childbirth educators in your area.

Here are some guidelines on choosing a class:

- A small, discussion-based class may suit you if you want to ask lots of questions and make your own decisions. If you are nervous about giving birth, ask friends to recommend a teacher who helps parents feel relaxed and confident.
- Look for a large class or arrange for an individual class with an independent teacher if you prefer not to discuss birth with virtual strangers.
- Make sure the class is geared to fathers if your partner wants to be involved. Some classes treat men as onlookers, divide you into separate groups or only invite men to one or two sessions.
- You might want a women-only class if you are on your own.
- Ask whether alternative approaches will be covered if you want a natural birth. Some classes assume everyone will have drugs.
- It can be easier to share experiences with other parents and perhaps make lasting friendships in smaller groups.
- Ask whether classes will continue after the birth. You may meet women who live nearby at classes run by a childbirth educator in your community. On the other hand, if you travel some distance to a class that friends have recommended, you're likely to meet people who share your outlook on life.

QUESTIONS AND ANSWERS

Q: I'm a single parent and wish I had somebody to share my pregnancy and birth with. I don't want to rely on my family, although they are very supportive. Where else could I get support?

A: Women often share the ups and downs of pregnancy and support each other, because some partners are not interested in the details of pregnancy or don't want to attend the birth. You may be able to develop a rewarding relationship with your midwife (see page 27), and you'll meet other women at prenatal classes. It may be easier to make friendships at exercise classes, or small birth-preparation classes rather than larger ones. If your family is supportive, letting them share your pregnancy can please everyone. You might want to attend a series of La Leche League meetings. They provide valuable information and support about breastfeeding and are a good place to meet other pregnant women and new mothers in your area.

Q: We plan to go on a vacation before our baby arrives. How can I make traveling easier, and how late in pregnancy can I fly with a scheduled airline?

A: Mid-pregnancy is a good time to go on a trip, and planning will make getting there and back less stressful. However you travel, wear loose, comfortable clothes and take plenty of snacks and mineral water.

In the car, a cushion to place in the small of your back or to sit on may help. Your seatbelt should fit below your stomach and across your chest, not under your arm. Sitting still for long periods makes you stiff, so allow extra time to stop every couple of hours and stretch your legs.

If you travel by plane, try to reserve a front or aisle seat so that you have more leg room and can walk around and visit the toilet more easily. Most airlines require a doctor's letter confirming you are fit to travel from 28 to 36 weeks, after which they will only carry you in an emergency. Individual airlines may vary, so check this. Remember to take your medical records with you, just in case you need a doctor during your trip!

Q: My brain cells are disappearing as fast as my waist expands! Why do I forget and lose things and what can I do about it?

A: Hormones cause some upheaval and part of your mind becomes taken up with the changes you are experiencing. Tiredness may also affect your ability to concentrate. The best solution is to accept the situation with good humor, rest more and use strategies to handle the overload. Start each day by listing things to do, putting a checkmark by the essentials and a question mark by the rest. Keep it on your bulletin board or in your purse. A checklist by the door will remind you of vital things, such as closing windows or locking up. Tie your keys to your handbag with a long ribbon. Write reminders on your calendar or the back of your hand, or put tiny, colored stickers where you will see them to jog your memory about appointments. If you streamline your life, it will be much easier to cope.

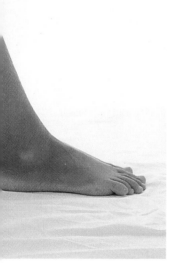

Plans and Choices

❝You don't have to make choices. You can go along with what other people decide. But I love the challenge of learning about birth and I'd rather decide for myself what I want. It's not that different from planning a special vacation. ❞

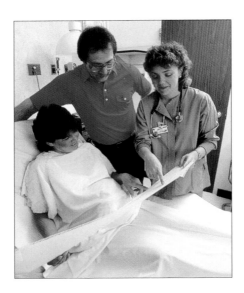

The nurse is explaining what the output from a fetal heart monitor means. You can share decisions about your treatment with her and your partner.

YOUR CHOICES FOR BIRTH

There are two, equally safe, basic approaches to care in labor. The first advocates intervention before a problem occurs in the hope of preventing it. The second favors watching carefully, but not intervening unless a problem actually arises. For example, if your labor was normal, but slow, a doctor who favored the first approach might want to speed it up using an I.V., in case you became too tired to push effectively. One who preferred the second approach might want to reassure you that everything was normal and help you conserve energy for pushing.

If a complication occurs, technology will be used to help, but if everything is normal, there is no evidence that it makes birth safer. Intervention is a matter of judgment, which depends partly on the philosophy of the staff. Some feel that intervening prevents a difficult or dangerous situation from arising. Others argue equally strongly that it can make further intervention necessary and actually cause problems that otherwise might not have arisen.

You may feel more confident giving birth using technology, or you may feel that nature knows best.

Birth in a hospital

The majority of births take place in a hospital. In every labor, a nurse or nurse-midwife will carry out routine checks such as listening to your baby's heartbeat and measuring your blood pressure. Beyond this, hospitals have different approaches to labor. Some expect their staff to follow so many rules that it considerably reduces your options; others are much more open to individual choices.

For a "high-tech" birth you stay in bed throughout labor, with a hormone I.V. to control the contractions, a fetal monitor to record your baby's heartbeat and perhaps an epidural (see page 122) to numb sensation. One intervention sometimes leads to others, so read chapter 10 to decide if this approach is right for you.

With a "low-tech" approach there is no active intervention as long as you and your baby are fine. You don't have to stay in bed but can walk around, use a rocking chair, kneel on a mattress on the floor or lean over a bean-bag chair to get comfortable. You can cope with contractions using relaxation and breathing techniques, but pain relief is always on hand if you need it.

"I decided not to give birth in my local hospital because it doesn't offer epidurals on request. I accept that there are some disadvantages to them but I don't see any point in suffering unnecessarily. If you wouldn't have a filling at the dentist without an injection, why give birth in pain?

I phoned a larger hospital 20 miles away to find out their approach, and then asked to be referred there. It's completely geared to using technology and I feel secure knowing that everything will be monitored very closely. It also has excellent facilities in its neonatal intensive-care unit, just in case. " MEGAN

Many hospitals have a mixed approach: basically low-tech but with rules regarding, for example, when an I.V. should be set up to speed labor, or how long you can push before having an assisted delivery. These rules are often set by a committee comprised of administrative, medical and nursing staff. If your labor is normal, you are free to accept or decline many established hospital rules, as long as both you and your baby are fine. However, in emergencies or in the event that an operative delivery is necessary, hospital rules will probably be followed without exception.

In most hospitals you can elect to stay for between six hours and a few days after your baby's birth. Even with a first baby, some mothers go home within hours, and most leave within a day or two. A pediatrician will check the baby before you leave the hospital and advise you on feeding and baby care.

The length of stay in a hospital is an individual decision, depending on how you feel, whether it's your first baby or you have other children at home, and what your insurance plan covers. As of January, 1998, insurance plans in the United States will be required to cover a hospital stay of two days following a normal vaginal birth, and four days after a Cesarean birth. If you plan an early discharge, make sure you have help at home so that you can concentrate on your baby at first.

The staff at the hospital

Staffing patterns vary, so the best way to find out who people are is to ask or look at name badges. Make a mental note of the color of the belt, shape of the

TO DECIDE WHICH APPROACH WILL SUIT YOU BEST

Check off the statements you agree with:

◆ *I don't mind being wired to machinery in labor. (a)*

◆ *People who choose to have babies at home must be crazy! (a)*

◆ *I prefer to move around and choose comfortable positions. (b)*

◆ *Labor is a natural event for most women. (b)*

◆ *I want my baby's heartbeat monitored by machine throughout the birth just in case anything goes wrong. (a)*

◆ *Relaxing in familiar surroundings should make labor easier. (b)*

◆ *Doctors and midwives usually know what's best for you. (a)*

◆ *I prefer no intervention as long as my baby is all right. (b)*

◆ *I want to avoid drugs if possible, because they have side effects. (b)*

◆ *Knock me out, please! I'd rather not feel a thing in labor. (a)*

The more "a" statements you checked, the more likely you'll feel reassured using birth technology. If you checked mostly "b" statements, you may prefer a natural approach. Staff in large hospitals may be more geared to using technology than those in small hospitals or birthing centers. Home births are least likely to involve intervention in labor.

cap or whatever distinguishes the ranks at your hospital. If everything is normal, you may not see your doctor until you are nearly ready to push out your baby. But there is always at least one doctor on duty whom you could ask to see. Check the name badge, which will normally have a doctor's status on it. Here are some of the people you may see in the hospital:

Obstetrician: A specialist in the medical problems of pregnancy, labor and birth.

Family physician: A specialist in a broad range of family-health matters, including pregnancy, labor and birth.

Staff nurse or nurse-midwife: She is qualified to care for you during pregnancy, normal labor and delivery. After the birth she helps you feed and care for your new baby.

Resident: He or she is a medical doctor undergoing specialized training in obstetrics.

Anesthetist: You'll see him or her if you've decided to have an epidural or need a Cesarean birth.

Pediatrician: A specialist in baby problems, who will also check your baby to make sure that she's healthy before you leave the hospital.

Lactation consultant: A mother who has breastfed her own children and who is trained to help other women. Not all hospitals have them.

Birthing centers

Birthing centers are run by local doctors and midwives. They can be separate institutions or attached to a hospital, and appeal to women who prefer a "low-tech" approach. They are not, as is sometimes thought, reserved for women having second babies, women who live in certain areas or for any other predetermined group.

You make your own way to the birthing center when you are in labor. Your doctor will be informed and may attend, although a midwife usually supervises labor and delivers your baby. If a complication occurs, you will be moved to an obstetric unit in a hospital.

Home birth

Home birth is as safe as hospital birth for most women, and it reduces risks such as infection and the negative effects of drugs and interventions. Even if you are over 35, small in stature, having your first baby or have a history of problems in pregnancy or labor, you may still be approved for a home birth. Some medical conditions, such as heart trouble, which could be stressed by labor, might make it unwise; but each case must be treated individually.

About a month before you are due, your doctor or midwife will give you a sealed delivery pack of things she'll need at the birth, and discuss arrangements, such as having a clear space where she can put her supplies. When labor starts she'll check you. If it's still early she may make other calls, but once labor is established she'll stay with you, contacting your doctor if he wants to be there. She'll have pain-relief medication and baby resuscitation equipment with her, although many women don't need them. She'll deliver your baby and stitch you if necessary. If a problem arises, she'll transfer you to a hospital. After the birth she'll visit you at home at least one more time. You may be expected to come to her office for two more checkups at two weeks and six weeks postpartum. You'll be given a phone number to use to contact her for advice.

Home birth is usually a positive choice, reflecting confidence in your ability to give birth, your midwife's skills and your family's support. You do need help—there's no vacation at home, no nurses to take over if you want a rest! Getting everything ready before the birth takes effort and you'll need someone to keep the household

"Some people prefer not to think about the birth in advance and just take things as they come, but I feel more confident if I've thought everything through.

I'm going to have my baby at my parents' house, where I usually stay while my husband is away. The midwife seems very happy about it, and my mother will look after my 2-year-old daughter. When she was born, my labor was quite short—only six hours—so if this labor is faster, as second ones sometimes are, I'd worry about getting to the hospital. " WENDY

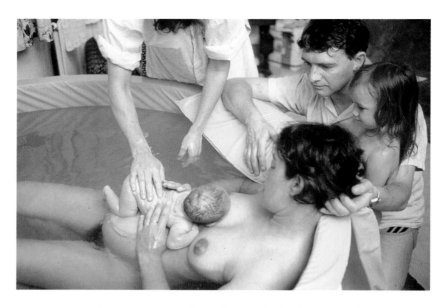

running. To find out more about home birth, buy a book or contact Informed Home Birth (see Appendix).

Water birth

Laboring in water can help you feel relaxed and make it easier to cope with the pain. Some hospitals and birthing centers have a pool installed, or you can rent a birth pool. But water isn't the answer to every problem! It can help labor progress but it cannot reduce problems such as dangerously high blood pressure. If a problem arises, intervention may still be needed.

Water birth usually means using water to relieve pain and reduce the need for intervention during labor.

Some babies are born underwater because the birth is very fast, but most mothers leave the pool before delivery. It is thought to be very safe if guidelines about water temperature and things like the use of aromatherapy oils, how far dilated you must be before you enter the pool and when you must leave it, are followed.

❝I knew nothing about water birth until I was 33 weeks pregnant, when a friend mentioned it. It sounded just right because I want as little intervention and as much privacy as possible during labor.

The midwives left us to find out about it for ourselves, so I borrowed books from the library. My partner was supportive but he insisted that I have the baby in a hospital.

I've rented an oval pool so that I can stretch out or brace myself across it. When my contractions start, we'll go to the hospital and my partner will put up the pool. It's been such fun planning the birth that I'm really looking forward to labor! ❞ RACHEL

Left: Using a birth pool can be an effective way of relieving pain in labor. *Right:* You may find it easier to relax in the familiar surroundings of your own home.

Most practical difficulties can be overcome, although you may have to search diligently to find a supportive birth-care provider. Women have had water births with twins or breech babies, when they normally use a wheelchair or after a previous Cesarean section. They have been arranged at a week's notice and have taken place in mobile homes. For more information, look for a book at your library or bookstore, or ask your midwife.

If you cannot arrange a water birth, don't forget the bathtub! It may be too small to allow free movement, but the water could still help relieve pain.

Getting the birth you want

The easiest way to get the sort of birth that's right for you is to choose carefully where to have your baby. Listen to your doctor's advice, read Chapter 10 about help in labor and discuss all the possibilities. When you and your partner have weighed everything, you're entitled to have your baby wherever you feel is right.

If you decide to have your baby in a hospital, ask your healthcare provider, midwife and friends who have had a baby recently for their views about different hospitals. One institution might be so accustomed to using birth technology that you'd find it hard if you wanted a natural birth, but another might not offer epidurals on request if you prefer this. You can phone a hospital prenatal clinic directly to find out what they offer. The staff should have time to discuss their approach with you or to arrange for you to visit. Think about asking some of the following questions.

For a high-tech birth:
- Can my baby be monitored electronically throughout my labor?
- Can I have an elective epidural even if I go into labor at night or during the weekend?

- How long would I be left before an I.V. is set up to increase the strength of my contractions?
- Would the technology be available even if the unit was busy?

For a low-tech birth:
- Provided the baby and I are both all right, how long can I go through labor without intervention?
- How will the staff help me to have a natural labor? What is the episiotomy rate here, and will the staff help me deliver my baby without an episiotomy (see page 151) or tear?
- Can I use whatever position I like for the delivery?

CHOOSING BABY EQUIPMENT

Choosing baby clothes and furniture is fun, but don't buy everything before your baby arrives. You may receive gifts or change your mind in light of experience. Here's a guide to the bare necessities you'll need for the early weeks:

Four T-shirts: Wrap-over styles are easy to put on, but ties can be tricky. Look for wrap-around T-shirts with snaps. Crewnecks fit well, but pulling them over the baby's head takes a little practice. Bodysuits don't ride up but they may be outgrown more quickly.

Four stretchsuits/nightgowns: Stretchsuits are neat and easy to care for; nightgowns may make diaper changing easier at first.

Two cardigans/sweaters: Loose sleeves make dressing easy.

Two shawls: Wrap your baby snugly in a cotton shawl to sleep at first. Draping a warm shawl over the car seat is easier than putting a snowsuit on your baby in the early weeks.

Snowsuit, hat, mittens (for a winter baby): A snowsuit with zippers down both legs or right under the diaper and wide armholes makes dressing easier. Hats with ties stay on better.

Diapers: Disposable ones are more convenient. Buy small packs until you know what suits you, then shop around to find the cheapest supplier and buy them in bulk. Reusable terry-cloth squares or shaped diapers are environment-friendly but need sanitizing powder. Cloth diapers need liners and pants, too. Some areas have inexpensive diaper-washing services.

Changing equipment: You'll need a changing table or a changing mat to put on the floor, or on a table or chest of drawers at the right height. Cotton rolls are cheaper than balls. Buy small amounts of diaper cream until you find what suits you and your baby's skin.

Car safety seat: Birth-to-nine-months seats with handles are easy to carry around. Two-way models (birth to four years) can be heavy and cumbersome in the early weeks. Some car seats do not fit in all cars, so check that the model you choose fits your vehicle. Most hospitals won't let you take your baby home unless you have a car seat installed.

Carrier/basket: A carrier can be useful; baskets can be lighter and easier to carry around.

Stroller: Choose from traditional or collapsible types and try pushing, folding and lifting different models. You could delay buying a stroller by using a baby sling at first.

Four bassinet or crib sheets and two blankets: Look for easy-care labels. A shawl could double as a blanket, and vice-versa.

Bath: A basin or plastic washtub is fine at first. A simple plastic bath (with or without a stand) is heavy to lift when filled with water; one that rests on the sides of the bathtub may be outgrown quickly.

Breast pads (for breastfeeding): Shaped pads are more expensive but may be more comfortable and stay in place better.

Six bottles and sterilizing equipment (for bottle-feeding): Wide-necked bottles are easier to fill but may be more expensive. To sterilize them, cold water with sterilizing tablets or liquid is cheapest; electric steam sterilizers are convenient and use no chemicals; microwave sterilizers are compact.

BREAST- OR BOTTLE-FEEDING?

Many parents believe, incorrectly, that formula milks are so sophisticated that there is little difference between them and breast milk. Breast milk contains hormones and enzymes that are not in formula milks because nobody knows what purpose they serve, plus substances to help fight bacterial and viral infections and combat childhood illnesses. Breast milk has all the right nutrients in the right amounts for your baby to grow healthily.

Breast milk adjusts to compensate if a baby is premature and alters as your baby grows and her needs change. It even dilutes in hot weather to satisfy a baby's thirst. There can be no doubt that breast is best for your baby.

Whether you breast- or bottle-feed, the most important thing is a happy, rewarding feeding relationship with your baby. If you can't breastfeed, or choose for various reasons to bottle-feed, there are compensations. It can be discouraging to feel that your baby is completely dependent on you, and other people can take over when you bottle-feed.

PARENTING WITH DISABILITIES

Parents with disabilities have needs as varied as their conditions, but pregnancy can seem especially discouraging if your doctor or midwife has little practical experience with your particular disability.

You may feel it's hard to plan ahead when you don't know the problems you are likely to face, but all parents discover how to handle pregnancy, birth and child care by trial and error. Small children seem to adapt easily to a parent's disability, perhaps because disabled parents spend more time over each task and talk to their baby more, so that a cooperative relationship develops.

PREPARING A TODDLER

Parents who are delighted to be having another baby want their other child to feel the same. But small children have little idea of time, so announcing the arrival of a baby six months beforehand is like talking about Santa Claus in June! Usually, the younger the child, the closer to the birth you can wait before telling her.

Get your child used to the general idea of families first. Point out babies, read stories, and talk about her friends' brothers and sisters so that she begins to understand what will happen.

Make changes in her life, such as starting preschool, well in advance. If she is moving to a new bedroom, let her settle in before setting the crib up in her old room! In the last month, she may enjoy helping to wash baby clothes or clean the stroller. Get her used to a routine that will make life easier when you have less time after the baby arrives.

Looking after a baby is a challenge. Together you and your child will find ways to overcome your disability.

QUESTIONS AND ANSWERS

Q: I don't think I'll get the sort of birth I want at the hospital my doctor uses. My first baby is due in three weeks. Is it too late to have a home birth?

A. You can always change your mind. But talk to your doctor first. If he or she feels home birth is risky in your case, listen to the reasons. Making a decision means taking responsibility for the outcome, so be sure in your own mind about what you want.

However, don't be put off by initial opposition. No one wants to fight, especially when pregnant, but opposition often melts away when you show you've thought something through and are determined. You don't need your doctor's agreement to have a home birth. But you *will* need to be accepted by a home-birth practitioner in your area. If you don't know of any, contact the American College of Nurse-Midwives (ACNM) or the Midwives Alliance of

North America (MANA) for referral to a certified midwife who can give you total care and any necessary backup. With just three weeks remaining in your pregnancy, however, it will remain up to the individual midwife to examine your medical records, determine if your prenatal care has been adequate and decide if you are an acceptable candidate for a home birth.

Q: What should I look for when choosing a nursing bra?

A: It's best to delay buying nursing bras until your baby's head has engaged (see page 52). When the head is high, your ribs expand to allow more space, so a bra that fits well then may be loose around the ribcage after the birth.

A nursing bra should be comfortable and substantial enough to play an effective supporting role. Look for a broad band to give support under the cups. The bra should fit without gaping, but with space to slip your hand between the top of the cup and your breast, to give room for expansion after the birth. Stretch straps are too bouncy when breastfeeding, and elastic loses shape with repeated washing. Cotton fabric allows your skin to breathe. Zippers or front openings are a matter of taste, but avoid seams that press and mark your skin, because they could lead to pressure problems during breast-feeding.

Q: How much equipment do new babies really need? We are not well off and I'm worried about spending too much.

A: Not as much as many people imagine, and there are ways to economize. Look through catalogues and collect information, but delay spending until you really need something. You may find you can borrow equipment from friends or relatives, or improvise after your baby arrives.

Most large towns have stores that sell nearly new clothes and equipment, but do check out *Consumer Reports*® magazine on safety standards before you buy. Economy is often a necessity, but if your heart really longs for something a little extravagant, consider the lift it could give you in return for economizing sensibly the rest of the time. Treat yourself if possible. Babies are fun as well as a responsibility!

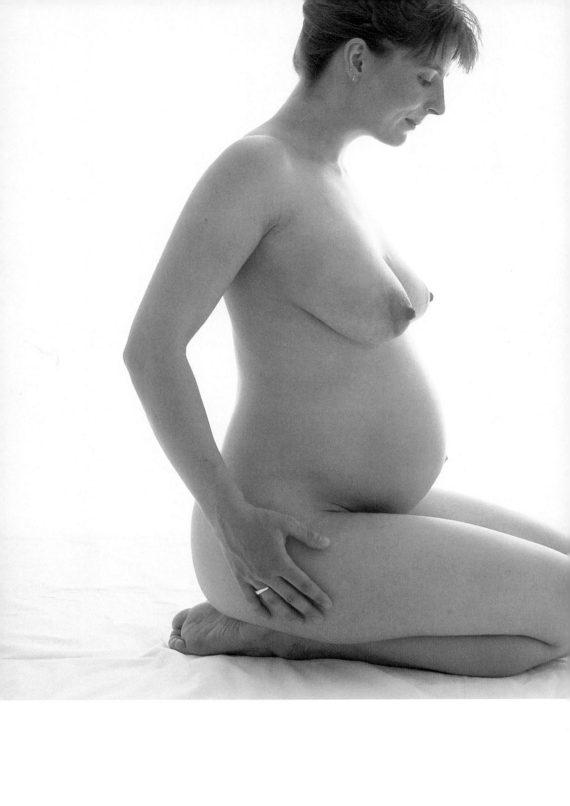

7

Late Pregnancy

(MONTHS 7 to 9)

"The last few weeks, and the end is almost in sight. I feel a mixture of terror, excitement, boredom and elation. The days drag, yet I want to hang on and savor every last bit of them. Once they're over, life will never be the same again."

Seventh month: *This baby is already lying head down, but about 25% of babies will be breech at this stage.*

Eighth month: *Compare this picture with the one on page 36 to see how much space your baby takes up, moving internal organs to make room.*

Ninth month: *Your baby stores fat under his skin in the last month so he looks much rounder and plumper.*

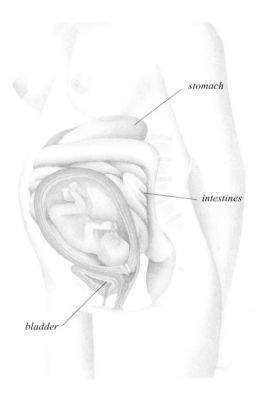

stomach

intestines

bladder

SEVEN MONTHS

HOW YOUR BABY DEVELOPS

In the last three months of pregnancy, your baby's breathing and swallowing rhythms become increasingly well regulated. Cartilage develops to give shape to his ears, his eyelids open, his fingernails grow, and the soft dark body hair (*lanugo*) disappears. Fat stores build up to provide energy and regulate his temperature.

Your baby receives antibodies to common bugs and childhood illnesses, such as chickenpox, through the placenta, which also produces gamma globulin to help both of you fight infection. Up to 1-3/4 pints (1 liter) of constantly renewed amniotic fluid filters out waste products from the uterus, and his skin is protected with creamy vernix to keep it from getting water-logged.

At 28 weeks, the average baby measures about 14 inches (35cm) and weighs 2 pounds (nearly 1kg). Each week for the next month he grows roughly half an inch (1cm) and puts on half a pound (225g), although this

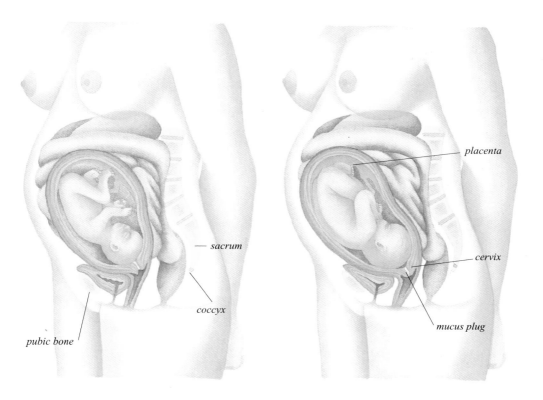

placenta

sacrum

cervix

coccyx

mucus plug

pubic bone

EIGHT MONTHS   NINE MONTHS

growth pattern gradually diminishes and almost stops a week or so before birth. Hormone levels in the placenta change, the uterus is fully stretched and the baby has little room to move. It's time to start the short journey into a new and independent life!

The majority of babies born after 32 weeks survive nowadays, and delivery after 37 weeks is considered normal. By this time the baby's lungs have matured and *surfactant,* a soap-like substance in the amniotic fluid, makes breathing easier by preventing the lung surfaces from sticking together. After 40 weeks, a baby is well equipped to enter the world, although he will still need loving care for months and years ahead.

HOW YOU MAY FEEL

Most women slow down a little but, if you are fit and experience no complications, late pregnancy can be very enjoyable. You may feel at your happiest and most relaxed. A large tummy usually elicits well-intentioned support and

"My pregnancy has changed our lives in little ways. I haven't stopped doing anything, but I've pulled over from the fast lane and I amble along in the slow lane. My husband has given up his share of the mattress and sleeps right on the edge of the bed because I've taken over the rest.

He has to keep a sense of humor and think for both of us. Last week the ceiling of a room we were decorating needed painting and he was going out. I asked him to get the stepladder for me before he went. He refused, and came home with a ball of wool and a pair of knitting needles! With three weeks to go, I reluctantly took the hint. " KAREN

kindness from other people, not to mention relieving you of unwelcome social obligations!

Many women have mixed feelings about giving up work; some count the days until they leave, while others dread the loss of income, stimulus and companionship. Every change in life has good and bad aspects. You will be able to rest more, but you may find that time passes slowly without the rhythm of work and you may become bored with your pregnancy. The last few weeks can seem to stretch ahead endlessly if you are already uncomfortable and heavy. See the next page and page 70 for suggestions on how to stay well.

You may feel increasingly worried about your baby's health and feel vulnerable to casual, throwaway comments, especially from health professionals. You may be panicky about birth and motherhood as they draw nearer, or you may swing wildly from depression to euphoria. By the ninth month this is usually overtaken by a positive longing to see your baby and to have your body to yourself again.

To create and give birth to a new human being is very special, but the last few weeks can be uncomfortable. As your baby grows, your uterus takes up space under your lungs, which can leave you short of breath. When your baby's head drops (see page 52) you'll breathe more easily—but will probably need to go to the bathroom more often! Your uterus may cause pain under your ribs, or an itchy or tight, stretched feeling in the skin over your tummy. Some women feel a sharp pain when the baby butts their bladder.

By now, most babies have definite waking periods with stronger kicks and movements. Some seem less active, while others knock a book off your lap or wake you up at night. You may have difficulty sleeping because your pelvis aches. The hormones that soften your ligaments to make the birth easier may also contribute to cramps, varicose veins, hemorrhoids and heartburn (see pages 72-3).

Your breasts will enlarge and they may leak *colostrum*, a creamy fluid present in your breasts before milk is produced. Some women experience nasal congestion, nose or gum bleeds, thrush or a copious but inoffensive vaginal discharge. Others find their ankles start to swell (see page 102) or they suffer from carpal-tunnel syndrome, where fluid compresses the nerves in the wrist, causing tingling or numbness. Your healthcare provider may suggest an orthopedic wrist support for this problem. These late-pregnancy symptoms can be tiresome, but see your doctor if they seem excessive.

You may feel your tummy become firm for about 30 seconds as Braxton-Hicks contractions tone up your uterus. These practice contractions may be barely noticeable, or so strong (especially if it is not your first baby) that you have to stop and breathe gently over them as though you were in labor. If you're fed up with your appearance, a new hairstyle or a good cut could give your morale a boost and save time later on.

RELATIONSHIP WITH YOUR PARTNER

Your relationship with your partner will change during pregnancy, especially if this is your first baby. Discuss the future, so that you can find common ground that allows each of you to get something of what you want from your partnership. When a baby arrives, a cozy twosome does not change magically into a cozy threesome! You will both be concerned about your baby's welfare but will also have individual needs to be fulfilled by negotiation.

It's normal and healthy for a woman to focus on her changing body and the birth, but not to the exclusion of all else. If you are too self-absorbed, it can be tedious for your partner. He will support you in many little ways, so try to respond to his needs too. If he attends classes or listens to "baby talk" for your sake, show equal interest in something that primarily concerns him.

When you are adding to your family, or your partner has children from a previous relationship, he may show less interest in your pregnancy. This can be disappointing if it's your first baby, so tell him how you feel. Some men need reminding to give extra help in late pregnancy, although many fathers willingly take on responsibility for other children. On the other hand, if this is your partner's first baby, give him the chance to enjoy being a first-time father by going to prenatal classes with him, even if you don't feel the need.

Taking pleasure in your partner's company helps fan the flames of love. Try to find activities that you both enjoy, can do together and can keep up after your baby arrives. Family life is challenging; pregnancy is an opportunity to deepen your understanding of each other's needs and strengthen the bond between you.

STAYING HEALTHY

The extra weight, softening hormones and gymnastic ability of your baby can make late pregnancy uncomfortable. You will feel better if you use your body well and conserve energy. Maintaining good posture (see page 44) prevents unnecessary muscle tension and painful strains to softened ligaments.

It can be frustrating to tire quickly, especially if you have work to do, but you'll help yourself if you listen to your body and rest before you become over-tired. Fifteen minutes of complete relaxation is worth an hour of half-resting with your mind spinning with things you feel you should be doing instead!

COPING WITH LATE PREGNANCY

◆ *Never stand when you can sit down, or sit when you can lie down. Make sure you stand, sit or lie without twisting your body.*

◆ *A V-shaped pillow can provide comfortable support when you are sitting in a chair or propped up in bed.*

◆ *To relax completely for five minutes, sit comfortably with your shoulders down and hands palm-up in your lap. Concentrate on the sensation in one hand and imagine it gradually growing warmer.*

◆ *For a quick pick-me-up, mash a banana and blend it with a glass of milk, a little honey and two tablespoons of natural yogurt.*

◆ *Try to make some friends you can rely on after your baby is born. Exercise and prenatal classes are good places to meet other pregnant women.*

◆ *If your pregnancy seems endless and you feel low, lift your spirits with an outing, or treat yourself to a massage or a special luxury to keep up your morale.*

Relaxing and sleeping

Most women sleep less soundly at the end of pregnancy. You might be awakened by night sweats, but more often it is the baby's movements and the call of nature. Keep a glass of water beside the bed, because your body needs extra fluid during pregnancy and dehydration can cause slight headaches.

If you and your partner sleep badly because you are restless, perhaps he could use the spare bed or sofa occasionally to get an unbroken night's sleep. A small package of cookies, a thermal container of hot cocoa or a good book within reach may help if you can't get back to sleep once you have awakened. On the positive side, at least insomnia prepares your body for night feeds after your baby arrives!

When you are really exhausted, you will sleep soundly in any position, but if you are having difficulty relaxing or sleeping you may find some of the positions illustrated on the next page comfortable.

PRENATAL CHECKUPS

From 28 weeks you'll probably have prenatal checkups every two weeks, and in the last month they'll be weekly. If you see the same staff each time, you can build a relationship with your doctor, midwife or members of her team, so that you feel able to ask questions, seek advice or discuss any worries you might have.

The checkups will be familiar by now, but your healthcare provider will also determine your baby's position (although this can change), make sure that he is growing well and look out for potential problems, such as pre-eclampsia (see page 102).

Relaxing and Sleeping: *Try lying on your side with a pillow between your knees to reduce the strain on your ligaments. You may prefer to put another pillow under your abdomen.*

Prop yourself up using a bean bag or two pillows under your knees to take the strain off your lower back. This position can help you avoid heartburn.

Sit in a chair with a V-shaped pillow supporting your head. You could put another pillow on a small stool to support your legs.

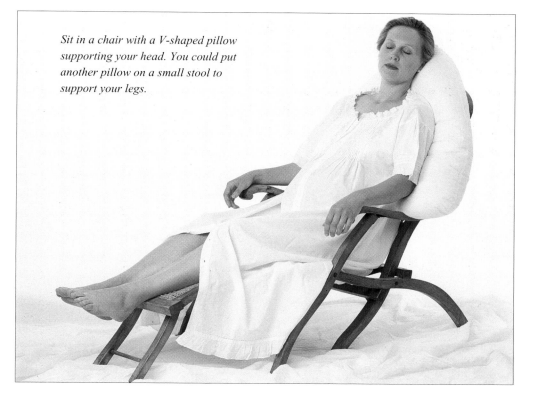

	KICK CHART						Name: **Sue**						
	Week: **34**						Week: **35**						
Day:	M	T	W	Th	Fr	Sa	Su	M	T	W	Th	Fr	Sa	Su
9.00														
9.30														
10.00														
10.30														
11.00														
11.30														
12.00														
12.30														
1.00														
1.30														

"Count to 10" kickchart: Start counting at the same time each day and mark the time of the tenth kick on your chart. A baby who is kicking happily as usual is thriving.

A kickchart is sometimes given towards the end of pregnancy to check that the placenta is working well. The midwife will explain what to do, but tell her if it worries instead of reassuring you.

You record your baby's kicks over a given period. After a few days, a pattern emerges so that you know what is "normal" for you. If you don't feel your baby move one day, or there's any marked change, such as less frequent kicks, tell your healthcare provider. Don't leave it until the next day!

Swelling

At least three-quarters of women suffer from fluid retention at some time in pregnancy. Your legs or ankles may swell in hot weather or at the end of the day. You may wake up to find your fingers tingling or your rings feel tight. If you can't get your shoes on, or your hands or face become puffy, contact your healthcare provider.

Don't restrict your intake of liquids or salt unless you are told to. Wear support stockings and sit with your feet up whenever possible. If your fingers swell, wriggle them to help ease discomfort; gently wind dental floss around your finger from the tip so that a ring will slip off when you unwind it.

Mild swelling can result from the normal fluid increase of pregnancy. If a hollow remains when you press the skin for 30 seconds and let go, you have edema. This is not dangerous in itself, but it can be a symptom of pre-eclampsia, which needs medical attention, so consult your healthcare provider.

Pre-eclampsia

This illness affects both mother and baby and is cured by the delivery of the baby and placenta. Early in a normal pregnancy your arteries adapt to accommodate an increasing blood supply so that your baby gets more food and oxygen as he grows. For an unknown reason (possibly genetic, with an environmental trigger), in about one in 10 pregnancies the blood vessels fail to adapt. The placenta gets insufficient blood, the baby doesn't grow well, the mother's blood pressure rises, and she may suffer symptoms such as edema and impaired kidney function.

In most cases, pre-eclampsia does no lasting harm. Worry and stress do not cause it; rest and relaxation do not cure it. A diet with adequate protein and calories may help prevent pre-eclampsia or reduce its severity (see page 39). In very mild cases, extra rest may help and your blood pressure might be checked daily at home.

However, for one-in-100 first pregnancies and fewer subsequent ones, the illness is serious enough to lead to convulsions or even coma unless it is treated. Pre-eclampsia can appear any time after 20 weeks, although it is more common in the last 12 weeks of pregnancy. It is usually suspected at a routine prenatal check and you will then be checked more frequently. If your blood pressure rises to about 140/90 and your urine contains protein (a trace is no problem but a "+" or more is cause for concern), you may be advised to go to the hospital for closer monitoring. Depending on the severity of the illness, you may go into labor spontaneously and have a normal delivery, or you might be induced or delivered by Cesarean section.

In rare cases where the illness comes on suddenly, there may be pain in the upper abdomen, vomiting, visual disturbances or a very severe headache. Contact your healthcare provider about such symptoms, although they don't necessarily mean you have pre-eclampsia.

Poor growth

A baby may fail to grow properly if his mother is ill, smokes or has an unhealthful lifestyle, or if the placenta fails to supply all his needs. The placenta reaches maturity somewhere between 32 and 34 weeks and then gradually becomes less efficient, although most will sustain all a baby's needs for more than 42 weeks.

If your baby seems smaller than expected for the stage of pregnancy you have reached, intrauterine growth retardation (IUGR) would be suspected. Ultrasound scans (see page 56), repeated at intervals, could confirm or refute the diagnosis.

Poor growth is more common in first pregnancies and fifth-or-later ones. Many individual factors probably contribute to it, but it is unlikely to happen if your weight is normal, you are well nourished, and you don't smoke. If you get regular prenatal checkups, any problem associated with poor growth, such as anemia or kidney disease, can be treated early.

If poor growth is diagnosed, you may go to the hospital for bed rest or medication to improve placental blood flow. In extreme cases, your baby would be delivered early. Although prevention and treatment of poor growth are preferable, even when they are unsuccessful such babies often eventually catch up.

"To be perfectly honest, I'm fed up with pregnancy. I can't sleep well or eat a decent meal or walk more than a few yards before sitting down to rest. My ankles swell every night and I haven't felt like going out for weeks. I know it's well-intentioned, but I've found it hard to adjust to being 'public property.' Sometimes people I hardly know come up and pat my stomach and I resent it. Pregnancy is not my favorite time of life. I can't wait for the baby to arrive."
SUSAN

YOUR BABY'S POSITION

Somewhere between 34 and 40 weeks most babies turn head-down and settle deeply in the pelvis. But babies are individuals: Some wait for extra softening hormones produced at the beginning of labor before they drop (engage) and others just stay bottom down. Once a baby is head-down and fully dropped, he rarely changes position.

If you feel a firm area down one side of your tummy, it may be your baby's back. Ask your healthcare provider if your baby is lying in an anterior position. This is a good lie: with his back to your tummy, he can tuck his chin on his chest, fit neatly into your pelvis and turn slightly to emerge at the birth.

If he lies with his back towards to your back (posterior), his chin may not tuck in so well and he has to rotate more to pass under your pubic arch, which could make the birth longer. Try kneeling on all fours as often as possible so that gravity helps his spine, which is heaviest, to move around. It sometimes helps to gyrate your hips whichever way feels most comfortable, to encourage him to rotate.

A baby who lies bottom-down and refuses to budge by the recommended turn-by date may simply be a late starter. Sit up straight to give your baby more room. Keep a bottle of baby lotion in the refrigerator to soothe the sore spot where his head lies. Try the remedies for heartburn (see page 73) if it is a problem.

If your baby does not turn head-down spontaneously by 34 weeks, you could encourage him using the methods described on page 106. Your doctor might also try, especially if it is not your first baby. You will be asked to lie on your back with your knees up and relax while the doctor massages your tummy, helping your baby to slip around. This is called *external version*; no force is used and the attempt will stop if your baby clearly does not want to move. After 36 weeks it's sensible to discuss breech birth (see page 160) with your healthcare provider in case your baby doesn't turn. Only 3% of babies remain in a breech position at birth.

Your baby's position has quite a lot to do with how your labor goes. If he lies well curled up and with his spine to one side of your tummy, your labor may be easier. But remember that being well-prepared can also make your labor easier. Learning to relax and being realistic about labor (see page 132) will help you cope if your baby takes a less favorable position.

" *Being pregnant again is great! I haven't had time to worry about every little thing and I've enjoyed sharing it with Emily, my 2-year-old, who loves babies. She's very knowing, so we had to tell her quite early because everyone else knew, but she has no idea of time and I'm sure she thinks we're making it all up! Now I'm almost there, I can't wait to see her face when she finds out we're not.*

We bought bunk beds for her bedroom and left her crib up. The first night she slept in it. Then she decided she was a big girl and wanted to sleep in the bed, so we went to buy a mattress and she chose the bedspread. Now she happily tells people the crib is for her baby. " ZOE

PRESENTATIONS
FOR BIRTH

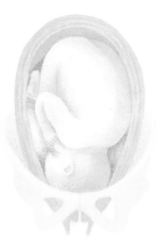

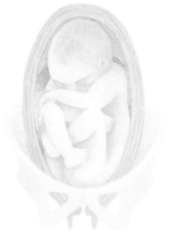

Above: Right occipito posterior (ROP), where the baby faces the mother's abdominal wall.

Above: Left occipito anterior (LOA) is the most common presentation. The baby faces the mother's spine.

Below: Frank breech, where the thighs are flexed but the legs are pointed upwards. The arms wrap around the legs.

Below: Footling breech, where the thighs are only slightly flexed and baby's foot is born first.

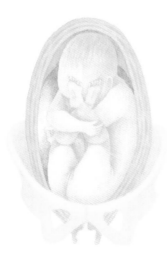

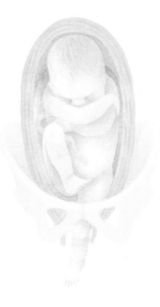

Above: Full breech presentation, where the thighs are flexed against the body and the knees are bent.

YOUR PREGNANCY PLANNER—MONTHS 7 TO 9

- *Prenatal checks are every two weeks; weekly for the last month.*
- *Find out if your employer needs a letter from your healthcare provider if you want to continue working after you become eligible for maternity leave.*
- *See an experienced fitter for nursing bras (see page 93).*
- *Rent maternity wear for any special occasions. Look in your local paper or phone book for advertisements.*
- *Pack your suitcase (see page 116) about six weeks before your due date. Buy or rent a car seat (see page 90) to bring your baby home in.*
- *If you have a toddler, make arrangements (with backup) for his care while you are in labor. Buy a small present for him, ready for his first meeting with his sister or brother.*
- *Write your birthplan (see page 118). There's still time to alter your plans if you want to have your baby somewhere else.*
- *Rent a pager to insure you can contact your partner when you go into labor. Look in phone book or at small advertisements in parenting magazines.*
- *Arrange day trips for after your due date because you might be overdue!*
- *Record a message on your answering machine if you need a rest from too many phone calls before and after the birth.*

QUESTIONS AND ANSWERS

Q: I am 35 weeks pregnant and my baby is lying in a breech position. Should I ask my doctor to turn him, or can I do anything myself to encourage this?

A: Your doctor would only decide to intervene after considering your history—for example, whether you have had other children, how firm your muscles are and the position of your placenta. You could certainly try to encourage your baby to turn using positions or alternative therapies, although babies are individuals and some prefer being bottom-down.

Put a bean bag or a pile of pillows on the floor and make a hollow in them for your abdomen. Lie on your front with your bottom higher than your hips for about 20 minutes. Relax and try to "will" your baby around. After a while (not always at the first attempt) your baby may float free of your pelvis and do a somersault. Get up slowly (you may feel rather shaken) and walk around or squat to help fix your baby's head in your pelvis. Alternatively, you could lie back with your hips raised on pillows and your knees bent and roll gently from side to side for 10 minutes three times a day. Stop if you feel lightheaded or uncomfortable.

If you want to try alternative therapies (see page 73), consult a qualified practitioner.

Q: Last week a van driver failed to yield to me at an intersection and almost hit the side of my car. I was unhurt but very shaken and later that day my baby kicked wildly for two hours. Could the accident have harmed him, and should I stop driving?

A: There's no reason to stop driving short distances right up to delivery day, provided you feel fine, fit behind the steering wheel and can comfortably fasten your seatbelt. You should not drive yourself to the hospital when you are in labor. You may find long journeys tiring in late pregnancy whether you are the driver or a passenger (see page 81).

A baby may react with a period of greater-than-normal activity after any sudden shock, such as an accident or upon your receiving bad news. Rest for a few hours to give your body a chance to recover, and if you are worried for any reason, contact your healthcare provider.

Q: I'm 34 weeks pregnant and my healthcare provider says my baby's head has engaged. I thought this happened at 36 weeks, so does it mean that my baby will be born early?

A: It suggests that your baby is lying in a favorable position and your pelvis is roomy. First babies engage on average at 36 weeks, but later babies may not do so until you're in labor. Once your baby has dropped, he has resolved the question of whether your pelvis is big enough for this. Every baby has to drop at some stage in order to be born normally, but it doesn't predict when you will go into labor. The timing depends on the size of your pelvis, how firm your abdominal muscles are, the amount of hormones flowing and your baby's position.

Q: My teenage daughters from my husband's first marriage want to be present at the birth. We have asked my mother-in-law to look after our 3-year-old son, who adores his grandma. How can I prepare my stepdaughters for the birth and make sure that my son does not feel left out?

A: Your daughters might like to look at books or a video with you, and they should be aware of the realities of birth. Tell them they can leave at any time if they wish, and explain circumstances when they might not be able to be there. Make sure that your healthcare provider is happy for them to be present, so they will feel welcome.

If a day spent with grandma's undivided attention is a treat for your son, he probably won't feel left out. He will not be at the birth but he can still be part of the celebration. Suggest that your mother-in-law might like to help him draw on balloons with thick felt tips and decorate a card for the baby. Pack a small surprise in his suitcase for him to find—and don't forget one for grandma, too!

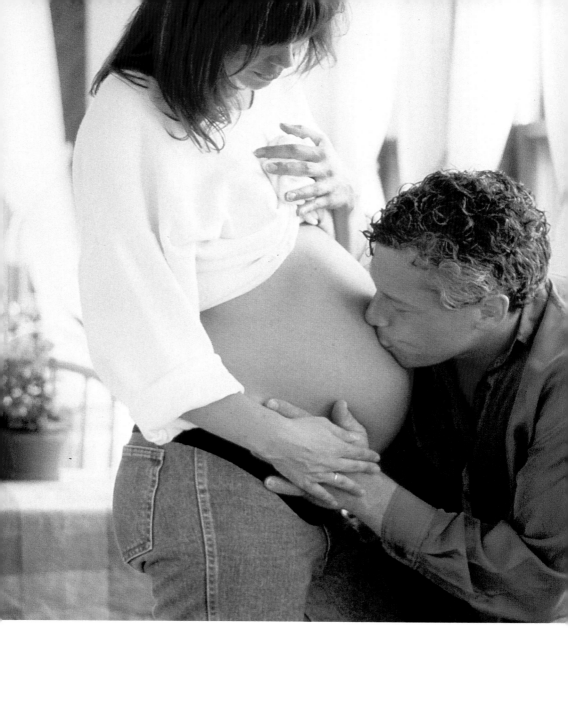

8

Preparing for the Birth

❝There's so much to think about when a baby is born. It's not just learning to relax and help yourself to handle the birth; it's all the practical little details like remembering to pay the gas bill and feed the dog! ❞

WHAT MAKES LABOR EASIER?

Labor is easier if you have room to relax and privacy so you can let go of your inhibitions and flow with the rhythm of the contractions. Intrusions, or distractions such as moving from one place to another, may disturb this rhythm. Darkness or subdued lighting can help you use instinct rather than rational thought. You need to feel safe and at ease in the place where you give birth, and with the people who care for you. Otherwise, the delicate mechanisms of the natural birth process may be upset.

Preparing for the birth will help make your labor easier by giving you confidence in your body and trust in your instincts so that you cope in the way that feels right to you at the time.

TOUR OF THE LABOR & DELIVERY FACILITIES

Most hospitals provide tours of their facilities, often on evenings or weekends so that partners can attend. Phone the hospital to check details, or ask at your next prenatal visit. Here are some things you could find out:

- What facilities are available? Is there a mattress for the floor, a bean-bag chair, rocking chair or large bath?
- What are the arrangements for refreshment and what are the car-parking regulations?
- What use could you make of the furniture in the room you'll be in during labor? A cupboard might be the right height to lean on; moving the bed might give you more space, for example.
- How does the staff feel about monitoring (see page 148), episiotomies (see page 151) or delivery positions (see pages 114-15)? Are there hospital policies regulating them, and can these be varied?
- Does the hospital have a night entrance? Hospital security procedures may mean the door you use during the day is locked.

RELAXATION AND BREATHING FOR LABOR

Labor is a physical task, like running a marathon. If you run stiffly, the race is harder. When your uterus contracts strongly other muscles tend to join in, but if you relax it works more effectively and your body's natural pain-killing hormones flow. During labor you'll need to keep checking so that you can release tension before it engulfs you. Pull your shoulders down and let them go, part your lips to loosen your jaw, turn your hands palm-up.

"I ignored the birth at first. Now I've started to face up to it and it seems like a huge wall. I'm like a yo-yo, one minute whining that I'll never cope and the next minute feeling like labor's no problem and everything will be all right! I'm going to prenatal classes and taking a tour of the labor and delivery suite. Once I put labor in perspective, I know I'll be fine. " SARA

Relaxation and breathing are intertwined—if you relax deeply, your breathing will adjust to the best level for you. Some women prefer to concentrate on breathing control to help them relax and give them something to think about. Use slow, gentle breathing, pausing slightly between breaths and letting your breathing rise to your middle or upper chest during the contractions if it's more comfortable. Your body will tell you what feels best. Always concentrate on the "out" breath to avoid hyperventilation, but if you do start to feel light-headed, cup your hands over your face and breathe into them slowly until the sensation passes.

Breathing for labor

Ask your partner to help you practice breathing for labor until you feel confident using different areas of your chest.

Right: *Full chest: Relax consciously and aim your breathing towards the warmth of your partner's hands, so that he feels a slight movement below your waist. During labor use full-chest breathing unless your contractions make mid- or upper-chest breathing easier.*
Below: *Mid chest: Breathe so that your bra gets tighter and your partner feels the movement with his hands.*
Below right: *Upper chest: Breathe lightly with little puffs, using the top part of your chest.*

POSITIONS FOR LABOR

The mechanics of giving birth suggest that some positions will work better than others in certain circumstances.

As your uterus contracts it rises up and forward, so leaning in this direction enables the contractions to work with gravity. Lying back makes them work against it. If you're upright, your baby's head presses against your cervix, speeding up dilation. Positions where your thighs are flexed and wide apart stretch the ligaments that join the three bones of your pelvis, thereby giving your baby extra room.

When your body is horizontal, gravity moves your baby away from your cervix and toward your spine, abdomen or side, depending on your position.

Sit reversed on a chair padded with a pillow. Relax onto another pillow placed on the chair back.

Stand, leaning onto your partner, the wall or a piece of furniture during contractions.

Sit with your knees apart, leaning onto your partner.

Some women find their contractions are more effective when they lie down because they are able to relax better; others find that lying down eases the pain of a very fast labor.

Adopting positions that use gravity and open your pelvis, such as the ones illustrated below, often makes labor easier. You could use pillows to reduce pressure on your knees or thighs. The positions suggested for relaxation on page 101 may also be comfortable.

There are no hard and fast rules—women are different and what works for one may not help another. Don't feel that you ought to use certain positions because they're supposed to be best. Just experiment to find those in which you can relax well.

Sit on the padded rim of a bucket. Place your feet squarely so that you can rock or move your body freely.

Spread your knees to make space for your tummy and lean forward onto your hands.

Kneel on something soft and lean onto your partner's lap or the bed.

Stand to deliver while your partner holds you under the arms. He could lean against a wall and bend his knees to protect his back.

Stand or semi-squat, supported by your partner or a healthcare provider. They should bend their knees as they take your weight.

POSITIONS FOR DELIVERY

Many women deliver on their backs because no one suggests anything else. This isn't ideal because your baby moves against gravity and puts extra pressure on the *perineum* (the delicate tissue around the birth canal) as it thins out. To move from your back to your knees, ask your partner to stand beside the bed to help you. Slide the outer side of one foot towards your bottom. Push on the bed with your arm to raise your body. Roll over to kneel facing the side of the bed, with your arms around your partner's neck. The midwife will help you deliver from behind.

Pushing is easier in upright positions because gravity helps and your tail-bone swings back, giving your baby more room to move. If the birth is rapid, you could move onto your side. Women who stand to give birth often report less damage to the perineum. It's up to you to choose your position. You will not know what's right until the time, but try out these positions in advance.

Lie on your side with your knees bent. Your partner supports your upper leg during contractions.

Kneel on the bed, leaning onto the headboard, pillows or a bean bag. This position helps prevent a tear.

Squat and lean into your partner's lap with your feet flat and your arms over his knees.

YOUR LABOR KIT

Your hospital will provide a list of things to bring with you, but here are some practical suggestions from mothers for what to take:

- *Light clothing, because hospitals are very warm.*
- *Paper fan or mineral-water spray to keep cool.*
- *Crushed ice in an insulated flask (to suck); ice chest with mineral water or fruit juice for your partner.*
- *Flannel or natural sponge to moisten lips; lip balm.*
- *Squishy ice pack, package of frozen peas or wooden back massager to ease backache; oil or talc for massage.*
- *Cassette recorder, music or audio tapes, headphones; jigsaw puzzles, games, books to pass the time.*
- *Treats to keep your spirits up; snacks for your partner, peppermint tea bags for gas (especially after a Cesarean).*
- *Cushion, bean-bag chair, small stool or bucket to sit on.*
- *Socks for cold feet.*
- *Poster or calendar to focus on; camera; money for the phone.*

YOUR PARTNER'S FEELINGS ABOUT LABOR

Most men are excited at the thought of being present at the birth, but they may be worried about not knowing what to do, or perhaps fainting at the sight of blood. Films and videos often give a false impression of labor because, like holiday programs on TV that always show happy people and sunny weather, they are selective in what they present. The birth of your own baby is usually less dramatic but much more emotional and exciting. If your partner is anxious, it will help if he attends prenatal classes with you.

YOUR BIRTH PARTNER/LABOR COACH

Your labor coach could be anyone close to you, although it's usually your baby's father. Midwives have more than one woman to look after, so his role is to make your labor easier by offering comfort, encouragement and loving concern. Even if your birth partner/labor coach only stays close to you, you'll value his (or her) presence. Sensitive support, freely given at the right moment is an added bonus because it raises your pain threshold and makes it easier for you to cope.

"I've never been afraid of giving birth. I'm more worried about losing control and not being able to make my own decisions. I read everything I could about birth, right from the beginning. I've learned to be more flexible because now I understand why things happen that can't be avoided." ANNE-MARIE

Here are some suggestions for birth partners/labor coaches:

- Take care of her physical needs. Help her change position, keep her cool, provide her with chips of ice when she wants them, change the music tapes and generally give her your attention. Never appear to be bored, or more interested in the newspaper or the labor machinery than in her!
- Keep up her morale if labor is long and her energy flags. Think of labor as a series of short intervals, not one long stretch of time. In the early stages, you could read funny stories or poetry to her, play "I Spy," choose your baby's name, walk around the corridors with her or produce an unexpected treat.
- Create a positive atmosphere, however her labor goes. She cannot relax if you are tense, so assume an air of calm, like a swan gliding on the surface while paddling hard underneath!
- Help her relax. Watch for tight face muscles or clenched teeth. Keep reminding her to relax her shoulders. Some women can't bear to be touched during labor; others like their shoulders massaged or their hair stroked. When the contractions are strong, redouble your efforts to keep her relaxed.
- Help her focus on something other than the contractions. Describe a place you both know so that she can imagine it; stroke her palm, or name groups of muscles so that she can relax them one by one. Most women find idle chatter distracting but counting can be helpful: Look into her eyes and count slowly aloud from the beginning of the contraction until it's over.
- Act as a physical support. Put your arms around her so that she can lean on you, if necessary, during contractions. Let her drape herself over you when she's kneeling, or sit on the floor using you as a sort of armchair. If she asks for support when she's pushing, protect your back by bending your knees.
- Act as her spokesman. Interpret her wishes to the staff, and vice-versa. She'll rely on you when the contractions are strong and may appear not to hear anyone else. Be sensitive to her wishes. She may genuinely change her mind about some things, like accepting pain relief.
- Remind her to breathe gently, emphasizing the "out" breath. Tension causes changes in breathing rhythm and rate, so concentrating on quiet breathing will help her relax.
- Massage her back, mop her brow, praise her efforts. Encouragement is more helpful than sympathy when a woman is trying hard to cope without any drugs. Stay supportive even if she gets mad at you—she really wants you there! After the birth, reassure her that she has coped well.

MAKING A BIRTHPLAN

Most women form a general idea about the sort of birth they hope to have by reading books on the subject and talking to other parents, relatives and friends, their partner or doctor, midwife or childbirth educator. Regardless of what other people think, you have to balance out what you see as the advantages and disadvantages of the different approaches to labor (see page 84).

Some women prefer the experts to take charge and make most of the decisions, believing that they know best. If this leads to the sort of birth that suits you, there's no problem. However, many parents are disappointed because decisions made by other people turn out to be wrong for them. Ideally, you'd discuss your wishes with your doctor or midwife beforehand, but it's not always possible in busy hospitals. The healthcare provider you see during pregnancy may not look after you in labor.

A birthplan makes you think about what's important to you. It can make you more realistic about labor, or even prompt you to change your hospital (see pages 92-93), as you come to realize that certain things in childbirth go together. For example, it may be easier to achieve a natural birth in a low-tech hospital or at home, because the staff in a high-tech hospital may see the need to use technology—speeding up labor with drugs, for instance—where a midwife at a home birth might not consider it to be necessary.

A birthplan conveys your wishes to the staff even if you're too busy coping with contractions to discuss them. Your hospital may provide a form, or you could simply write a letter that can be attached to your medical records, briefly describing the approach that suits you best and specifying three or four things that are really important to you. A birthplan isn't written in stone—you can always change your mind later.

There are many ways of giving birth safely. Your healthcare provider will make sure that what you choose is safe, so in the end it comes down to what makes you feel happy and confident, and only you can decide that!

PAIN IN LABOR

The amount of pain you experience in labor is determined by physical factors, such as the shape of your pelvis and the position of your baby, and psychological factors, such as fear. You may describe contractions as strong sensation, or you may find them agonizing.

Some women feel intimidated by the thought of pain and have an epidural at the earliest opportunity; others accept severe pain rather than using any drugs. Being realistic, able to relax and be positive, raises your pain threshold. Women who attend prenatal classes use fewer drugs for pain relief. They either feel less pain or handle it better. Pain in labor doesn't have to be overwhelming—you decide how much you're prepared to tolerate.

◆ **Companions in labor:** *Do you want a friend or relative instead of or in addition to your partner, to share support if labor is long? Do you want your partner to stay throughout labor or to leave during certain procedures? Can he stay for a Cesarean birth?*

◆ **Your stay in the hospital:** *Do you want to know the healthcare provider who delivers you, do you prefer to be examined by a female doctor, or do you have special needs because of a disability, a language difficulty, your religion or diet? Do you mind students being present during labor and delivery? Enemas are rarely offered but you can ask for one if your bowel is full.*

◆ **Positions for labor and delivery** *(see pages 112 to 115): Upright positions work with gravity; they tend to speed up labor and help you push, but you may get tired. Lying down lets you rest but may prolong labor.*

◆ **Pain relief:** *Meperidine (Demerol®) and epidurals help severe pain but may have side effects, and it may be hard to move about or change position. Other drugs with less potential for respiratory suppression of the baby may be preferred. Self-help methods do not affect your baby but are only effective for moderate pain. If you prefer not to use drugs, you could ask the staff for help and support.*

◆ **Speeding up labor:** *Breaking the water (see page 147) may shorten labor, although labor may be more intense and more painful. If it fails, a hormone I.V. (see page 147) may be needed. This also shortens labor but can be harder on the baby. Your baby may become distressed, so you'll be continuously monitored and movement may be restricted. If this fails, you might need a Cesarean section.*

◆ **Monitoring the baby by machine** *(see page 148): Having a continuous record of your baby's heartbeat may give you confidence, but the trace can be hard to interpret, leading to unnecessary anxiety or intervention. Belt monitors restrict your movement; scalp electrodes allow more movement but are also invasive.*

◆ **Episiotomy or tear** *(see page 151): An episiotomy could be bigger than a tear but neater to repair. Women who express a strong desire not to have either are more likely to achieve their wish!*

◆ **Delivery of placenta** *(see page 138): Leaving the cord to pulsate may mean up to an hour's wait for the placenta, but the baby gets extra blood and a gentler transition to independent breathing. Cutting the cord immediately saves a few minutes, but forces the baby to breathe on her own before she may be ready. Say if you prefer a "gentle birth" (see page 137).*

◆ **After the birth:** *Do you prefer to hold your baby immediately or after she's been cleaned and wrapped up? Do you want to breastfeed immediately?*

Self-help methods of pain relief

Most people learn to handle moderate pain in everyday life, for example, by simply ignoring a headache or using a hot-water bottle for a stomachache. Distraction, temperature changes, movement and touch are thought to work by stimulating larger nerve bundles. Like shutting gates, these nerve bundles intercept pain messages as they travel along fine nerves to the brain. When your body gets used to the stimulus, you feel pain again as the gates swing open, but changing the stimulus shuts them again. This principle can help you cope with labor pain. Try these self-help methods:

Problem: In early labor your contractions hurt and you feel apprehensive.

Self-help: Distraction: Watch TV or a video, beat your partner at a board game, or sort through family photos.

Problem: Your stomach aches during or between contractions.

Self-help: Touch: Massage under your stomach with a relaxed hand. Warmth: Use a hot-water bottle wrapped in a towel. Movement: Change position and rock your pelvis gently.

Problem: You have a constant backache, peaking at each contraction.

Self-help: Change the temperature: Press your back to a heating radiator padded with a towel, use a small towel wrung out in ice water or a bag of frozen peas wrapped in a towel. Touch: Ask your partner to massage your back.

Problem: Contractions are overwhelmingly strong.

Self-help: Focusing: Ask your partner to count slowly through each contraction with you. Movement: Rotate your pelvis gently, change your position, rock your body, make yourself walk to the bathroom.

Backache Massage: Your partner places his hands on either side of your spine, keeping his elbows straight while he applies pressure.

Alternatively, you may find it comfortable to stand with your feet apart, leaning onto the bed or another piece of furniture.

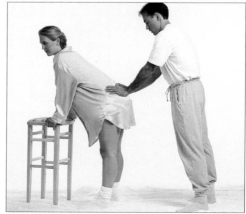

Backache massage in labor

Firm massage or pressure can help if you feel the contractions in your back. Your partner should use body weight, not muscle power, so that he can keep it up as long as necessary. Use corn starch or oil to prevent soreness and tell him the best position—usually it's about halfway between the base of your spine and your waist. Practice the techniques on page 120 and below beforehand.

Your partner supports himself on his hands and presses the balls of his feet against your spine.

Sit or lie with the base of your spine against your partner's, while he gently leans back to apply pressure.

Your partner supports his elbow on his hip bone, leaning gently forward. It may be easier if his body is at an angle.

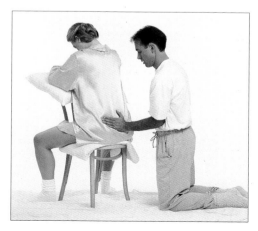

Other methods of pain relief

Each method of pain relief has advantages and disadvantages. For example, Demerol and epidurals are effective for severe pain, but you have to consider their potential side effects. Think about it beforehand, but choose the most appropriate method of relief available at the time.

Epidural: A pain-relieving drug is passed through a fine tube into the space around your spinal cord, eliminating sensation in your abdomen. It can be increased as needed. You may have an I.V. to accelerate labor and counteract low blood pressure, a monitor for your baby's heartbeat and a catheter in your bladder. About half of all women who have epidurals need an episiotomy and an assisted delivery (see pages 149-51). Occasionally women who have a epidurals get severe headaches afterwards. Research evidence is conflicting as to whether more women suffer long-term backache. However, an epidural is the most effective method of relief for severe pain.

Meperidine (Demerol): Merperidine is a muscle relaxant that helps you handle severe pain. This is given by injection once or more during labor or through an I.V. If you are small, a vegetarian or someone who rarely takes medicines or alcohol, a small dose may be adequate. You'll stay in bed because it makes you drowsy; most women say it distances the pain rather than taking it away. Women react differently. Some suffer nausea or vomiting, but another drug can stop this. If you have pethidine too close to delivery, your baby may need an antidote or be sleepy, so that breastfeeding is difficult at first.

Fentanyl: This is given by injection or through an I.V. Its effect on women is similar to that of pethidine, above. However, fentanyl is increasingly preferred over merperidine because it is a shorter-acting medication with less potential for respiratory suppression of the baby.

Acupuncture, electro-acupuncture and acupressure: Needles, electrical stimulation and pressure (respectively) can reduce pain when applied to specific points on the body. In labor you may be able to use electro-acupuncture or acupressure yourself. Acupuncture requires the presence of a specialist, and treatment may begin before the birth.

Hypnosis: Most prenatal classes teach some form of relaxation technique. The hypnotist takes this to a deeper level and helps you narrow your attention until you are ready to accept the suggestion that you will feel no pain during labor. The hypnotherapist may be present

"It's surprising how much you can decide for yourself in labor. I want to move around, so I hope I don't need Demerol or an epidural. I don't look forward to a crowd of students coming in to gawk at the last minute, but they have to learn, so I wrote on my birthplan that I prefer one student to be there the whole time instead. The most important thing is to have my baby with me after the birth, not taken off to some nursery, because I'm partially deaf, and I'd worry about not hearing her if she cries." JUSTINE

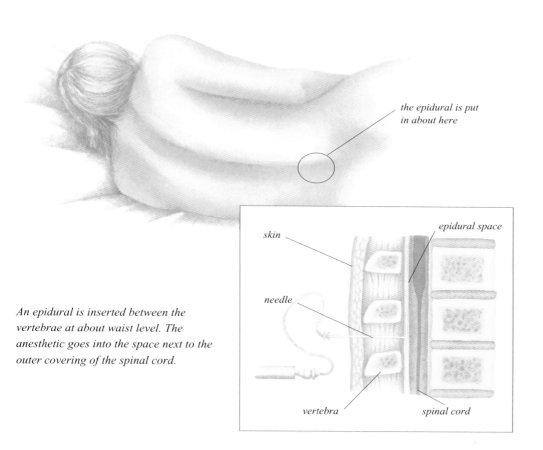

*the epidural is put
in about here*

skin

epidural space

needle

*An epidural is inserted between the
vertebrae at about waist level. The
anesthetic goes into the space next to the
outer covering of the spinal cord.*

vertebra

spinal cord

during labor, or you may learn self-hypnosis or auto-suggestion. Several sessions are needed, starting some weeks before the birth. Hypnosis may work by altering your emotional response to pain. Only about 25% of women can be fully hypnotized, but others may find some help from the technique.

- *Arrange for someone to feed any pets at home while you're in labor.*
- *Remember to stock up the freezer, buy frozen prepared meals or canned goods for the early days.*
- *Stock up on household basics like detergent, snacks for visitors, and food, soap, and so on if relatives are staying.*
- *Buy batteries for a cassette recorder, film for a camera, thank-you notes and small surprises to keep toddlers occupied.*
- *Pack a bag if your toddler is going away; write a list of what she does each day to help whoever looks after her.*
- *List phone numbers—doctor, midwife, hospital, partner, friends, neighbors, relatives—on a bulletin board and write down all offers of help.*

QUESTIONS AND ANSWERS

Q: I want to use upright positions in labor. Is there a new epidural that you can walk around with, instead of having to lie in bed all the time?

A: Some hospitals offer mobile epidurals, a combination of a spinal block (similar to an epidural but placed lower down the back) and a conventional epidural. At present they are not widely available, but their use is increasing. They are given in the same way as ordinary epidurals. Less anesthetic is used but they have disadvantages similar to ordinary epidurals. The anesthetist makes sure that you have full use of your legs before letting you walk around. On the whole, women like them, although some do not get full mobility.

Q: I assumed my husband would be with me at the birth but to my dismay he has refused suddenly. I feel rejected and worried about coping alone. How can I persuade him to change his mind?

A: Twenty-five years ago, few fathers were present when their children were born. Today most men are there, a revolution that is bound to suit some people better than others.

If he refused because he's anxious about his role, finding out how to help you may be the answer. But some men simply don't want to witness labor and delivery and this attitude isn't a betrayal. Relationships work in different ways and there's more to being a good husband or father than attending the birth!

You won't be alone when your baby is born. Your midwife will provide some help and companionship as part of her professional duties. Single mothers or women whose partners work away often ask close relatives or girlfriends to be their birth partner. Why not consider this? It's a privilege for the person you choose and it can also be something you both can enjoy sharing. She can attend prenatal classes with you and share your experience in a way that complements your husband's involvement. If he feels there is no pressure on him, you may find your husband's feelings change and he wants to be more actively involved, perhaps staying for the early part of your labor. You might even end up with two birth partners working together!

Q: I am determined to avoid stitches after the birth and have heard that massaging the tissue around the vagina can help. How should I do this?

A: Nobody can guarantee that you won't need stitches, because it depends to some extent on factors like your baby's position and whether the delivery needs assistance. However, you can help avoid damage to your perineum (the tissue between the vagina and anus) by gently massaging it.

In the last few weeks of pregnancy, massage vitamin E or wheat-germ oil (these are particularly suitable although any pure vegetable oil would do) into your perineum for about five minutes each day. Immediately after your bath is a good time. When it's completely absorbed, gently stretch the tissue with your fingers until you feel a slight burning sensation.

In time you'll find your perineum stretches farther before you feel this sensation, proving that it's becoming more supple and less likely to be damaged during the birth. When you are in labor, ask your healthcare provider to help you avoid the need for any stitches, and write this on your birthplan (see page 118).

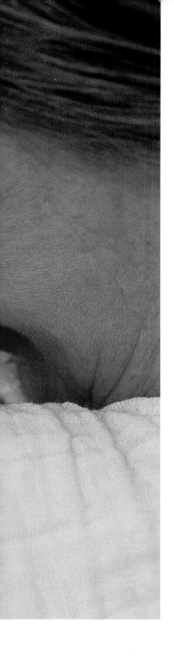

9

Labor and Birth

"When my contractions started, it felt like I was being launched into space. I bubbled with excitement and elation and couldn't wait to see my baby but at the same time I was terrified! After all the theory and the preparations, I had to jump and trust that I could fly."

WHEN WILL THE BABY ARRIVE?

About 85% of babies are born within two weeks around their due date. When the date is calculated from the first day of your last period, about 10% (mostly first babies) are two weeks overdue. When the birth date is estimated by ultrasound scan, only about 2% of babies arrive two weeks late.

The timing of labor may be inherited from your baby's father, as some women go into labor consistently early with one partner but become overdue with a new partner. His family may be a better guide to whether your baby will be born on time than your own family, although babies do mature at different rates and tend to come when they're ready!

If you notice signs of labor starting three weeks or more before your due date, seek help right away. Many babies come early without problems, but some will need a specialist's care. If you have several weeks to go, your doctor may try to delay your labor to give your baby more time to mature. Take your medical records with you when you stay away from home and contact the nearest hospital if labor does start.

If you go a week or more overdue it can be stressful, and after two weeks your healthcare provider may want you to be induced (see page 146). Receiving concerned phone calls and comments from friends or relatives when your due date passes with no signs of labor may make you feel inadequate, like a performing seal who can't perform! On the other hand, the last few days before your baby's birth could be a very special time for you and your partner. Arrange special occasions to look forward to together instead of just sitting around waiting for contractions.

WHAT CONTRACTIONS FEEL LIKE

If you tense your leg, the muscles in your thigh contract and become hard. When you relax they soften again. You tighten your leg muscles voluntarily, but hormones make your uterus contract involuntarily to open your cervix. Your baby's head (or bottom) then holds it open and the next contraction stretches it slightly more. As more hormones are secreted during labor, the contractions become stronger, dilating your cervix more effectively.

Did you wonder what the baby's movements would feel like when you were first pregnant, only to find the sensation strangely familiar when you felt it? You may notice the same about your contractions, although women clearly do feel the sensations differently as the following quotes show.

"At first the contractions felt like menstrual pains down at the bottom of my tummy. Then they intensified into a hot, cramping sensation. My whole body went rigid with each one."

"Nobody told me that you sometimes feel the contractions all in your back, so that was a shock. I kept waiting for something to happen in my tummy but it never did."

"The sensation started in my back and radiated around to my tummy and down my legs. It felt like the ache you get if you have cramps. I could still feel it when the contraction was over."

"My contractions felt as if someone was hugging me so tightly I couldn't breathe. They weren't very painful but there was this tremendous sensation of pressure that almost overwhelmed me."

BEFORE LABOR STARTS

The first stage of labor lasts from when your cervix begins to open until you're fully dilated, ready to push. Before dilating your cervix softens and thins out. Some women experience diarrhea, or have a "show" of bloodstreaked jelly — enough to cover the top joint of your thumb. This is the mucus plug that seals the cervix and it means that your cervix is softening. If there's fresh bleeding, tell your healthcare provider, but otherwise do nothing. You might not feel contractions for some hours, or even days.

Sometimes the "waters" leak and you keep finding that your pants are damp; or the waters may break (see page 141). Phone your healthcare provider for advice—she will probably want to check you. Even if you have no contractions for several hours they may become strong quite quickly once they start.

Many women have regular contractions as the cervix thins and the baby's head moves deeper into the pelvis. You may feel bothersome pains that come and go over several days, or you may have painful tightenings that continue for hours, or even a day. The length and strength of the contractions is usually more significant than the interval between them. If they last 30 to 40 seconds and you feel normal enough to chat or drink a little juice in between them, it's unlikely that you're about to give birth, even if they are five minutes apart. Doing something different may make these contractions disappear for a while. Have a bath or go out for a walk if you've been resting, or lie down if you've been up and about.

The "pre-labor" phase before true labor begins can be tedious. It's best if you can ignore it for as long as possible. Try the following ways of passing the time:

- Ask a friend to keep you company.
- Rent videos (and a video recorder if necessary).
- Go for a walk or window shopping.
- Start doing a large jigsaw, reading a new novel, making an outfit for the baby.
- Clean out a cupboard, re-cover the ironing board, bake a cake.
- Address birth announcements, write letters or phone friends.
- At night have a bath, a milk drink, a couple of acetaminophen tablets (such as Tylenol®), if necessary, and try to sleep to conserve energy.

TIME FOR THE HOSPITAL OR HELP?

If you have fresh bleeding or your water breaks, your doctor or midwife will probably want to check you out, so phone her or the hospital immediately. With contractions, it's a matter of how you feel. If you're happy and confident, that's fine, but don't hesitate to phone if you're worried about anything or just need reassurance that all's well. An experienced healthcare provider can usually tell if you're in labor just by talking to you.

EARLY LABOR

To decide whether you're really in labor, compare your contractions with the ones you have been having. As they build in length and strength, you'll be more certain that true labor has started. Strong contractions last about 40 to 60 seconds, come regularly and definitely feel as though they mean business. Some women are elated to know they're in labor, while others get butterflies, as though they have stage fright.

If you're going to a hospital for the birth, phone to let them know that you're coming in. Get your partner or a friend to drive you there. When you arrive, a nurse will take your information and do the routine checks that you're familiar with from prenatal visits. She may examine you internally to check if your cervix is dilating. If it's still thinning, you'll be reassured and sent home or put in a prenatal unit. Don't let this upset you. Contractions can sometimes feel more urgent than they are, even if it's not your first baby.

If you're in labor, you'll probably be given a single room. You may be offered a bath or shower. It is not common practice now to offer an enema unless you ask for one. An electronic fetal monitor may be put on your abdomen for half an hour to get a "base reading" of your baby's normal heartbeat. You and your birth partner will then be left together with a buzzer to summon help if you need it, and a nurse will check from time to time to see how you're doing. Every three to four hours she may examine you to check dilation. If progress is slow, she may suggest breaking your water or setting up a hormone I.V. to strengthen the contractions (see page 147). Try not to get discouraged if early labor takes a long time.

Here are some ways to pass the time:

- Sort through the family photo album, look at travel brochures and plan a real or imaginary vacation.
- Give yourself a treat—smooth a luxurious cream onto your face, take a shower using a fragrant shower gel, or use some special massage oil.
- Play audiotapes or music, ask your partner to read to you or to give you a shoulder or foot massage. Try out different positions for labor (see page 112), remembering that stronger contractions help you make more progress.

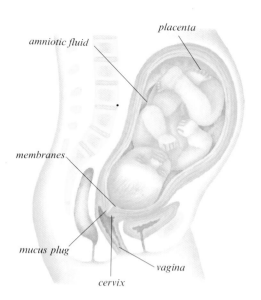

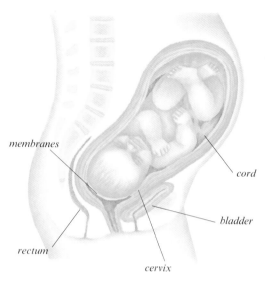

amniotic fluid

placenta

membranes

mucus plug

vagina

cervix

membranes

cord

bladder

rectum

cervix

Pre-labor phase: Before labor begins your contractions draw up your cervix so it becomes shorter and eventually thinner.

First stage of labor: Your uterus tips forward with each contraction as your cervix opens. This helps your baby into the birth canal.

ACTIVE LABOR

As your cervix dilates your contractions will become even longer, stronger and closer together. They may last 60 to 90 seconds and come every two to four minutes. You'll be making good progress, but you'll probably need to concentrate hard on relaxing both during and between them. You may feel calm and very peaceful; or you may feel weary and anxious to get the birth over with.

In the final stages of dilation, or "transition," there's often almost no space between contractions. Some women feel angry or panicky, or find themselves weeping tears of frustration or despair; others feel deeply calm, confident and so detached that they actually doze off between contractions.

Your healthcare provider will continue to listen to your baby's heartbeat and make sure you're all right. She may ask if you'd like to be given medication for pain (see pages 122-3). It can be hard to cope with the intensity of active labor, but you're nearing your goal and it's worth remembering that the stronger the contractions, the sooner you'll reach it.

"I couldn't decide if I was in labor, so we went to the hospital when I thought traveling would be uncomfortable if we left any later. I had a backache all the time, but my partner gave me lots of emotional support. I needed his strength and was glad that he was very firm with me."
ANGELA

" *I didn't realize that labor could go on for over 20 hours. It was much longer and more tiring than I'd expected, but less painful. I tried every position in the book, and some that weren't.*

My husband massaged my back and played music tapes for me, but most of all he kept my spirits up. When I was pushing I kept thinking I was going to mess the bed and so I held back when I should have gone for it. But the moment the nurse put Louisa in my arms for the first time it was magical. I forgot all about labor and felt like a star. **"** MONIQUE

Be realistic about labor

It's claimed that there are about 150 contractions in the "average" first labor, while a second or third baby takes about half that number. A textbook first labor lasts about 12 hours, including the delivery but not the pre-labor phase when the cervix is thinning out. So the average rate at which the cervix dilates is 1cm per hour.

Of course, this tells you very little about *your* labor, because women are individuals and are not so conveniently predictable. Some labors start and stop over several days. Some babies take their time to turn to a better position. Some women take many hours to dilate to 4cm and then the uterus gets the hang of it and finishes in less than an hour.

Whether it's your first baby or your fifth, you don't know beforehand what your labor will be like, so be realistic. Some women have an easy time. Others, including well-prepared or experienced women, find themselves struggling for reasons beyond anyone's control. Keeping calm and relaxed always helps, but it does not guarantee labor will be normal. Nor is a normal labor necessarily an easy labor.

Accept your labor for what it is, not for what you would like it to be. Your doctor, nurse or midwife can offer help if you need it, so be flexible. Labor will be a positive experience if you feel you made the right decisions in the circumstances.

Most problems in labor are unpleasant rather than dramatic, but nobody can prepare you for a real emergency. It happens rarely and you just have to cope as best you can and rely on the hospital team for help.

COPING WITH CONTRACTIONS

- ◆ *Relax with a sigh at the start and end of each contraction.*
- ◆ *Breathe slowly and gently, emphasizing the out breath.*
- ◆ *Keep checking that your shoulders and jaw are loose.*
- ◆ *Rest your palms upwards.*
- ◆ *A deep, warm bath may help you relax.*
- ◆ *Using imagery may help. For example, think of feeling heavy and soft, or imagine riding over the contractions on a surfboard.*
- ◆ *Ask your partner to count aloud to help you to pace yourself through each contraction.*

Long labor

About 80% of first labors are over within 12 hours, without any intervention. A slow labor, although it can be normal, may be hard to handle. It can be exhausting and your morale may plummet when there's little progress, but it can also be much gentler and more enjoyable than a very fast labor. These suggestions may help you to cope better:

- Try to deal with each contraction without thinking about those in the past or still to come.
- Walking or squatting often stimulates contractions. Have short rest periods lying down, then get upright and moving again.
- Have several deep, warm baths.
- Go to the bathroom every hour to keep your bladder empty.
- Ask for guaranteed privacy for half an hour if concerned staff make you feel tense. Kissing, cuddling and breast stimulation can help to release contracting hormones.
- Send your partner out for 10 minutes of fresh air every hour. He needs energy to keep up your morale.

Back labor

If your baby faces your front rather than your back, it's harder for him to pass under your pubic arch during the birth. Because of the shape of his head, it's like an egg trying to fit sideways into an egg cup. About 10% of babies start labor in this position. The contractions turn them gradually into a better position for the birth. This rotation is progress even if you are not dilating, but labor may be longer and pressure may cause severe backache.

Try these helpful remedies:

- Kneel on all fours, gently rocking your pelvis.
- Have your partner or friend put firm pressure on your back or massage you during contractions (see pages 120-1). Some women prefer feather-light massage.
- Use hot or cold compresses, renewed frequently.
- Ask for an epidural, if the backache seems to be more than you can handle and nothing else helps.

Very fast labor

It may seem like a good idea to get labor over and done with in a few hours, but if your cervix opens three times as fast as most women's, your contractions may also seem to be three times as strong! In a very short labor, there may be barely time to catch your breath before the next contraction is upon you. On the other hand, a short labor is usually not complicated.

Some women are disappointed that they were not more in control but felt swept along in a raging torrent, unable to do anything but bob along for the ride. You may feel shocked and shaky after such an experience, although you will probably also feel pleased that your labor did not last any longer!

Left: Pushing is hard work but it can also be very satisfying, because you are actively helping your baby to be born.

Below: This mother is upright, supported between her partner's knees. As her baby's head emerges, the midwife gently guides it to prevent a tear.

THE BIRTH

The second stage of labor lasts from when your cervix is fully dilated until your baby is born. Pushing contractions are shorter and less frequent. They feel different from those that open your cervix. You may think you need to go to the bathroom, you may feel a downward movement in your abdomen and pelvic floor, or find yourself making deep sounds in your throat. Your knees may feel weak or buckle so that you need support.

Press the buzzer if your doctor or midwife isn't there. She'll check that your cervix is fully dilated. If you push when there is a rim of cervix in front of the baby's head, it could swell like a bruised lip and take longer to dilate. To

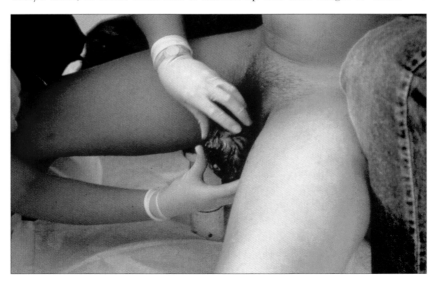

prevent this, breathe slowly and blow out sharply on each out breath, as though you were blowing a feather off your nose. When you are fully dilated you may need to push immediately or there may be a pause when you can rest. Get into an upright position so that gravity will help your baby move down the birth canal until you get an urge to push.

Your birth attendant will put on a plastic apron. If you are in a hospital, she'll bring her equipment in or move you to a delivery room. She'll stay with you during the birth, guiding you and making sure that your baby is coping well.

Many women find that the pushing action is a welcome relief after the tumult of final dilation, although this depends on the baby's position and

Above: *The mother helps deliver her baby. The birth attendant supports the baby's head as it turns to help his body slip out easily.*

Right: *A wonderful reward for all that effort! The mother cuddles her newborn baby for the first time, her face full of love.*

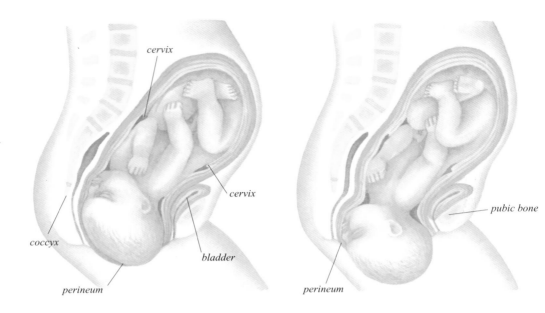

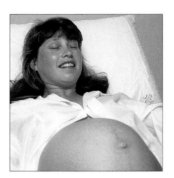

Your baby's head follows the curve of your pelvis, moving your coccyx (tailbone) aside. Notice how thin the perineum is—your birth attendant may ask you to pant instead of pushing at this point.

Your baby's head flexes up underneath your pubic arch and emerges, releasing pressure on your coccyx and perineum. At this point the back of your baby's head is towards your front and you'll be able to feel his hair.

whether the pelvis is roomy. It can be hard work and you may feel too exhausted to be bothered; alternatively, you may feel full of energy, excitement and joy.

Try beforehand to find a birth attendant who is happy to deliver you in any position. If you choose an upright position, gravity will help your baby to descend, but if the birth seems fast or you've already delivered a baby quickly, you could try lying on your side to slow it down. Ask your birth attendant to help you deliver your baby's head without a tear, and listen to her instructions.

Your baby's head will turn to fit under your pubic arch and you may feel a burning sensation as the perineum (tissue around the vagina) stretches. The birth attendant will support your baby's head to protect your perineum and tell you when to stop pushing and pant instead. She'll perform an episiotomy

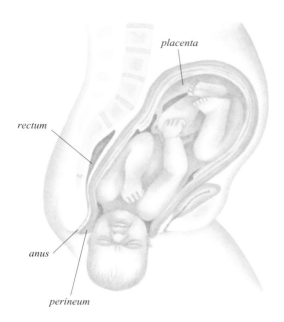

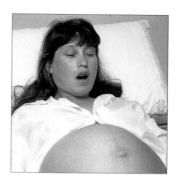

Your baby turns to face your thigh, so that his shoulders fit more easily through your pubic arch and pelvic floor. When his shoulders emerge his body tumbles out.

placenta

rectum

anus

perineum

if needed. Many women suffer no damage at all or only have a very small tear in the perineum.

Your baby's shoulders will turn to fit under your pubic arch and his body will tumble out, to be placed on your abdomen or in your arms. He can be cleaned and wrapped up first if you prefer. You may have an injection to prevent too much bleeding after the placenta is delivered.

Gentle birth

Have you ever thought about what birth feels like for your baby? He's squeezed through your bony pelvis, thrust from warmth and security into space, bright lights and unmuffled sounds.

If the birth is normal, you and your birth attendant could help make it a gentler experience for your baby.

- Ask your birth attendant to deliver your baby onto your abdomen or into your arms and leave the cord to pulsate before cutting it (see page 138).
- You can provide a particularly soft wrap to keep your baby warm while you cradle him after the birth.
- Ask if the lights can be dimmed and unnecessary noise avoided.
- Bathe your baby in warm water soon after the birth.
- If the birth has to be assisted, make up for any distress suffered by you or your baby by being especially gentle and loving with him afterwards.

HELPING WITH THE BIRTH

To actively help the birth of your baby:
◆ *Choose the position that feels best at the time.*
◆ *Think of the entrance to your vagina and direct your pushes down there. Involuntary grunts are normal and can be helpful.*
◆ *Open out your birth canal and "give" birth. Some women hold back for fear of emptying their bowels, a sensation that's caused by the pressure of the baby's head.*
◆ *Listen to your birth attendant. She'll guide you and tell you when to stop pushing so that she can ease your baby out gently.*

Your newborn baby

When you see babies with perfectly shaped heads and silk-soft skin in movies or television dramas, they are usually a few hours or days old! Some truly newborn babies look like that, but others look purple, blue or gray and covered with vernix, a substance that stops the skin from becoming water-logged in the uterus. You may or may not think your baby is beautiful!

Some babies have puffy eyes, blue hands and feet or fine black hair (lanugo) on their bodies. Others have lumps and bumps from the pressure of your pelvis, or streaks of blood from a tear or episiotomy. Don't be alarmed; many babies look vulnerable and birth-bruised at first. All this changes quite quickly and in a few hours or days he'll look as perfect as any cherub!

After the birth

The third and final stage of labor is the delivery of the placenta. Your birth attendant may clamp and cut the cord immediately, or she may wait until it stops pulsating. Your partner can cut the cord if he wishes. Some babies are put on a sloping table to have their airways cleared.

Identity bracelets will be attached to your baby's wrist and ankle and you can cuddle and breastfeed him if you wish.

You may well feel a tremendous elation, a rush of love for this new person and pride in your achievement. You may feel wide awake and full of energy. But it's equally normal to feel curiously detached, rather disappointed in your baby and simply relieved that the birth is over.

"Labor wasn't what I'd expected at all. I had a show but then nothing else happened for several days. I had contractions every night and then they'd die away again. After a week of this I couldn't stand it any longer and went to stay at my mom's house. That night I felt a little strange. By the time we got to the hospital, the contractions were so strong I couldn't walk and they had to bring a wheelchair to take me to the ward. After three quick pushes, Kiara was born. I'd go through a birth any day. I can't believe I was so lucky!" DENISE

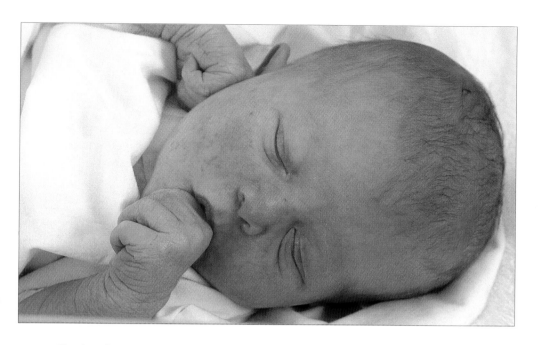

Don't judge your initial reaction harshly; just accept it for what it is.

You'll be asked to push again to deliver the placenta, although you might not want to! It feels like delivering a slippery wet sponge after the firmness of a baby's head. A midwife or doctor will stitch you if necessary, and you can wash up or shower and put on a clean nightgown. Later, your baby will be weighed, measured and checked by a pediatrician. You and your partner will be offered a glass of juice and left alone to get to know your new arrival.

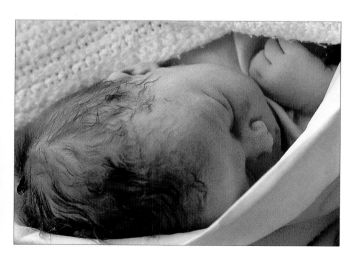

Above: This baby has wrinkled skin and slightly puffy eyes. In a few days he'll fill out and the swelling will subside. His skin is blotchy, which is very common in newborn babies.

Left: This newborn has an elongated head. It molded to this shape to pass more easily through the mother's pelvis, but in a few days it will become round again.

Some hospitals give every baby vitamin K, either orally or by injection, to help prevent a rare disease in which the baby's blood fails to clot and bleeding occurs. You may want to discuss this with your healthcare provider before the birth so that you can make a considered decision. Ask the staff to explain the pros and cons of any treatment they suggest, because responsibility for making decisions on your baby's behalf lies with you.

After an hour or two you'll probably be transferred to a postnatal ward and your partner may go home. Hospital routines vary but the staff will show you the ropes. By now you may be feeling calm and confident, like the cat that drank the cream; or wobbly and unsure of yourself, like a new girl at school. Remember there's plenty of help available and there's no "right" or "wrong" way of caring for a baby. Just give your feelings time to settle down.

The Apgar score

This is a standard method of ensuring that babies who need it receive special attention. One minute after the birth, the midwife checks your baby's appearance (color), pulse (heartbeat), grimace (reflex), activity (muscle tone) and respiration (breathing). Each measure is awarded zero to two points. A total score between seven and ten means your baby is fine. The assessment is repeated five minutes after the birth, and by then a low score has often improved. If the score is still under seven, your baby will be watched carefully for a while, but even then most babies turn out to be fine.

Bonding

Babies have no idea of other people's needs and are very demanding. Bonding is the process of emotional attachment that makes parents put their child's needs first. You'll know it's happened when you feel a rush of love or heart-stopping anxiety as someone else picks up your child!

Bonding is easier if you can hold and feed your baby soon after the birth, but don't worry if you're separated for some reason. Like falling in love, you may bond instantly or over time. Sooner or later it happens to all parents!

BIRTH AT HOME

If you have your baby at home, the birth will proceed much the same as in the hospital. Call your doctor or midwife when you feel you need her help or reassurance. You'll be free to do what you please and she'll observe you, checking your blood pressure and your baby's heartbeat and examining you occasionally.

After the delivery, you can shower while she cleans up and collects any dirty laundry for your partner to deal with later. She'll dispose of the placenta, although some couples prefer to bury it in the garden and plant a tree in the baby's honor. When you're settled and everything is cleaned up, your doctor or midwife will leave a phone number in case you need her. She may return in a few hours.

QUESTIONS AND ANSWERS

Q: I'm prepared to accept pain in order to have a natural labor but I'm no superhero! How can I cope with the pain without using drugs?

A: Try lots of different positions until you find what's most comfortable. For example, kneel on something soft and lean onto a bean-bag chair, or sit back-to-front on a chair and lean on a pillow placed over the back. Stand with your arms around your partner's neck; rock your body or circle your hips to ease any discomfort. Massage can help: Lightly stroke the skin around and under your abdomen to take away surface tension, or ask your partner to press firmly on your lower back (see pages 120-1). Try sitting in a deep, warm bath; some women find it helps if their partner pours cool water over their stomach or down their back during contractions.

Think of contractions as rushes of warmth and energy; or as exhilarating waves that build up, tumble over and recede. Some women imagine riding waves on a surfboard, or climbing a hill and sliding down the other side.

Keep your breathing slow and gentle, emphasizing the out breath and trying to let the contractions flow over you without resistance. Concentrate on relaxing so deeply that you feel as if you are inside a glass ball, aware of what is going on outside but not distracted by it. Remind yourself that the pain is caused not by injury but by muscles working hard to deliver your baby. There are lots of ways to cope and it will not go on forever.

Q: I'd feel so embarrassed if my water broke in public. Is it likely and if it happens what should I do?

A: Fewer than 15% of labors start with the water breaking, and it mostly happens at home where you spend most of your time. Even if it happens, it's unlikely your baby will arrive immediately. If you are upright and your baby's head is engaged, gravity makes it act like a cork in a bottle, preventing liquid from escaping.

Put a child's rubber sheet over your mattress for the last month or so of your pregnancy. When you're out, wear a couple of sanitary pads, or even a gel-filled incontinence pad (available from a drug store). You can be sure that if anybody noticed a gush in public (which is rare) they would either look the other way or want to help you out.

Q: Do I have to wear a hospital gown in labor and can I eat anything? I'm worried about running out of energy if I have a long labor.

A: You may be offered a gown but in many hospitals you can wear what you like in labor. If you're admitted early and want to walk around to get your contractions going, keep wearing your ordinary clothes. When the contractions become so strong that you want to stay in your room, change into something cool and comfortable like a nightgown, a large T-shirt or one of your partner's shirts. Some women feel best wearing nothing; others feel inhibited if there is a lack of privacy.

In the past, women were often only given sips of water or ice chips during labor. When you're in strong labor you may not want to eat. However, withholding food and drink does not guarantee an empty stomach should a general anesthetic be necessary. If you are hungry, have something light such as toast, soup, scrambled eggs, stewed fruit or plain cookies. Many hospitals provide small meals of this sort to give you energy.

Q: I live an hour away from the hospital. My first labor took three hours. What should my husband do if we can't reach the hospital and are alone with our toddler?

A: Start without delay when you think something is happening, but if there is no time, don't panic. If you are on your way to the hospital and you can feel your baby coming, your husband should pull over safely and stop the car. At home, he should stay with you, reassure you and use common sense.

Most babies deliver themselves and breathe very competently. They are wet and slippery when they are first born, so they need to be held firmly and kept warm. If your baby has mucus in his mouth, your husband could wipe it away before giving him to you, still attached to the cord, to put to the breast. He could get a blanket to keep both of you warm, and phone for help if there was no time earlier. Your doctor or midwife will come immediately to cut the cord and deliver the placenta or advise you to come to the hospital. Don't worry about the cord. It doesn't have to be cut right away. Quick births are usually uncomplicated and toddlers are rarely upset if you stay calm.

Q: I want to have a natural birth but I'm worried that my doctor might not let me. I don't want to be difficult but how can I make sure that I will be allowed to cope with labor my own way?

A: Provided everything is going normally, your doctor will probably be happy to go along with your wishes and you should be able to do whatever feels comfortable for you at the time.

Communication can be a problem when you're under stress, so write a birth plan (see page 118), discuss it with your doctor at your next prenatal visit and have a copy attached to your medical records.

Remind the staff that you want to have a natural labor when you phone to say you're coming to the hospital. Nurses differ in their approach to birth, just as mothers do, and this gives the staff on duty a chance to assign you a nurse who feels the same as you, if possible.

Q: I have had several colds during pregnancy, which interfered with my breathing. During a recent bout of the flu I worried about the birth. What can I do if I go into labor feeling ill?

A: Minor illnesses like colds and flu are usually either suppressed during labor or labor is delayed until you have recovered. This also tends to happen with asthma or migraine attacks, sinus headaches and the like. That's not to say that women always feel at their best during labor, but the body seems to decide its priorities instead of overburdening you. If you feel run down or under stress, it makes sense to try to improve your general health. Perhaps you could modify your diet or rest more, so your body gets a chance to recover its full strength.

Q: I've been to classes and read a lot about labor but I'm not confident that I'll cope when it comes to the real thing. What happens if I can't relax and breathe properly, or if I make a huge fuss?

A: Women often worry that labor is too big a job for them to handle, only to find hidden strengths they never knew they had. Relaxation and gentle breathing will help you cope with contractions, so they are worth learning. However, there are no rules such as "you have to relax all the way through . . . don't make a noise . . . you have to breathe like this or that . . ." You'll automatically give your best, so forget about setting targets for yourself. It's not a competition and nobody wins prizes for breathing perfectly or suffering stoically. All you have to do is let it happen.

Giving birth is more like crossing a field full of molehills than climbing a mountain. You may not know how many there are and some may be harder to get over than others; but if labor is normal, the task is not impossible. If it isn't, help is available. Take one contraction at a time, deal with it and let it go. Try to cope—not according to any rules, but in whatever way feels right and works best for you.

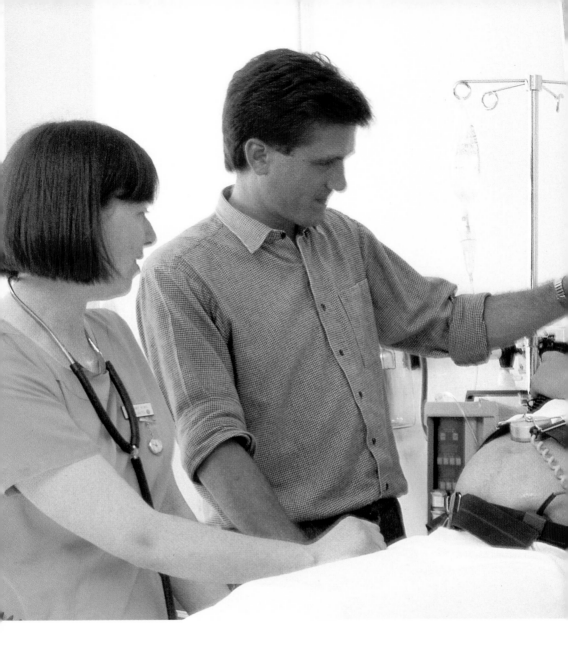

10

Help During and After the Birth

"You never know what might happen at the birth. Doctors are like lifeboats— you're glad they're there but you hope they won't be necessary. I'm nervous, but I can relax knowing help is always at hand, although I probably won't need it. "

HELP IN LABOR

If things don't go as smoothly as everyone hopes, intervention can make the birth easier or safer for you or your baby. It isn't something to be dreaded; it can provide a positive solution to a problem. Sometimes it is essential because you or your baby are at risk. In any rescue situation you should simply let the staff take control and tell you exactly what to do.

In other cases assistance is not essential but could help. The decision depends on the professional judgment of the staff (see page 84) and on what you feel is best for you and your baby. You could leave it up to the staff, but if you want to share the decision you need to think about the issues.

Intervention usually comes in a "package." For example, if your labor is speeded up you will be monitored to make sure the baby copes well, so you may have less freedom to move about and seek comfortable positions; labor may be more painful, so you might need more pain relief. If you or your baby are at risk, you will want to accept help without question. Thinking about the pros and cons of the various elements of a "package" will help if you want to share the decision when intervention is optional.

Induction

Labor may be started artificially if your baby is clearly at risk. For example, treatment might fail to improve pre-eclampsia (see page 102), or there might be concern because the baby's normal pattern of movements changes dramatically or she stops growing.

Induction might also be suggested when you are overdue, to reduce the risk of the placenta failing or of a more difficult delivery because your baby is bigger and her bones are less pliable.

You might *want* to be induced, but the procedure carries some risks so the decision should be made individually and only for a good reason.

Some doctors induce women routinely 10 to 14 days after their due date. Others allow three weeks, so if your baby is kicking happily you could ask whether this would be safe in your case. If you are given a date for induction, try gently stimulating your breasts and nipples the day before to increase the release of oxytocin, the hormone that causes contractions. It may just get the labor started!

Practice patterns differ, but typically if it's your first baby you'll be asked to go in the previous evening. You'll be examined and a suppository or some gel will be inserted in your vagina to soften the neck of the uterus.

Prostin may start your labor easily so that it progresses normally. If not, you may be given further doses at intervals, until your cervix starts to dilate. You may experience some colicky "hormone" pains, especially with higher doses of prostin, and with second or later babies. These pains usually settle down after an hour or two. True labor contractions are easier to handle. With a second or later baby your cervix may be so thin and soft that it's not necessary to use suppositories or gel.

Your water may be broken using an *amnihook* (similar to a plastic crochet hook) or an *amnicot* (a finger covering with a tiny plastic hook on the end). This procedure shouldn't hurt because there are no nerves in the amniotic sac, but the internal examination may feel uncomfortable. Breaking your waters often establishes effective contractions but if not, they will be stimulated using an oxytocin (Pitocin®) I.V. This will be set up immediately if there is an urgent reason to induce you, such as pre-eclampsia. The medication will be increased gradually until contractions begin.

Induced labor does not affect most babies, but you'll be monitored throughout to make sure. If your baby is distressed, a tiny drop of blood may be taken from her scalp and analyzed to double-check her oxygen levels, and she'll be delivered quickly if necessary.

How painful you find induced labor depends on how easy it is to establish your contractions. If you're overdue, or have already had a baby, it may be no more than mildly uncomfortable. It can be painful if your uterus is not ready for labor. Comfort sometimes has to take second place to your own or your baby's safety, but pain relief is always available if needed.

Speeding up labor

If your water breaks but the contractions still fail to start, or start very slowly, your labor may be speeded up. The risk of infection, which could be serious for a baby, rises slowly after about 12 hours and more rapidly after 24 hours. A compromise has to be reached between allowing the contractions to start or strengthen spontaneously, which could take some hours, and insuring that your baby is delivered without risking infection.

Sometimes contractions start and stop, or continue for many hours with little progress. Sometimes they are strong but fail to dilate your cervix, although they often become more effective as you relax. Slow labor is tedious but not abnormal in itself; every contraction helps you towards your goal. If your baby is fine you may prefer to accept this pattern of labor.

When labor is accelerated your water is broken, which usually strengthens your contractions. Your baby is monitored and an oxytocin I.V. is put into your arm to stimulate stronger contractions; this remains until after your baby is born. Your contractions may be more painful, but labor will be over sooner and you can have pain relief, if you want it. Unless speed is essential, the I.V. can be started slowly and increased gradually to avoid overwhelming you.

Some doctors offer "active management" to guarantee that your labor will be over in 12 hours. Once you're in labor your water is broken and internal examinations are performed every two hours or so to check progress. If your cervix dilates slowly, an oxytocin I.V. is set up and increased until the contractions dilate your cervix at the rate of about 1cm an hour. Your baby is

"The birth didn't go at all as I'd hoped. I had pre-eclampsia, so there were drugs to control my blood pressure, an I.V. to speed up labor and I wasn't allowed to push. They tried to deliver Sam by vacuum extraction followed by forceps. I felt cheated. It was total technology when I wanted a natural birth! If I could do it all over again I'd prepare in exactly the same way. I understood what was happening, so I felt in control. Some decisions were hard to make, but others were very easy. It wasn't a good birth, but I coped well and I certainly produced a lovely baby! "DEBBIE

monitored in case she becomes distressed. Recent research suggests that this active management shortens labor by an average of one hour but does not make an assisted delivery less likely.

Many women have mixed feelings about speeding up labor unless it is essential, so you may want to discuss it first with your doctor or midwife. Often it's possible to delay the decision for a few hours, to see how things go. However, although an I.V. increases the risk that other intervention may be necessary, it can also be a safe way to speed up a prolonged labor.

Monitoring the baby

During labor the birth attendant listens to your baby's heart rate through a hand-held or electronic stethoscope. The beat changes as the uterus contracts, returning to normal when the contraction ends and blood flows freely again. If a baby is short of oxygen, her heartbeats increase or decrease too much, or return to normal too slowly after a contraction. This gives early warning of distress so that action can be taken immediately.

An internal or external electronic fetal monitor can give a continuous record of your baby's response to contractions. Most hospitals record a "base reading" of your baby's heart rate in early labor and fetal monitors are used routinely in "high-tech" births. They are also used as a safeguard when there is intervention in labor (such as an I.V.) and if there is any concern about your baby's heart rate.

An external monitor has two electrodes, held on your abdomen with soft belts made of webbing. One picks up the strength of the contractions and the other records your baby's heartbeat. The information is fed into a machine with digital and auditory displays (which can be turned off if they worry you), and recorded as a readout on paper. Your movement may be restricted because every time you move, your baby also moves, so the electrode may need to be repositioned. The monitor could be attached while you sit in a chair and moved each time you want to change position, but it obviously makes it harder to move freely.

An internal monitor provides similar information but an electrode is attached to your baby's scalp through your cervix. Scalp electrodes are less restrictive; if you had a backache, for example, you could still kneel to have your back massaged. However, many women feel they are intrusive to the baby. Occasionally they cause minor scratches or hair fails to grow at the spot where the monitor was attached, although this is unnoticeable when the baby's hair grows thickly.

The readout from a monitor needs skilled interpretation. If it is not absolutely clear whether your baby is distressed and action is required, you could ask for a second opinion. However, if there is a problem with your labor, a fetal heart monitor can reassure you and improve safety for your baby.

Forceps or vacuum delivery

Ideally, your baby needs time to gently negotiate the contours of your pelvis, but no great delay during her delivery. Forceps or vacuum extraction can help ensure that her birth is neither too fast nor too slow.

Forceps are shaped like spoons, curved to fit the birth canal, with different types according to need. They are lubricated, inserted individually into the vagina and locked together at the handles like old-fashioned salad servers, so that they cradle the baby's head without harming it.

Vacuum extraction equipment consists of a cup, similar to a large bath plug or plunger, that fits on the baby's head and a pump to create suction to hold the cup securely in place.

Vacuum extraction is becoming more popular than forceps (which take up more space) but the decision depends on the actual circumstances and the experience of the doctor. The method he or she feels most confident using is likely to be the most successful.

Your baby might become distressed if the birth is too slow. Normally her head aligns with your pubic arch, moves down the birth canal with each pushing contraction and slips back a little between contractions. Some babies make no progress because they slip back too far after each contraction, or they try to pass under your pubic arch (which is shaped a little like a wishbone) at an angle. Using forceps or vacuum extraction, the doctor can gently turn your baby's head to fit the arch, or stop her from slipping back after each contraction. If you've been pushing for an hour or two without progress and are exhausted, it may be a great relief when such assistance is offered!

Forceps or a vacuum extraction can also help a baby come out quickly. For example, a baby might be distressed because her cord was compressed or her mother's pelvis was a very tight fit. Adopting a different position or using extra effort might help, but if the distress continues, an assisted delivery could solve the problem. A premature or breech baby might be delivered with forceps to guard against too rapid a birth, to protect the baby.

About one birth in 10 is assisted, always by a doctor. Most doctors prefer you to lie with your feet in *stirrups*, adjustable canvas slings attached to short poles at the foot of the bed. Your legs will be lifted into stirrups together, not one at a time, which could strain your pelvic joints. Relax at the hips and ask the staff to adjust the stirrups if they are uncomfortable.

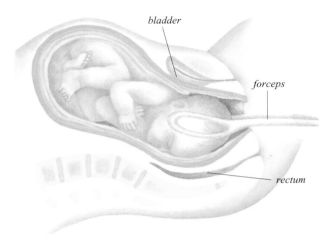

bladder

forceps

rectum

Forceps are curved to fit the pelvis. Without causing damage, they hold the baby's head securely so the doctor can turn it slightly or stop it from slipping back into the birth canal.

Unless you already have an epidural in place, you will be given an injection that numbs the nerves around the birth canal, so that you feel sensation but no pain. An episiotomy is usually performed to enlarge the opening to the birth canal and give the doctor extra room to deliver your baby.

When you feel a contraction or the staff say one is coming, you can help by pushing so that the forceps or vacuum extractor make the contraction more effective. The doctor uses a slow and steady action, like easing out the cork from a bottle of fine wine. A pediatrician will be there, but most babies need no help. You may see pressure marks from forceps or a swelling on your baby's head

A vacuum extractor looks like a shallow cup. It fits onto the crown of the baby's head and is held securely in place by suction. A forceps or vacuum-extraction delivery can make a difficult birth easier.

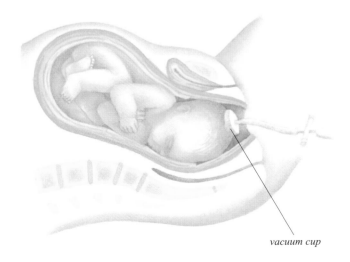

vacuum cup

that matches the vacuum cup. These can look alarming at first, but they disappear within a day or two. Long-term problems are very rare because difficult assisted deliveries have been replaced by Cesarean sections. If your baby is irritable for a while, as though she has a little headache, she will be comforted if you are especially gentle and loving with her in the early days.

"I handled my contractions using nothing but breathing, but the delivery was difficult. Emily's head kept rocking to and fro under my pubic bone. I tried various positions but ended up with my feet in stirrups. The nurse mentioned getting the doctor, which motivated me to push like mad, but even so I had a vacuum-assisted delivery. It was very tense and confusing at the time, but as soon as Emily was born I was euphoric."
JANE

Some assisted deliveries are easy; the baby is simply lifted out, and you may feel little different afterwards from a mother who had a normal delivery. Sadly, others are very hard work for everyone concerned. This is sometimes unavoidable, and you may feel considerably bruised and sore afterwards. You will be grateful that your baby is safe but may also feel distressed at what happened (see page 153), even though it solved a problem and was not your fault.

Episiotomy

This is a cut made in the outlet of the birth canal, to enlarge the opening and provide extra speed or extra space to deliver a baby safely. You might have one if your baby is breech, premature or in distress, or if you need an assisted delivery. A tear may be smaller and heal faster, but an episiotomy is preferable to a tear that damages muscles controlling your anus. Although an episiotomy may sometimes be needed, it may increase the chance that you will have a tear. Just like fabric, your tissues tear more easily once they have been cut.

An episiotomy is usually performed and stitched afterwards by whoever delivers your baby. Some birth attendants perform more episiotomies than others. Hospitals that set a time limit on how long you can push, or don't encourage you to choose your delivery position, tend to have higher rates. If you use perineal massage (see page 125) and you tell your doctor or midwife that you want to avoid an episiotomy or a tear, you are less likely to have either.

Although an episiotomy sounds nasty, most women say that they were hardly aware of it at the time. Imagination is often far worse than reality! You may be given a local anesthetic, but in most cases the midwife or doctor waits until a contraction has reached its height. A short cut is made with round-ended scissors. The tissue is naturally numb as it is stretched by your baby's head.

A local anesthetic is usually given for stitching the incision, although some staff put in sutures immediately after the placenta arrives, while the area is still numb, because they feel that the anesthetic makes the tissues swell and this contributes to later discomfort. There is no need to suffer—just ask for more pain relief if you need it.

"I had an I.V. because Thomas was badly positioned and the doctor wanted stronger contractions to help turn him. I pushed for about three hours because he hadn't turned enough. Having an episiotomy and a forceps delivery was a relief. You view everything differently if there's a problem. At that moment I didn't want choice, just a baby!

Thomas went to the neonatal intensive care unit right away because he'd inhaled something and they wanted to make sure his lungs were all right. He weighed 10 pounds, a giant compared to the tiny premature babies. He looked silly being there and he cried so loudly that I was embarrassed! But he was out soon and neither of us was the worse for wear." CAROL

Most women say that the pain of stitches came as a shock. Some discomfort is caused by bruising and swelling, which subsides in a day or two, but you'll feel very sore for a few days and the incision will take about a couple of weeks to heal (see page 175 for ways to cope). Be especially careful about hygiene to avoid any infection. Clean the tub before you use it as well as afterwards, and wipe toilet seats carefully. If your stitches are extremely painful, tell your healthcare provider. Stitches inserted after a difficult birth or that become infected can cause more severe pain that lasts much longer.

HELP AFTER THE BIRTH

When your placenta detaches from your uterus after the birth, bleeding is inevitable. Heavy bleeding that is difficult to stop (postpartum hemorrhage) can be serious. However, it's not common and when treated promptly is rarely as dangerous as it used to be.

A hemorrhage might occur if the uterus failed to contract properly after the birth because it had been over-stretched by more than one baby, or if labor was prolonged and exhausting, or the mother was weakened by anemia or illness. The uterus would be massaged and an injection of a drug such as oxytocin would be given to contract it.

For even faster action, the drug could be delivered straight into a vein. If the cause of bleeding is an injury to the cervix, this would be repaired. Blood-clotting agents, intravenous fluids or a transfusion could be given if necessary.

Occasionally, the placenta is not delivered normally after the birth because it is particularly firmly attached to the wall of the uterus. This can happen whether or not the mother has had an injection of oxytocin. A retained placenta is a potential source of heavy bleeding. You would be sedated or given a general anesthetic so that it could be removed successfully.

Any emergency during labor or after delivery is frightening for you and your birth partner. Nevertheless, if you have a postpartum hemorrhage, the chances of successful treatment with no aftereffects are high these days.

FEELINGS AFTER THE BIRTH

If you consider the fantastic feat nature performs during birth it's no surprise that a mother or baby sometimes needs a helping hand. It's a relief to come through a difficult situation safely and know that your baby is all right. Many women can then put the experience in the past and enjoy their baby.

For some women, however, the memory of a birth causes great sadness. This is often linked to insensitive treatment they've received, lack of support from the hospital team or feelings of powerlessness when events have been taken out of their hands. Some women blame themselves, or feel their body let them down. In reality it was probably nobody's fault—giving birth, especially for the first time, can be difficult sometimes. Flexibility is essential when coping with an unknown experience, but if you wanted a natural labor you will feel upset, even when you know that intervention was unavoidable. Occasionally both fathers and mothers can be haunted by feelings of anger and despair, almost to the point of obsession.

You may feel that it could have been different, that help wasn't needed, or that it should have come sooner. However, any decision has to be made with the information available at the time; judgment without the benefit of hindsight will be fallible. You may feel guilty if you can't come to terms with what happened. Other people often think a healthy baby is all that counts. Of course this is important, but it's no compensation for a difficult birth.

Strong emotions are always better brought out into the open and not ignored or buried. You will feel grief at the loss of your expectations, but you have to accept what happened and how you feel about it. Sometimes there is no answer to the questions: "Why did this happen?" or "Why me?" How long it takes to heal, emotionally or physically, depends on the individual. In time you will be able to assign the past to its rightful place and move forward confidently to enjoy the future.

OVERCOMING A DIFFICULT BIRTH

Here are some strategies parents have found helpful in coming to terms with a difficult experience:

◆ *Talk to your partner or sympathetic friends until you don't need to talk any more. Find people who will listen to you, not just brush your worries aside or say that what matters is a healthy baby.*

◆ *If you were not able to discuss the birth with the staff involved, make an appointment to do so later. Write down all your questions in advance because it's easy to forget something at the time.*

◆ *Write down your experience, with comments about what made it better or worse. Send a copy to the hospital to help them handle similar situations in the future.*

HELP FOR YOUR BABY

Your baby will go to the neonatal intensive care unit (NICU) if she needs extra attention after the birth. For example, she might be premature or very small; she might have breathing problems after a difficult delivery and need to be observed for a few hours. If she is ill or has a handicap she might need some treatment. You will be transferred with her, if necessary, to a center that can deal with her particular problem.

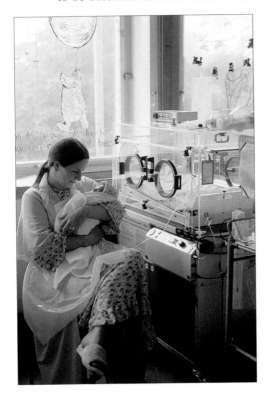

You can often stroke or cuddle your baby even if she has to spend some time in the neonatal intensive care unit.

The machinery and equipment in the NICU can be frightening at first, and your baby will look tiny and frail, heightening your feeling of unreality and anxiety. But the tubes and winking lights provide extra security for her, and all the photos of past patients now doing extremely well indicates the success of most treatment.

The NICU is the best place for a baby with a problem. The wards are usually bright and attractive, with staff who care deeply about babies and parents. You'll be taken to see your baby as soon as possible (although you may have to sleep in a different unit) and you'll be able to talk to the pediatrician. In some hospitals, a Polaroid® photograph is taken of every baby who needs special care, so that the mother can have it beside her bed to look at between visits. Ask if this is possible; or if you own or can borrow a video camera, your partner may be able to take a video of your baby so that you can see what she looks like and feel closer to her.

Breast milk is the best food for a baby, especially one in the NICU. Make your wishes known to the staff and ask for any help you need. Depending on the problem involved you may be able to breastfeed normally. If your baby has to be fed by tube you can express your milk. Don't be frightened to do what you can for her yourself, in partnership with the staff. It will help you feel close to her. She will know she is loved if you touch her, stroke her and talk to her as much as possible.

QUESTIONS AND ANSWERS

Q: I really want to have a natural labor. How does the staff decide when to intervene and what help is needed?

A: A doctor, nurse or midwife's training and experience tell her when help is needed. For example, she feels your tummy to judge how your baby is lying. If she is unsure she can confirm it once your cervix has started to dilate because your baby's *fontanels* (two diamond-shaped soft spots where the skull bones join) are different sizes. She takes your blood pressure and listens to your baby's heartbeat and judges whether they are normal, whether they need watching, or require immediate intervention.

If you or your baby were at risk, a doctor would decide what action was necessary, because midwives generally deal with normal labor. Your consent to treatment would be sought, except in a dire emergency in which there is literally no time to spare.

Where intervention might or might not help, your midwife may seek a second opinion from a colleague. She should also find out your wishes. Think about the issues beforehand and refer the staff to your birth plan (see page 118) so that you can share the decisions confidently.

Q: Will my partner be allowed to stay with me throughout labor, or will he have to leave the room during internal examinations or if I need a forceps delivery?

A: If your baby is born at home you can have anyone you wish with you in labor. In the hospital your partner has no legal right to be present, although it is customary today for men to be welcomed. Most hospitals let you stay together throughout labor, including an assisted delivery or a Cesarean section performed under epidural. Some may ask your partner to leave for examinations, and many will not allow him to be there for a Cesarean section under general anesthetic. If there is an emergency, you will not want to question the rules, but in other circumstances exceptions have been made simply by talking nicely to the staff!

Q: Is it better to cut the cord right away or to leave my baby's cord to pulsate after the birth?

A: Your birth attendant may clamp and cut the cord immediately, making sure your baby is breathing. She or a colleague then puts one hand on your abdomen and gently pulls the cord to deliver the placenta within about ten minutes. An injection may be given after the placenta is delivered to reduce the amount of bleeding after the birth.

When the cord is left to pulsate, a jelly-like substance inside it swells up to cut off the blood flow. While this happens the baby gets oxygen and extra blood through the cord and there is less haste to encourage independent breathing. Some women prefer the more relaxed pace of such a delivery. If so, include this on your birth plan.

With few exceptions, there is no medical reason to cut the cord right away. It will stop pulsating on its own in a short while, anyway. Exceptions include twin pregnancies in which one twin may have received an excessive amount of blood, or when blood incompatibility is a concern.

Q: My older brother has no sensation down one side of his face and my mother said it was caused by forceps when he was born. I'm afraid of this, so what should I do if I need a forceps delivery?

A: How easy it is for a throwaway comment to make such a lasting impression! Your mother's forceps delivery would have been necessary to solve a problem at the time, and unfortunately the way they were used at that time sometimes caused minor nerve damage. Twenty or thirty years ago, forceps deliveries were performed in circumstances where today a Cesarean section would be performed, because it is now safer.

Forceps are usually only used today for a simple "lift out," when a baby is well down the birth canal. Talk to your doctor or midwife about your fears. She may suggest writing on your birth plan (see page 118) that you prefer a vacuum delivery if you need help delivering your baby.

The best way not to need an assisted delivery is to be well prepared for labor. Learn to relax and handle labor without unnecessary stress and choose positions that work with rather than against gravity. However, anyone might need help if the baby is in an awkward position or labor is excessively long. Try to look at it positively; if you need an assisted delivery, it will help you or your baby.

Q: My friend's baby had to go to the neonatal intensive care unit after he was born because he had inhaled something and his cord was wrapped twice around his neck. He's fine now but I'm worried about the same thing happening to me.

A: Your friend's baby probably inhaled *meconium*, the sterile, tarry substance that fills the fetus's intestines before birth. If a baby becomes distressed, meconium is often released into the amniotic fluid. It can irritate the lungs and cause breathing problems if the baby inhales it, although in practice most babies don't.

Many babies with a long cord are born with it around their neck. The umbilical cord is said to be the part of the human body with the greatest variation—measuring from just a few inches to over 4 feet (125cm), although the average is about 24 inches (60cm). The midwife checks for the cord during delivery, looping it over the baby's head or clamping and cutting it immediately to release it if necessary.

Often the baby seems untroubled by having the cord around his neck, even if there is more than one loop. This is probably because the blood pumping through the cord prevents it from pulling tight. However, some babies need extra oxygen or other care, and others are not interested in feeding immediately but prefer to wait a while, to get their breath back. Most babies do not need special care; your friend's baby may have gone to NICU for a combination of factors, but the main thing is that he's fine now.

Q: I'm having my first baby at home with a midwife I really like. If I have to go to the hospital because a problem arises, will the staff blame me for wanting a home birth?

A: It won't be your fault if a problem arises. It could happen in any labor, but it's less likely if you're relaxed and confident. Presumably you chose to have your baby at home because you feel more at ease there, with a midwife you know and trust. These things are important for many women.

If you need help, your midwife will take you to the hospital and she'll probably stay with you until your baby is born. She'll know the staff and they'll be aware of your disappointment that the birth hasn't worked out the way you'd hoped. Hopefully everyone will work together to support you through a difficult time.

Afterwards you'll need time to come to terms with the experience—sometimes several weeks or months if it was very traumatic. It's unpleasant to be moved during labor, but women who have experienced it say they are glad they spent part of their labor at home; most would have a home birth again.

11

Special
Situations

> *"As soon as the twins were born
> I forgot everything that happened
> before. It didn't matter what labor was
> like. Their little heads rested on my
> chest and I was only aware of feeling
> great peace.* "

TWINS OR MORE

There are twice as many multiple births today as there were a generation ago, and they are safer because most are discovered early by scan. With good care and attention, more than 90% of twins are born healthy.

If you find out you're expecting more than one baby, make sure that you eat well. Small, frequent meals may be more comfortable in later months and some doctors will prescribe vitamins and minerals. You'll need extra rest, too, and may be advised to leave work early or to get help if you have other children. Pregnancy may be more uncomfortable but unless it's complicated you'll be treated much like anyone else, although you may have more prenatal checkups.

Many twins are delivered vaginally without complications. Both babies will be continuously monitored and the second twin usually arrives within 20 minutes of the first. If a problem occurs an assisted delivery (see page 149) or a Cesarean section might be necessary, even if the first baby has been born normally. Multiple births other than twins are usually by Cesarean section.

BREECH BABIES

Breech babies sit upright in the uterus rather than adopting a head-down position. About one baby in four is breech at 28 weeks, but only one in 40 at birth. Most have turned around by 36 weeks (see page 106).

A breech baby poses simple, mechanical problems at the birth. Usually a baby's head, his largest part, passes through the pelvis and birth canal first. He gets oxygen through his cord until his head and chest emerge and he can breathe. The rest of his body, being smaller, slips out easily.

If his bottom emerges first, his cord will be compressed (reducing his oxygen supply) while his head passes through your pelvis. There must always be plenty of room for his head to follow his body easily, because he relies on oxygen from his cord until his head is free and he can breathe. If your pelvis is roomy and your baby is small and well-positioned, there is unlikely to be any delay during the delivery. Otherwise a Cesarean section is preferable to risking a vaginal delivery that might cause him distress.

Some doctors use X-rays or CT scans (computerized tomography—a sophisticated X-ray) to help judge the chances of a trouble-free delivery. A pelvic diameter of 11cm might be considered adequate if your baby is small; a big baby would need extra room. A scan may be performed before or during early labor to determine your baby's exact

"The staff at the hospital was laid back about a breech birth and made me feel really safe. I had an epidural for high blood pressure, which would have been increased if I needed a Cesarean, but there were no problems. It was a wonderful birth.

They put a mirror where I could see to help me push, and the birth attendant just ran his finger around Jessie's head as she was born. My boyfriend kept me calm and the staff made a fuss of me and told me what was happening so I trusted them fully." LOUISE

position. Your labor may be induced (see page 146) around your due date so your baby's head is still soft enough to fit easily through your pelvis. A baby's bottom does not fill the pelvis, so go straight to hospital if your waters break. There's a tiny risk that the cord will be washed down first and get squashed, leaving your baby short of oxygen.

" I wrote a birth plan before my Cesarean section, asking the staff to talk to me during the operation and to help me breastfeed immediately after the birth. The operation was complicated and I was very frightened, but even so the doctors stuck to my requests. Looking back, I wouldn't have changed anything. It was an intensely personal experience for me and my husband. We learned a lot about ourselves. "
JENNIE

In the hospital you'll have blood taken to determine its type and an I.V. or a tube inserted for fluids, saving precious moments in an emergency. Your baby may be monitored continuously (see page 148). Some breech babies pass meconium, the tarry substance from the gut. This is usually no cause for concern.

You may have more examinations to check dilation during a breech labor because your baby's bottom may slip through your partly dilated cervix, making you want to push too soon. Some doctors suggest an epidural to reduce this urge.

Alternatively, you could kneel with your chin on your chest so that gravity takes your baby away from your cervix, or slowly and sharply blow out as you would candles on a cake, one by one in your imagination, to stop yourself from pushing too soon.

A breech delivery is usually performed by an obstetrician, with you lying back with your feet in stirrups. You may be given an episiotomy to create extra room. Some doctors use forceps to deliver the baby's head steadily while others cradle it in their hands to keep it well flexed. Then everything should proceed like any other birth.

CESAREAN SECTION

Close to half of all Cesareans are classed as emergencies, performed because a problem arises during labor, but only about 5% of problems occur without warning. Usually there's time to explain what's happening and to reassure you. An elective (pre-planned) Cesarean avoids the risk of an emergency arising and in some circumstances this is safer than a normal delivery. The staff can be more relaxed than they could be when responding to a crisis. You can also plan ahead and organize your family.

On average, about 24% of women have Cesarean sections today. However, studies conducted in both the United States and Canada have shown that at least half are unnecessary. Medical risk may not always be the primary reason a Cesarean section is performed. In the United States, for example, you are more likely to have a Cesarean section if you are over 35, white, married, live in the Northeast or in the South, have private insurance coverage, and go to a large hospital (with more than 300 beds).

One reason the incidence of Cesareans is on the rise is that the operation is safer than it was. Serious complications are rare. For an elective Cesarean section under epidural, the risks are only very slightly higher than for a normal delivery.

The World Health Organization (WHO) recommends an overall Cesarean section rate of 10% to 15%. How often they occur at individual hospitals varies considerably. It may be wise to make a few phone calls to find out local rates.

If you are worried about having a Cesarean birth, discuss the reasons for it with your doctor. Some people feel that anything other than a vaginal birth is second-rate, but a Cesarean birth can be a triumph, enabling you to avoid excessive trauma and helping your baby, who might not otherwise have survived, to be born safely. Here are some reasons why a Cesarean section might be recommended, although not all of them make it essential:

- You make little progress during labor. Your contractions may be long and strong but fail to dilate your cervix, or to move your baby's head down through your pelvis. They might be too weak to be effective, even with the added help of a hormone I.V.
- Your baby and your pelvis are the wrong shape or size for each other (cephalopelvic disproportion). Your baby could be too large or your pelvic cavity, too small or an unusual shape.
- Your baby becomes distressed and starts to pass *meconium* (waste products from his gut) into your waters, or his heartbeat may be abnormal.
- Your baby is lying in a breech or transverse (horizontal) position; or his face (instead of the crown of his head) is coming first.
- Your placenta lies across the cervix (*placenta praevia*), or detaches from the wall of the uterus (*abruptio placentae*), causing bleeding, or the cord *prolapses* (slips down in front of the baby).
- You have a pre-existing problem, such as pre-eclampsia, low-lying fibroids, diabetes, an active herpes infection, heart or kidney disease, or have had surgery to repair the vagina.
- Your baby is delicate. This might include premature or very small babies, and mothers who have had extensive fertility treatment or lost a previous baby.

A general or local anesthetic

In an emergency, a general anesthetic is routine, because there may not be time to set up an epidural or increase an existing one to the level necessary for surgery. For an elective Cesarean, you can usually choose the type of anesthetic.

An epidural (or *spinal block*, placed lower along your back) means you'll be awake and can share the birth with your partner. You'll avoid the small risks associated with general anesthesia, and most mothers say that the delight of having the baby lifted into their arms is well worth the apprehension before-

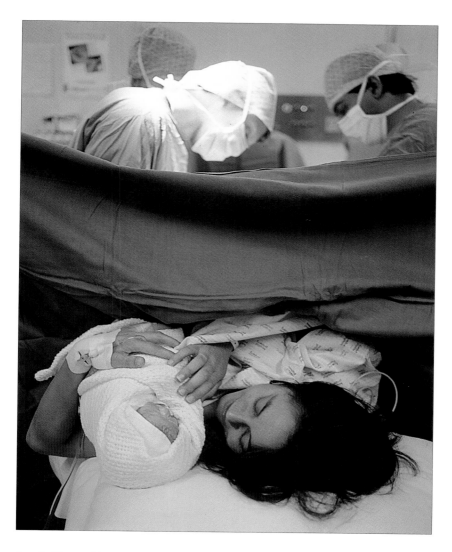

hand. If a problem arises or you feel at any time that you can't handle the operation, you can always opt for a general anesthetic.

A Cesarean birth under epidural. The baby is given to the mother to cuddle while the incision is repaired.

It is not possible or right for everyone to have an epidural. If you have a general anesthetic, your partner will not be present, but you could ask if the staff could take photos and if he can wait outside the operating theater so that your baby can be brought to him to cuddle while your incision is repaired. If he's there when you wake up, you'll see him and your baby first. Later, you could ask the staff to describe the birth to you.

A Cesarean birth

An obstetrician usually performs the operation and procedures are similar whether you have a general or local anesthetic. Typically, for an elective Cesarean you go into hospital the day before so the staff can complete routine tasks like taking blood for typing. After midnight you usually have nothing to eat or drink. Before the operation you'll be asked to sign a consent form. You'll also have to remove jewelry (a ring can be taped over), makeup and nail polish so the anesthetist can watch your color during the operation. You'll have an antacid to neutralize your stomach contents, even with an epidural, in case you need a general anesthetic instead.

The top part of your pubic hair is shaved and you have a bath or shower and put on a cotton gown. An I.V. for intravenous fluids is set up and a catheter inserted to keep your bladder empty. It may be uncomfortable but shouldn't be painful. Electrodes are taped to your chest to monitor your heart and pulse, and a blood-pressure cuff is put on your arm. A diathermy plate, part of the equipment used to control bleeding, may be strapped to your leg. Just before the operation starts, you breathe pure oxygen from a mask, for your baby's sake.

An epidural or spinal is set up in the usual way (see page 122). You may wear elastic stockings to help maintain your blood pressure. If your partner is present, he sits at your head dressed in a gown. The theater will be warm, so remind him to wear something cool underneath. A frame with sterile drapes is placed over your chest to block your view and the anesthetist makes sure that your tummy is numb. You won't feel pain but there may be sensations such as the waters being sucked out or tugging as your baby emerges. Sounds such as water flowing or instruments clattering can be masked if the staff talk to you, or you listen to music.

If you have a general anesthetic, it's delivered into your vein; a light one is used for the delivery, followed by a deeper one for repairing the incision. As you drift off to sleep, a narrow tube is passed into your windpipe and you may be aware of the birth attendant pressing gently on your throat to stop anything from going down the wrong way.

Most babies are delivered through a 4- to 6-inch (10cm to 15cm) "bikini" cut near the pubic hair line. When hair grows back, the scar barely shows. A vertical incision may be needed for triplets, a baby in an awkward position or a dire emergency. Your abdominal muscles are gently parted and your baby is delivered in about 10 minutes. It takes about 45 minutes to close the incision, using individual stitches, a single "running" stitch, or small metal clips.

"My first Cesarean section was an emergency for failure to progress. An epidural left a 'window' of sensation, so I had a general anesthetic. It left me feeling knocked out for a day or two but I got over the operation quicker than some friends got over normal births. After six weeks I was out playing tennis again."
CLARE

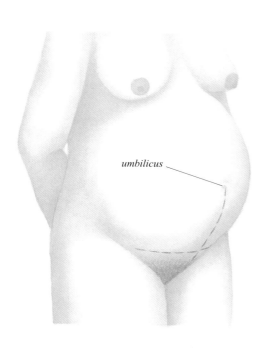

umbilicus

Vertical and "bikini" cuts (shown) are more common these days. Occasionally a "classical" cut is made to the side of the umbilicus.

A pediatrician is always present, because some babies need temporary help to breathe, although this is less likely if you have had some contractions. If your baby needs extra attention (perhaps for the reason that the operation was needed) you'll be taken to see him in the neonatal intensive care unit (see page 154) as soon as possible. Some hospitals take Polaroid® photos to show you your child immediately.

After the birth

If you were fit and healthy before the birth, you're likely to recover quickly, although you'll feel a bit wobbly to begin with. General anesthetics are much lighter these days, so you may feel few or no after-effects. After an epidural, your legs may be numb for several hours. The I.V. and catheter will remain in place for up to 24 hours after the birth. If a drain was used to remove fluids from the incision, it will come out after a day or two. Initially your incision may be covered by a dressing; the clips or stitches usually come out in about five to seven days.

Pain varies from person to person and can be severe at first, but adequate pain relief will help speed your recovery. You may be given suppositories to help reduce inflammation, plus an injection or additional painkillers through the epidural. Some hospitals use patient-controlled analgesia (PCA), where you give yourself pain relief through a machine with a device to prevent over-doses. Some women use the breathing techniques they learned for labor. After a couple of days, Tylenol® may provide sufficient pain relief. Tell the staff if the pain does not diminish or gets worse, because it could indicate an infection that needs antibiotics.

Moving will be uncomfortable at first but rotate your ankles and tighten and release your pelvic floor as soon as possible. Try not to hold your scar except to cough or sneeze, and remind visitors that laughing hurts!

When you are allowed up, ease your body to the edge of the bed using your arms for support. Lean forward as you stand, taking the weight on your thighs.

"Physically I was fine three weeks after my Cesarean, although I got very tired. But psychologically I lost confidence in my body. I couldn't take it for granted any more and was very fearful for about six months. Sex was difficult because I was afraid, and the longer I left it, the more of a hurdle it became. I worried about little things and felt I was fussing, but I needed constant reassurance that everything was normal." JENNIE

Try to walk tall instead of stooping and do not worry about the stitches coming apart—they won't!

An upright chair with arms is easiest to get into and out of and you may want someone with you when you take a shower. Don't take a bath! The physiotherapist may show you some helpful ways to move. Do as much as possible for yourself, but ask for any help you need and don't expect to do as much as someone who has had a normal delivery.

Cesarean babies are usually prettier-looking than vaginally delivered babies because their heads have not been crammed through the pelvis, so that's a bonus! Bonding may happen immediately or it may take time—as with any delivery. Your partner can help you to move, lift your baby, breastfeed and so on, but most of all he can be understanding and supportive if you hit a low spot, as everyone does occasionally.

The first week after any birth is full of emotional ups and downs, with negative feelings mixed up with joy and love for the baby. You may be euphoric because you came through the operation safely, or dismayed that the birth was not what you expected. Your feelings may see-saw wildly, or you may feel very tearful.

Be kind to yourself! Have a good cry if you want one. Rest as much as you can and be patient. A Cesarean birth is no easy option, but care and support from the staff and your partner will help you to recover both physically and emotionally.

AFTER THE BIRTH

You may find some of these items useful after a Cesarean birth.
- *Slip-on shoes and slippers—bending is painful at first.*
- *Small footstool for getting off a high bed. Earplugs to get some sleep in the hospital.*
- *Waist-high pants or boxer shorts that don't rub or irritate the scar. Fennel or peppermint tea bags to help combat gas.*
- *High-fiber bran cereal to help prevent constipation.*
- *Wet wipes beside the bed, to freshen up.*
- *A wire coat hanger to retrieve things that roll out of reach.*
- *A soft cushion to protect your scar from the seat belt during the trip home.*

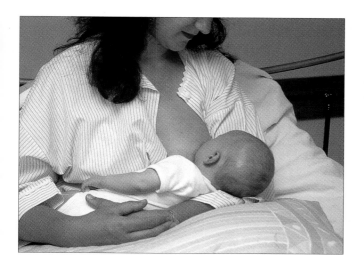

If you breastfeed your baby sitting up, make sure your back is well supported. Put a pillow over your scar and lay your baby on it, holding her close to your breast.

Breastfeeding after a Cesarean

You'll be able to breastfeed your baby as soon as you feel ready. Anesthetic drugs cause no problems and the milk usually comes in around the third or fourth day, although sometimes it takes a bit longer. If your baby is sick or premature you might need extra help, but any difficulties are more likely to be linked to the baby than to the type of birth.

Experiment to find a comfortable feeding position. It may be easiest to feed your baby in bed. You'll have to cope with discomfort from your incision, but other women may have painful stitches after an episiotomy. Take it day by day. You may need to ask for help at every feed because you have had major surgery. If you are patient and positive, you are almost certain to succeed.

You may feel much more comfortable if you breast-feed your baby in this position. Rest her head on a pillow and tuck her legs under your arms so that her weight doesn't press on your scar.

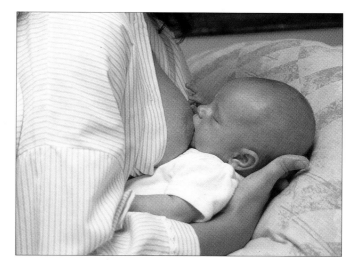

Going home

Most women leave the hospital three to five days after giving birth by Cesarean section. Going home can be unnerving and you may feel especially vulnerable at first. You'll recover faster if you take good care of yourself. Visitors can be tiring when you're recovering from an operation, so ask them to come back when you're feeling stronger. There are some ideas for conserving energy below and also on page 177. You'll need extra help for several weeks, but by taking life easy most women get over the birth fairly rapidly.

Try to avoid any task that pulls on the scar for four to six weeks. This includes lifting and also driving, because you may not be to handle an emergency that occurs while driving.

The physiotherapist at the hospital will supply suitable postnatal exercises. Start them when you feel ready, but be guided by your body and make sure you don't overtire yourself.

The normal discharge (*lochia*) lasts from two to six weeks. Some women feel ready to make love after a couple of weeks and others not for several months. It depends on whether your incision has healed, how tired you are and so on. If you adjust your position to avoid pressure on the scar, gentle lovemaking can be more enjoyable than after a normal delivery followed by stitches, but if it hurts you might have a slight infection that needs treatment. If you have attempted intercourse before your postnatal checkup, discuss any difficulties with your doctor. If not, you can see him or her for advice at any time.

CONSERVING ENERGY AFTER A CESAREAN

◆ *Delegate as much as possible. If in doubt, don't attempt a task immediately. Put it off until the next day or better still, the following week.*

◆ *Have a place for your baby to sleep and a set of diaper-changing equipment upstairs and downstairs to save trips. A table at the right height for changing diapers saves any bending.*

◆ *Keep an insulated flask of coffee or tea and a snack beside you to maintain your strength, especially if you are breastfeeding.*

◆ *Write down all serious offers of help and suggest specific jobs like vacuuming or taking an older child to play with others.*

◆ *Stock up your freezer, or buy takeouts or frozen foods for easy meals at first. Check that you have basics, such as soap, and keep a list of other items you need so that someone can shop for you.*

◆ *Wear loose clothing with large pockets to carry things.*

◆ *Advertise for a helper in your local store or through your religious organization. An extra pair of hands for a few weeks will be well worth the cost, especially if you have other children.*

Getting over a Cesarean birth

Full recovery after a Cesarean birth takes anywhere from a month to two years, but the average is about six months. Your scar will be red, then pink; finally it will fade to white or silver, possibly remaining numb for several months. However, physical healing is only part of the process. Many women have no problems coming to terms with a Cesarean birth, but others say that the hurt in their bodies healed faster than the hurt in their heart.

An emergency Cesarean tests your reserves of courage far more than a normal birth. Most women are overwhelmed with fear. Fear does not always disappear once a crisis is over; the reaction can be delayed.

Initial acceptance of a Cesarean section can be a way of coping, like covering your ears while they adjust to a loud noise. You may feel so grateful that you deny sadness about not having a normal delivery until it surfaces later, perhaps when a close friend has a normal birth. Sometimes it helps to talk about it with your partner, midwife or someone else who has experienced it.

Most women need to know the reason for their operation, to view it neither as their body's failure nor as unnecessary interference by the doctors. Try to find out before leaving the hospital but if that's not possible, make an appointment to see the obstetrician, however long ago the birth was.

In general it's wise to wait about a year before considering another pregnancy. "Once a Cesarean, always a Cesarean" is an old wives' tale. It depends on the circumstances—for example, fetal distress is unlikely to happen twice. Regardless of the reason for their previous operation, more than two-thirds of women go on to have a normal labor. After an uncomplicated operation with a bikini-line scar, your care next time would probably be little different from any other woman in labor. Discuss it with your healthcare provider.

DISABILITY OR LOSS OF A BABY

It's a shock to learn that your baby has a disability. You'll need time to adjust, to find out the extent of the problem, the prognosis and the help available (see Appendix). Most parents want honest information even if a definite diagnosis is not available immediately. Many disabilities are not as bad as they seem at first.

If a baby dies, you lose your hopes and dreams as well as your child. Such a tragedy can bring very negative emotions. You may feel angry and blame the staff or yourself for what happened, even when it was nobody's fault. You may search endlessly for reasons, and feel guilty about anything from a missed prenatal appointment to simply being too happy.

"Nobody knows why we lost our baby. It was just one of those things. He'd have been starting school now and I often wonder what he'd have been like. It was awful at the time but you come through and learn what really matters in life. You stop worrying about little things. We have two other children and John will always be a precious memory." TONI

This lovely baby has had a cleft palate and lip repaired. Although it is a shock to learn that your baby is not perfect, many problems such as this can be expertly treated. They're not the disasters they may seem at first.

Grieving is hard work and you'll feel exhausted and overwhelmed by the sadness at first. Later there will be short periods of respite when normal life takes over. These phases will become more frequent and longer, but for months or even years you may find something unexpected will trigger a flood of memories and your sadness will feel as raw as ever.

Some fathers find it is hard to talk about the loss of a baby, but this doesn't mean they don't care. There is no set way or time to grieve, but you often learn more from coping with sadness than you do from life's joys. If you feel the need to talk several weeks or even months later, when everyone else seems to have moved on, contact one of the organizations listed in the Appendix.

Life will never be quite the same. Just take one day at a time. Eventually you will come to accept what has happened and move forward again.

❝ *Joe is my first baby and it was a complete shock to be told that he only had one hand. I felt guilty, even though it probably happened before I knew I was pregnant. I wanted a reason and went through my diary looking for anything that could have caused it. One of the hardest things in the first few days was telling friends, when they were ready with their congratulations.*

I wish I could relive the time around the birth. We should have been so happy but we were upset because we didn't realize it would make no difference! Joe has an electronic hand now and he's quite a rascal. There's nothing he can't do. **❞**
JEAN

QUESTIONS AND ANSWERS

Q: I had a difficult first birth, which ended in a Cesarean section. For my second birth I've been offered a "trial of labor." What does this mean?

A: Cesarean births are very safe but in most cases a normal delivery is even safer. Most Cesarean sections are performed for reasons that aren't likely to happen again. Your previous birth may have been difficult because your baby was in an awkward position. If this baby is well positioned, the birth will be much easier, so you'll labor normally but will be carefully monitored to insure that you make good progress and that your baby copes well. Everything will be ready so that there's no delay if another Cesarean section becomes necessary.

A normal labor after a Cesarean is called a "trial of labor" because your previous scar could break down, although this is extremely rare if a bikini or vertical cut (see page 165) was made the first time. Occasionally it used to happen after a classical cut, which is seldom necessary these days. If a woman hasn't had a Cesarean section, but there is some doubt as to whether she will achieve a normal delivery, she may also be offered a "trial of labor."

Q: I have a spinal-cord injury and use a wheelchair. Will I have a Cesarean section or a normal birth?

A: You have a good chance of a normal delivery unless there's an obstetric problem unrelated to your disability. If a Cesarean section is recommended, make sure you understand the reason for it and feel happy with the decision. Women with disabilities often say that they were not sure why they needed an operation.

Q: My midwife thinks I could have a normal delivery for my breech baby. However, my obstetrician recommends a Cesarean section. Whose advice should I take? And what about external version?

A: A Cesarean birth is preferable to a difficult breech delivery, so it depends on individual circumstances. Research suggests that it's not necessary to deliver all breech babies by Cesarean, but risks are lower for births in which the baby's head comes first. Ask your obstetrician why he thinks you need one. If you don't like his answer, ask to be referred for a second opinion to someone who delivers breech babies vaginally unless there's a particular reason not to.

External version is a process that attempts to turn breech babies around through external manipulation before labor begins so that they can be born head first. When successful, it prevents unnecessary Cesarean sections and eliminates the increased risks of breech births. You will be given a medication that makes you drowsy and softens the uterus. Then an attempt is made to turn the baby. It is successful in as many as 50% to 60% of attempts.

Q: Can my husband stay if I need an emergency Cesarean section?

A: If there is plenty of time and you're having an epidural, he could probably stay, but in a dire emergency there might not even be time to explain what is happening. You'd be suddenly surrounded by doctors, whisked away to the operating room and given a general anesthetic to hurry things along. Neither of you would want any delay. You'd probably be in the recovery room within an hour.

12

The Early Days

"At first I was floating, as if I were in a dream. Feeding, bathing and changing my baby took all my attention. As the days passed, the tasks became familiar and comfortable. Within a month I couldn't remember life without a baby to love and care for. **"**

HOW YOU MAY FEEL

The days after a baby's birth are wonderful and exhausting. Excitement and elation may be mixed with bewilderment and frustration as your body undergoes rapid changes and your mind becomes preoccupied with your baby's needs. Take life slowly; give yourself space. Most women feel generally well, but emotional energy can mask physical tiredness. If you can't handle all the visitors at the hospital, ask them to visit when you get home.

You may feel afterpains for a day or two, a good sign that the uterus is returning to its nonpregnant size. Afterpains tend to be more pronounced with second and subsequent babies, and they are usually strongest during breastfeeding. If you prefer not to take Tylenol, just relax, breathe gently and focus your attention elsewhere until they pass, as you did during labor.

You will have a discharge of blood and mucus (*lochia*) similar to a heavy period at first. It usually contains clots, but if these are larger than a walnut, mention it to the birth attendant. Get out of bed slowly because you may have a sudden gush and feel faint. It is advisable to use sanitary pads rather than tampons to reduce the risk of infection. Breastfeeding helps reduce the flow because the uterus shrinks faster, sealing off the blood vessels. After the first week, the lochia becomes pink, then brownish and intermittent for between two and six weeks. Sometimes lochia lasts longer, but if it's not bright red and does not smell offensive it usually eases up eventually with no problem. A heavier flow may occur if you have been doing too much. If you're worried, contact your doctor.

It's important to empty your bladder to avoid problems such as infection, but that may be difficult for a day or two. If you can't manage it because of bruising or trauma, you may be given a catheter until the problem clears up.

Your first bowel movement may be uncomfortable, but try not to strain too much. It won't harm any stitches but can lead to hemorrhoids. As your system returns to normal your bowel movements will become softer and easier to pass. Drink plenty of fluids, eat roughage such as muesli, bran or whole-wheat bread, move around to tone up your system—and wait. Don't feel under pressure to perform—a few days' delay will make no difference and may be nature's way of giving your body time to heal. In the early days it's normal to have:

- Folds of loose skin and quite a "bump" where your baby used to be. This will shrink and become firmer as the days pass.
- Tiny broken veins, bloodshot eyes, small bruises, hemorrhoids or an aching pelvis, caused by the effort of pushing.
- Excess perspiration as your body gets rid of extra fluids.
- A feeling of unreality, whether it's your first baby or not.
- Mood swings or general feelings of inadequacy or anxiety.
- A slightly raised temperature of up to 100°F (38°C) for a few hours around the third or fourth day when your milk comes in.
- Discomfort sitting or walking; soreness and exhaustion, especially if the delivery was difficult.

174

Coping with stitches

You will probably feel bruised and sore after the birth simply because your tissues have been stretched. If your perineum is undamaged, the soreness normally fades in a day or two. Megapulse treatment is offered in some hospitals: the physiotherapist uses a device that passes an electrical pulse over the area to reduce bruising.

A small episiotomy or tear may take up to 10 days to heal; a large episiotomy could take longer. The birth attendant will check your incision frequently to make sure it is healing normally. Good hygiene is important to avoid infection, which increases discomfort and delays healing. Wash your hands before and after changing sanitary pads and use medical wipes on toilet seats in the hospital.

Here are some ways to help yourself:

- Tighten and release your pelvic floor muscles gently to help reduce the swelling.
- Let air circulate around your incision.
- Stand up to pass urine, so that the flow avoids any sore places. Gently wash yourself afterwards to reduce stinging. If you don't have a bidet at home, stand in the shower and use a jug or a shower spray (pointing downwards) with warm water. Dry yourself with soft tissues.
- Hold a clean sanitary pad over your stitches to support them when opening your bowels.
- Put ice cubes in a plastic bag, wrap it in a towel and hold the ice pack on your stitches.
- Stuff one leg of a pair of old tights with something soft and tie it into a ring to make a soft pad to sit on at home; or rent a "doughnut cushion" to sit on.
- Ask the midwife to help you to breastfeed lying on your side.
- If your stitches don't feel considerably better after a week to 10 days, ask your birth attendant to check them again.

CHECKS FOR YOUR BABY

While you are in the hospital, a pediatrician will examine your baby thoroughly in your presence. For instance, he'll listen to her heart and make sure her hip joints are stable. He may check the reflexes that help her to adapt to independent life, such as breathing, sucking and swallowing, "rooting" or searching for the nipple, grasping, "stepping" when her feet touch a firm surface, and the "Moro" reflex, in which she throws out her arms if startled. On the fifth day after delivery, a blood sample will be taken from your baby's heel to test for some rare disorders such as phenylketonuria.

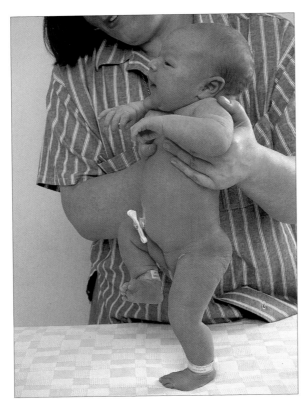

If you hold your newborn baby upright and let her feet come into contact with a firm surface such as a table top, she will lift each leg in turn and place it in front of the other as though she was going for a walk. This "stepping" reflex is automatic and fades within a week or two of the birth.

Over half of all babies develop jaundice, which gives them a suntanned look caused by *bilirubin*, a yellowish substance in the blood. Jaundice is usually mild but babies are watched carefully because occasionally it proves more serious. It usually fades after a week, or it may take slightly longer for a premature baby; meanwhile the baby needs frequent feeding. High bilirubin levels can be lowered by phototherapy in the hospital under a special light. Your baby's eyes will be covered for protection, but you can remove the blindfold when feeding.

A few babies suffer from low blood sugar (*hypoglycemia*). It's more common with low-birthweight or premature babies, and when the mother is diabetic or has had a difficult delivery. To avoid your baby becoming limp and apathetic, or perhaps jittery, the staff will want to be sure that she has a good feeding within a few hours of birth. Sometimes a baby needs extra feeding, or even intravenous feeding.

If you have your baby at home, the physical checks will be carried out by your healthcare provider, although your baby can be referred to a pediatrician if necessary. Your healthcare provider will take routine blood samples and keep an eye open for things such as jaundice.

GOING HOME

Most mothers normally leave the hospital within a day or two of the birth, although you may stay longer if there are any problems. Caring for your baby on your own can seem overwhelming, but your midwife, if you have one, will visit you for up to 10 days and longer if necessary. You will have postnatal checkups at your doctor's office, too.

Make rest a high priority for at least 21 days after the birth. You'll want visitors, but the most welcome ones will admire your baby, tell you how wonderful you are, drop off a little present—and leave! Unless they are really helpful, and you get along very well, having relatives stay can be tiring.

"When Freddie arrived, the love I felt for him was indescribable. We are a close family and everyone kept asking me to bring him over and show him off. It was tempting to refuse because he had not been inoculated or he might have caught a cold from one of my nephews or nieces. I had to make myself believe that a cold would not be a disaster.

"It would have been so easy to sit back and tell myself I didn't need my family, but I did; they gave me support and saw the funny side of life when I felt overwhelmed. My older sisters have children and they came up with suggestions I wouldn't have thought of, like not changing his diaper at night because it woke him up and he took another hour to settle again. Everyone threw in advice and I chose what I wanted."
LINDA

Although you may feel fine at first, you'll run out of energy quickly, so rest even if you feel energetic. If you have used up your reserves of emotional energy by trying to do too much, a problem like your baby waking frequently at night or a temporary feeding problem can get blown out of proportion.

Here are some ways to help you avoid exhaustion. (See also page 168 on conserving energy after a Cesarean.)

WAYS TO CONSERVE ENERGY

◆ *Put a sign on the door asking people not to visit between certain times because you will be resting.*

◆ *Don't offer visitors refreshments unless you want them to stick around and chat.*

◆ *Take the phone off the hook when you want to rest or feed your baby. Record a message giving details of the baby.*

◆ *Make a list of jobs that need doing such as shopping, taking a toddler to the swings, or ironing. When somebody offers to help you'll have an answer ready.*

◆ *Forget the usual chores. Grab an extra hour's rest in the morning and in the afternoon when your baby is asleep.*

◆ *Make sure everything (book, drink, remote control for TV) is within reach when your baby finally falls asleep in your arms.*

Most toddlers are naturally gentle with a new brother or sister, taking out any hurt feelings on Mom or Dad. Try to respond positively when your toddler wants to show affection for the baby.

RELATIONSHIP WITH YOUR PARTNER

A birth of a wanted child touches tender feelings in most men. After such a highly emotional shared experience, it may be hard for your partner to leave you in the hospital, especially at night if he has to return to an empty house.

If the birth was difficult he will have found it as upsetting as you. He will be relieved that it is over but may feel angry, blaming the staff or the baby for what you went through. He may feel responsible for putting you in the situation and need reassurance to shake off the guilt.

Men are expected to be strong and supportive during and after a birth but many new fathers feel uncertain about their role. As you adapt to the presence of a precious but demanding baby you'll need to find a new relationship that satisfies both of you. It takes time and can prove stressful.

The early days after a birth are unsettled. Enjoy the elation—it's a very special time in your lives—but be kind to each other.

RELATIONSHIP WITH YOUR FAMILY

A new baby subtly changes the relationships within a family, creating aunts and uncles from sisters and brothers, grandmothers and grandfathers from mothers and fathers. It's unrealistic to expect everything to go back to normal after a couple of weeks.

A toddler needs to get to know his new brother or sister. Small children sometimes behave badly because they are too little to handle the excitement of having a brother or sister, which can be overwhelming. It helps to keep to a normal routine as far as possible. Show that you love and understand your toddler in the few weeks while he is coming to terms with the new arrival.

Babies can unite families in a very positive way. Children from previous marriages are linked by a new baby who is a half-sister or -brother to each of them. However, some family relationships may need tactful handling. Older relatives may have more experience bringing up children but this is *your* child and it's *your* responsibility and privilege to make the decisions. It costs nothing to smile and thank them for their advice, while *you* decide privately whether or not to follow it. Instinct or experimentation will tell you whether something works for *you*.

CARING FOR YOUR NEW BABY

There is no single "right" way to bring up a baby and nobody, however experienced, finds what works the first time. Most parents use a mixture of guesswork and trial and error, trying different strategies without worrying. However, if you're new to parenthood, you may feel more confident following simple guidelines. The first guideline is to collect everything in one place before you start!

Diaper changes: You'll need a fresh diaper, something to clean your baby's bottom (baby lotion or warm water and cotton balls or pads) and petroleum jelly.

- Lay your baby on a changing mat or towel. Take off the dirty diaper, clean her bottom with a cotton ball and baby lotion or water, dry it carefully and apply petroleum jelly to help prevent diaper rash. Holding her ankles, lift her bottom and slide the fresh diaper underneath. Bring it up between her legs and fasten the tabs. If you are using a cloth diaper, pin it in place and put on plastic pants. Put the dirty diaper in a bucket with sterilizing solution, or a plastic bag for disposal.
- Wash your hands thoroughly.
- Babies with very delicate skin sometimes get red, sore-looking areas on their bottom. At the first sign of diaper rash, expose your baby to the air as much as possible. For example, lay her on her changing mat in a warm room, leaving her diaper unfastened.

Bathing: New babies don't need bathing every day. You can "top and tail" your baby, washing just her face, hands and bottom, some days. To bath her you'll need fresh clothes; diaper-changing materials; boiled, cooled water and cotton balls or pads; a soft towel; and soap or baby bath gel if you wish. Fill the bowl or bath with warm water and make sure the room is warm.

- Undress your baby except for her diaper. Wrap her in the towel.
- Wash her face with boiled, cooled water. Wipe each eye from her nose out, using separate cotton balls. Dry her face. Wash her head, rinse it using the bath water and dry it. Take off her diaper and clean her bottom.
- Lift her into the water by slipping your hands under her body and holding her arm and leg so that she is supported on your wrists. Keep an arm under her neck while you rest her legs on the base of the bath. Use the other hand to wash her.
- Slip the hand back under her bottom and hold her leg to lift her out. Dry her carefully. Put on a clean diaper and clothes.

Breastfeeding

Breastfeeding may be simple to establish, or it may be several weeks before you find it easy and rewarding. Babies are individuals: Some are eager and can't wait to get at the food, while others fiddle around and don't seem to know what's good for them. It helps to breastfeed soon after birth, when your baby's

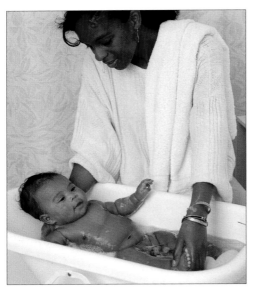

Hold your baby like this when you put her in the bath.

sucking reflex is strongest; if there's a delay or the first attempts do not go smoothly, perseverance and good support usually lead to success.

Your midwife or a nurse will help you with the early trials. Take time to find the right position for you. Good positioning helps avoid sore nipples and enables your baby to take a good feed. It will depend on the shape of your breasts, how big your baby is and what feels comfortable. You should feel relaxed, not hunched up or distracted by discomfort.

Your baby's chest should face yours, with her head tipped back slightly so that her chin is close to your breast and her lips are near your nipple. "Chest to chest and chin to breast" is an easy way to remember. Use pillows for extra support if necessary.

HOW TO BREASTFEED

- *Support your baby's shoulders and neck with your forearm, cradling her head gently in your other hand. Use whichever hand and arm feels more comfortable.*
- *Brush her lips with your nipple until she opens her mouth.*
- *Wait until she opens her mouth really wide, like a baby bird. Be patient; this may take several minutes.*
- *When her mouth is wide open, bring her head towards your breast so that she takes a good mouthful of breast tissue as well as your nipple.*
- *If she is latched on properly, her jawbone will move as she sucks. If not, slide a little finger into the corner of her mouth to break her suction. Relax and try again.*

You can help prevent sore nipples by making sure your baby is well supported and latched on properly. Wash your nipples once a day without using soap, which removes natural oils, and keep them dry. Cotton bras can help air circulate. If your nipples become sore, expose them to the air as much as possible. Nipple creams may be soothing, but occasionally they also cause soreness. A change of feeding position to even out pressure on the nipple or temporarily using a nipple shield may help.

Brief feedings as often as your baby will cooperate in the early days will give you both practice. You'll learn the positions that work for you and your baby will learn to latch on and feed well. This helps to minimize engorgement, where the rush of milk coming in on the third or fourth day leads to hard, swollen breasts. If you are engorged, expressing a bit of milk first may make it easier for your baby to latch on. You can encourage the milk to flow by applying warm compresses, or try cold compresses to reduce swelling. Sometimes alternating hot and cold compresses works, and some women swear by wearing a firm, supportive bra with cooling cabbage leaves inside for a few hours!

If you have any breastfeeding problem, ask for support right away. Your midwife, healthcare provider or another mother who has breastfed successfully may be able to help, or contact one of the groups listed in the Appendix, such as La Leche League, who are happy to give advice and support.

"I lived on excitement after Bianca was born. The birth was great and I felt fantastic. I lost weight and everyone said how good I looked, but I wasn't eating enough extra calories for breastfeeding. Bianca was always hungry and I never saw any milk, so she was on a bottle by the time she was six weeks old. I suppose I wanted to prove that parenthood was fun and that it didn't need to make any difference to your life. Breastfeeding failed because I did too much. I've learned to be more laid back!" NICKI

Make sure you are sitting comfortably and that you hold your baby close to your body when you breastfeed.

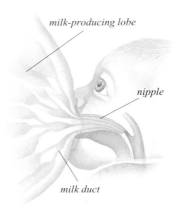

milk-producing lobe

nipple

milk duct

This baby is latched on well, taking a good mouthful of breast with her bottom lip curled back. In this position she has plenty of room to breathe.

When your baby is well positioned, with a good mouthful of breast tissue, your nipple will reach the back of her tongue and palate.

Bottle-feeding

If you are unable to breastfeed or choose to bottle-feed instead, there is no reason to feel guilty. It can be a very satisfying experience. Cuddle your baby, and when it's practical, open your shirt so that she can feel the warmth of your skin as she feeds.

Some babies like formula straight from the refrigerator. Others prefer the bottle warmed in a bottle warmer or jug of hot water. Keep the bottle tilted throughout the feed so that the nipple stays full of liquid and your baby doesn't suck in air, which could give her colic.

Hygiene is especially important when you bottle-feed because your baby will not gain the immunities that breastfeeding offers. Germs multiply rapidly in stale milk, so be sure to clean all bottles and nipples thoroughly before sterilizing them.

Instructions may vary slightly, so read the label on the formula package, but in general make up bottles like this:

- Wash your hands and boil enough tap water for the number of bottles you intend to make.
- Cool the water and pour the correct amount into each bottle, using the measuring marks on the side.
- Measure the formula using the scoop provided. Don't pack it down, because too much powder can be harmful. Level it off with the back of a knife.
- Add the powder to the bottle, screw on the cap and shake to dissolve it.
- Store bottles in the refrigerator, but throw away any unused formula after 24 hours.

"I'd never thought about the intensity of caring for a baby before I had Kathryn. She knows nothing of the world and what I teach her will form the basis for her attitudes in life.

I couldn't breastfeed because I had drugs for blood-pressure problems, so at first she had bottles. When my milk came in, she wouldn't latch on; sometimes she screamed solidly for a couple of hours. It would have been so easy to bottle-feed, but I really wanted her to be breast-fed, and eventually I succeeded. I was surprised at the warmth she brought from unexpected places. An old friend I hadn't seen for years brought me a rose to plant in the garden in her honor. A friend of my mother's sent a little dress. " ROSEMARY

Enjoy your baby!

If you decide for good reasons to bottle-feed, you may agonize that your baby will suffer and others may judge you—but other mothers will be busy agonizing over their own supposed failings.

For many years you'll worry about making wrong decisions. Just as you gain confidence in your own sound judgment, your children will reach their teens and tell you all over again that you're wrong! Life is for living, and mistakes are inevitable. It's best to accept this basic fact of life early and get on with enjoying your baby.

QUESTIONS AND ANSWERS

Q: My baby is five days old and I'm finding breastfeeding is agony, especially at the start of each feed. I don't want to give up but I've begun to dread it. What am I doing wrong?

A: Some women experience sharp pain at the beginning of a feed, when the milk lets down. It usually disappears after two or three weeks, as the ducts get accustomed to the sudden rush of milk. Anticipate it and deliberately relax your shoulders and take your mind elsewhere for a minute, until it passes.

If pain continues throughout the feed, ask your healthcare provider, a La Leche League member, or a friend who has breastfed her own baby to check that your baby is latched on well. Don't push your nipple between her lips so that she has to haul herself onto the breast; wait until she opens her mouth wide before you latch her on. She should take a good mouthful of breast with her bottom lip curled back.

Most babies come off the breast by themselves when they have finished feeding but some doze, wake up when they slide off the nipple and then jerk back on for another feed! This can make your nipple sore, so put your baby on your shoulder if you think she has finished. Cuddle her until she settles. Sore nipples usually heal within a day or two once the problem has been identified.

Q: My baby is 10 days old and has been in intensive care since birth. We are ready to go home now but I'm afraid I won't be able to cope. There's always a nurse to help me here so I feel secure. Breastfeeding still isn't easy. Could I ask to stay longer?

A: It's easy to lose confidence in yourself when your baby needs the care of highly trained professionals, but the staff will reassure you that now she is better you can provide everything she needs to thrive. Breastfeeding is sometimes harder to establish when a baby is ill. With time and patience it gets easier. When you go home, contact a lactation consultant or your local La Leche League (see Appendix) for breastfeeding help. Your confidence will quickly return once you find out that you really can cope!

Q: I thought life would be wonderful once my baby arrived, but he's three weeks old and I still feel completely overwhelmed. All he does is howl and I feel trapped. I wanted him so much but now I long for my old life. Do other mothers feel this way, or am I not suited to motherhood?

A: More mothers than you might guess feel like this at first, but nobody likes to admit it. Try telling your healthcare provider or a sympathetic older relative who will understand and support you.

You also need some practical help. It's not your fault that your baby cries so much. Ask a friend or relative to take him out for a walk so that you can have a shower or a rest without worrying about him. Plan to get out of the house on your own, leaving your partner to cope at home.

Anyone could feel trapped in your situation but getting out is wonderful for the morale, even if it is only for a couple of hours between feeds. This difficult phase will not last forever. In time, your baby will settle down and become more contented and rewarding and you will adjust to your new life and get your energy back. Then you'll find that life with a baby can be fun.

Q: My baby's skin was beautiful when he was born but now that we're home, his face is covered with spots. My doctor didn't seem concerned but was it something I ate?

A: Your baby simply has especially fine, delicate skin, and the spots may come and go for a few weeks until his system matures. They are probably not linked to anything you ate or did. Red spots appear sometimes if a baby becomes overheated and sweaty, but babies who are not too hot also get them. Tiny white spots (*milia*) are caused by temporary blockage of the glands that secrete sebum to lubricate the skin. They disappear after a few days and you should never squeeze them.

Just when you want your baby to look his best because everybody is coming to admire him, he develops spots! They look awful to you, but visitors are more likely to notice his tiny fingers, delicate ears and sweet expressions.

13

Getting Back to Normal

❝I never thought parenthood would make me feel so protective. Of course there are bad times when she won't stop screaming and I've really had enough. But then she smiles at me—and I forgive her for everything!❞

ADJUSTING TO PARENTHOOD

Parenthood is a truly intense experience. It involves a lot of giving in situations that arouse rather primitive emotions. At times your baby will fascinate and delight you; at other times you'll feel anxious, angry or inadequate. You may worry that his well-being lies largely in your hands and that you'll never be good enough for this responsibility. The ideal of a perfect mother is born of love and raised on other peoples' expectations, but a baby's ever-changing needs make perfection impossible.

Most mothers take several months to get into any sort of normal routine. Congratulate yourself if you manage to achieve one thing per day in addition to baby care. Breastfed babies often want to suckle happily all evening, every evening, and the cumulative lack of sleep sneaks up on you until you may find yourself operating in a daze. Most people believe they need eight hours' sleep every night, but your body will soon adjust to less. You won't feel really great while this happens, but if you're exhausted you will probably sleep anytime and anywhere!

For many months ahead you'll be a willing slave to a pint-sized boss. You may long for your baby to sleep, to give you a little space of your own—but when he does, you'll think about him constantly!

Babies sleep as long as they need to and are happy or miserable, according to their temperament. There is little you can do to influence this. If your baby cries despite your efforts to comfort him, you may worry that he dislikes you or has failed to bond to you, but it will probably have more to do with his nature than your relationship or how you handle him. Follow his lead until a routine evolves naturally after a few months. When you have a baby, your life takes on a slower rhythm. Somewhere within you you'll find the patience to respond to the day-to-day demands a baby makes, although you may also grieve for a "lost" part of you—the independent woman who could do what she wanted, when she wanted.

If you use a wheelchair or have another disability you may already live at a slower pace, so the change when a baby arrives is not so great. Physically able mothers often have to learn the hard way that rushing around is neither desirable nor comfortable. Slowing down can actually be a source of great vitality. It gives you time to enjoy your baby.

> **Before I had Lucien, everybody warned me I'd get no sleep. I expected to look like a zombie with toothpicks keeping my eyes open, but Lucien fed and went straight to sleep. Everyone said that by the time he was six months old my time would not be my own, but he happily watched me puttering around, or the washing machine going around. I returned to work part time and went on vacation without him and he was fine!**
>
> **Now I'm pregnant again and the doom-and-gloom brigade are saying. 'You won't have another one like Lucien, you know!' The awful things they warned me about never happened, and anyway he wasn't a baby for long. It's best to take each day as it comes and enjoy motherhood.** YASMIN

Who can help you?

There are many experts, supporters and other parents to help you make the most of parenting:

- Your healthcare provider can check your baby's growth and discuss immunization, feeding and baby care. She may be able to help you contact other parents if you have a special situation.
- Relatives and friends can give advice, boost your confidence and look after your baby when you need a break.
- Childcare books can give you information and answer some questions.
- Baby magazines publish informative articles on baby care written by experts. Keep copies for reference as your baby grows. The voluntary organizations listed in the Appendix provide a range of services.

CRYING BABIES

If your baby cries constantly it's neither your fault nor your sole responsibility. After two or three months he'll be more settled. Meanwhile, here are some things to try that might help:

- Check with your doctor to establish that there's no physical reason for the crying, and then stop worrying about it.
- Ask friends and relatives to help by taking your baby out for an hour or two to give you a regular break. This is essential for maintaining a sense of perspective.
- Take your baby out in the car, or walk around the block. You won't be the first parent to do this in pajamas at 3 a.m.!
- Contact Friends' Health Connection (see Appendix), which may put you in touch with someone who has had a similar problem.
- If your baby has colic at roughly the same time every day, accept it and don't plan activities for this time.
- If you think you might harm your baby, put her in a safe place, such as her crib, and go away for 10 minutes to calm down; contact a La Leche League leader, the American Academy of Pediatrics, or Child Help (see Appendix). They will offer practical support, not condemnation.
- If you are breastfeeding your baby, try eliminating all dairy products from your diet. If the dairy products in your diet have been bothering your baby, you may have to wait several days after eliminating them from your own diet to see a result.

RELATIONSHIP CHANGES

A small baby changes life for both you and your partner. Here's what some fathers say about their new role:

"It's difficult to reconcile the demands of my job and the desire to be a good father. I'm not always there, so I can't fall into Lucy's routine because I don't know what's going on."

"I love being a father. It's much better for you than a few beers and a burger, a pleasure that has had to take a back seat recently! But I worry about my financial responsibility now that Carla isn't working."

"Ben is growing and changing all the time. I really want to get back to see him each evening, but I feel slightly jealous of the time Abby spends with him. She seems closer to him than to me."

If you look after your baby most of the time, you'll go beyond following general advice (which only works up to a point) and start fine-tuning, adapting subtly to your baby's likes and dislikes. When your partner returns to work he may lose his confidence in being able to take care of the baby because he hasn't had much practice. Give him time and space to find his own ways to cope. Don't constantly tell him how to do it or demonstrate your superior skills too readily!

Sadly, the most loving of mothers can be possessive over a baby, while even supportive partners often don't do as much as they think they do. There's the fantasy of domestic bliss where everyone has their needs met while chores are shared harmoniously. The reality of family life finds a demanding baby and adults who have feelings of power and vulnerability.

Potentially, parenthood means being on call for 24 hours a day with no days off! Any division of labor is fine if both partners are happy with the situation. If not, creeping resentment can easily sour your relationship. There can be no change if one partner keeps his or her feelings a secret. Start by being as open as you'd like to be: Talk to each other and negotiate agreements that suit you both. Close relationships always involve conflicts. Resolving these through compromise will both challenge and strengthen your partnership.

Your baby should become a happy part of your lives, and not take over completely. Once a week it's a good idea to sit down with your partner and review the situation. On the opposite page are some ideas to help you balance everyone's needs.

"Having a baby should change your life, and parenthood is rewarding, but my husband and I found the adjustment wasn't easy. If you want to work things out you really have to communicate. Our relationship has always been good because we had time to spend together.

When Sophie arrived, we couldn't keep up all our activities without getting frazzled, so for six months we decided to concentrate on looking after her and not expect much for ourselves. Every few weeks we made ourselves sit down and set some time aside for each of us. We used a baby sitter so we could spend time together alone. It sounds very planned, but it worked for us." JULIA

BALANCING NEEDS

◆ *Time management: Some jobs must be done every day; others, such as bathing your baby, could be done less frequently.*

◆ *Weekend sleep-in: One partner looks after the baby while the other stays in bed for as long as he or she likes on Saturday morning. On Sunday, reverse the roles.*

◆ *Advance planning: Once a month, sit down and plan chores and time off for each partner.*

◆ *Talking time: Every week, you each spend five minutes listening without interruption while your partner talks and 20 minutes discussing any issues that come up.*

◆ *Regular night off together: Hire a baby sitter and spend time doing something you both enjoy.*

◆ *Team work: Take turns with other couples or single parents looking after the children while the others have a break.*

Your sex life

Some women feel ready to make love again as soon as a week or two after giving birth, but most take somewhat longer. If there has been a lull in your sex life, perhaps starting in late pregnancy and continuing after the birth, you may find that the spontaneity is lost and it is necessary for you and your partner to make a positive decision together to resume sexual relations. Sex may be painful or remind you of a negative birth experience. Full breasts may feel uncomfortable or messy when they leak milk, or you may need reassurance about your appearance.

You may be exhausted because your baby does not sleep through the night, or distracted by his demands for attention. You may be so preoccupied with parenting that you forget about your adult relationship. It's not always easy to communicate if guilt or resentment is present, but talking with your partner may help you to find ways to set your sex life on course again.

Discomfort can often be improved by using a different position or a vaginal lubricant. Having extra help at home could insure that you are less tired or that you get a break from your responsibilities. Good humor and a willingness to communicate are essential. Your sex life will be different but it need not be less good; remember that penetrative sex is not the only form of lovemaking—there are many different ways of giving and receiving affection. Stroking, kissing and cuddling are all important ways of demonstrating your love. If you continue to show each other warmth and tenderness, and explore other means of providing each other with erotic pleasure, a full sexual relationship can follow in its own time when you both feel ready for it.

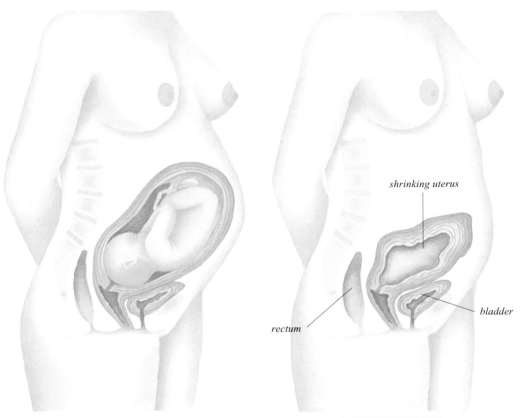

shrinking uterus

rectum

bladder

BEFORE THE BIRTH   AFTER THE BIRTH

POSTNATAL BODY

Your figure may look much the same as before pregnancy or you may notice some subtle changes. Your uterus will be slightly bigger than previously and your tummy may have a more rounded outline. It will feel flabby at first, becoming firmer after a few weeks. Your breasts may be larger if you are breastfeeding. If not, they'll be smaller and softer for several months while the fatty tissue that shapes them builds up, replacing the milk-producing tissue that developed in pregnancy.

Your pelvic floor is stretched during a normal birth and you may suffer stress incontinence when you cough or laugh. The muscle tone can be improved with pelvic floor exercises (see page 45), but it may be several months before you feel confident again.

The scar from a tear or episiotomy may feel strange and it can be reassuring to take a look using a hand mirror. Your periods might return in a few weeks, or not for a year or more if you are fully breastfeeding. You can conceive

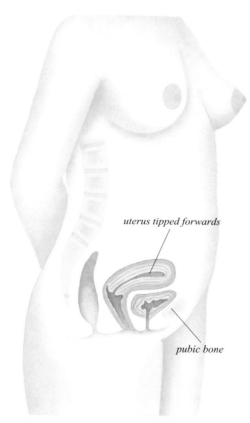

uterus tipped forwards

pubic bone

Far left: Your uterus takes up a lot of room at the end of pregnancy, stretching your abdomen and compressing your internal organs.
Center: After your baby is born, your uterus shrinks rapidly but you'll still look about five or six months pregnant. Your intestines have more room and they'll gradually resume their normal place.
Left: Six weeks after the birth your uterus will have contracted to the size of a small pear and returned to its normal position in your body.

SIX WEEKS LATER

before your first period. Becoming pregnant soon after giving birth could strain your body, so use contraception unless you are sure you really want another baby immediately. Breastfeeding is not contraceptive.

Some women rapidly return to their pre-pregnancy weight, although this depends on body type. It's unwise to diet while breastfeeding, but after several months you'll naturally lose the extra fat stores laid down during pregnancy. If you bottle-feed and want to lose weight it will probably be necessary to watch what you eat and exercise more.

When you're heavily pregnant, you can't see over your tummy and you may be dismayed to discover stretch marks. These are red and unsightly at first. There's nothing you can do about them (they depend partly on skin type), but they fade to pink and eventually to a barely noticeable silvery cream.

Some women find their joints ache, especially after lifting or standing too long. Rest more and take care not to strain yourself—your joints will stabilize as your hormones settle down.

Back and Buttock Exercise
1. Lie on the floor with your knees raised.

2. Tighten your buttock muscles and lift your hips. Hold for a few seconds, then slowly lower your back down to the floor.

Postnatal exercises

In the early months, general exercise classes may be too strenuous because your ligaments will still be soft and easily strained. Buy a video or find out about special postnatal exercise classes.

If you cannot join a class near home, here are some exercises you could try. Warm up gently before you start and relax afterwards. Repeat each exercise six times to start with, working up to 10 or 12 repetitions. Ask your health-care provider or a physiotherapist for advice if you have any doubts—for example, if an exercise feels too strenuous or you have a previous back or neck injury.

Don't push yourself; short, regular sessions are better than a marathon that tires you out. However eager you are to get your figure back, respect your body and put your baby's needs first.

Abdominal, Back and Buttock Exercise
1. Kneel on all fours with your hands pointing forward and your knees hip-width apart.

2. Drop your head forward and try to touch your face with one knee. Hold in your abdominal muscles and round your back.

3. Stretch your leg out behind you and hold it for a few seconds, feeling your buttock muscles tighten. Repeat the exercise using your other leg.

***Exercise for Diagonal
Abdominal Muscles***
*1. Lie with your knees raised and
hands by your sides.*

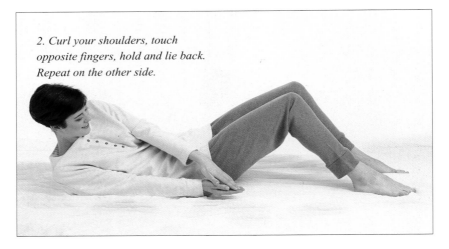

*2. Curl your shoulders, touch
opposite fingers, hold and lie back.
Repeat on the other side.*

Your postnatal checkup

About six weeks after the birth you'll be offered a checkup with your health-care provider. Your blood pressure and urine will be checked, and your breasts and abdomen may be examined. You may be weighed, although many women will not have returned to their pre-pregnancy weight. You'll have an internal examination to make sure that everything is normal, including stitches and the muscle tone in your pelvic floor. A cervical smear may be taken and you'll be asked about your health in general.

Many women have minor discomforts after childbirth. You should discuss anything that is worrying you. On the opposite page is a list of some common postnatal concerns that you might wish to talk over with your healthcare provider.

Exercise for Straight Abdominal Muscles

1. Sit with your knees raised and a little apart and your arms stretched out.

2. With your back rounded, curl down a little, hold for a few seconds and curl up again. Keep your muscles controlled.

- Any questions you have about what happened at the birth.
- How you really feel. Your doctor cannot be of any help if you smile brightly and say you're feeling fine when you actually feel ill or depressed.
- Uncomfortable tear or episiotomy, sore nipples or any other pain.
- Stress incontinence. Your healthcare provider may suggest more pelvic floor exercises (up to 100 or more a day). If there's little improvement in another six weeks, further treatment, such as small weighted cones that you hold in your vagina, may be offered.
- Any difficulties that you're experiencing with your sex life.
- Contraception. You may need a different size diaphragm or intrauterine device, or a different pill if you are breastfeeding.

POSTNATAL DEPRESSION

About 80% of women experience "baby blues" or some degree of temporary weepiness a few days after the birth. Some women go through a phase of feeling "down" a few weeks later, when the novelty and excitement surrounding the birth have worn off, sleep deprivation has built up, and there is less practical help from family and friends.

About one woman in 10 suffers moderate postnatal depression, sometimes several months later. Severe depression requiring hospitalization or a long course of treatment affects fewer than one in 500.

Postnatal depression interferes with your enjoyment of life and should always be taken seriously. It's an illness, not a sign of inadequacy, and it's easier to treat if it's caught early. Don't struggle along, failing to recognize the symptoms or feeling too ashamed or lethargic to seek help.

It can be hard to admit to yourself that you feel depressed, especially if you have nothing to be depressed about. There's tremendous pressure to keep up the appearance of coping when everyone else seems to be doing so. If you don't fit the fantasy and nature has not come to your aid and turned you into a competent, contented mother, you may feel many negative emotions. These are not signs of an unfeeling monster but of a mother who needs help.

Treatment might include individual or group psychotherapy, sessions with a counselor to talk over your feelings, or a course of antidepressants. These are not addictive but they usually have to be taken for some time to be effective. When suggesting treatment, your doctor will take into account your symptoms, your preferences and whether you are breastfeeding. Support groups for new parents may be found within many churches and community-based organizations and Depression After Delivery (see Appendix) may also provide support.

POSTNATAL DEPRESSION SYMPTOMS

You may feel low for a few days without being clinically depressed, but it's important to seek help if you're worried or if you experience any of these symptoms for two weeks:

- *An increasing loss of confidence so that you can't face meeting people, even friends, or you need to stick to a rigid routine because you cannot cope with the slightest change.*
- *Negative thoughts, feelings of worthlessness or hopelessness.*
- *A loss of interest in food, your baby and life in general.*
- *Butterflies in your tummy all the time, or a general feeling of panic every time your baby wakes up.*
- *An agitated feeling so that you have to keep busy all the time.*
- *A feeling of exhaustion—but you're unable to sleep when you get the chance.*

Friendship is very important. You and your baby will enjoy sharing the company of other mothers and babies.

MEETING OTHER MOTHERS

The companionship and support of other mothers makes all the difference when you have children. Friends will discuss your baby's development over and over again. They'll understand the joys and difficulties of family life. They'll laugh with you, offer suggestions, reassure you that a phase will pass and find your toddler lovable at times when you secretly find him impossible.

In these early stages, it is important to meet and make some new friends. Invite some women from your prenatal class over for coffee—someone has to start the ball rolling. Try looking on your clinic notice board for details of a local parent-and-toddler group (babies are included). Think about joining a class at your local college, club or church—there may even be a crib for your baby. Spend time watching the toddlers playing at the local park and chat with the other parents. Ask your healthcare provider to introduce you to some other mothers.

It's easy to stay at home and tell yourself that you don't need anything else in your life; to use the possibility that your baby might catch a cold as an excuse for not meeting people. But sooner or later you'll feel lonely and wish that you and your baby had some friends.

"I thought I'd work freelance from home, but I hadn't realized just how much time a baby takes. I hated the thought of someone else looking after Ben and realized my career was less important to me than I'd thought! Now I live at a child's pace, not by the clock. I make decisions according to events at the time and ignore the five-year plan that used to rule my life. We can't afford vacations, but now our quality of life is good. "* KATE

RETURNING TO WORK

Returning to work has both positive and negative aspects; just accept this without feeling guilt or any regrets! The popular image of an organized woman with her family life under control so that it never interferes with her work is a myth. The best you can hope for is that your arrangements hold up most of the time. You'll juggle work and motherhood and may feel that you are doing neither job well, but your baby will probably be perfectly happy!

Even if your employer has never considered it before, it's worth trying to negotiate a work schedule that suits you. Decide what you want, work out how it could benefit your company, and present your plan to the personnel manager. You have nothing to lose by taking the initiative.

Local social services (look in the telephone book) keep lists of nurseries and registered child babysitters. Make arrangements for your return to work in plenty of time and plan a phased-in changeover, because peace of mind is very important. Many women continue breastfeeding night and morning, but do allow a week to drop each feeding time before you start work so that your body can adjust. If your baby won't take a bottle, talk to his caregiver. He may accept one from her, or he may start to drink from a cup.

QUESTIONS AND ANSWERS

Q: I worry about my baby all the time. I even wake him up to make sure he's breathing. I fret over every decision in case it turns out to be wrong. Why am I so concerned?

A: You worry because you care so much and because your baby still feels part of you. Call it love—or just motherhood!

These feelings can be overwhelming, especially the first time around, when each stage your baby goes through is new. You'll gradually learn to relax over day-to-day events as they become familiar, but you may go through phases of intense, stomach-churning anxiety as each new stage arrives.

Babies respond individually so it's rarely possible to be sure that you've made the right decision except in hindsight. This applies whether it's your first baby or your fourth. Experienced moms watch what happens and have no hesitation in changing their mind if a decision proves wrong. If you do your best you'll be right most of the time.

Q: My hair has been coming out in handfuls since my baby was born. When I brush it more falls out and my pillow is covered with it every morning. What can I do?

A: Hair has growing and resting phases. Pregnancy hormones encourage growth, but when they stop circulating some women's hair stays in the resting phase until the normal growth pattern reasserts itself. Hair loss may start around three to four months after the birth but it usually stops by about six months when the hormone levels stabilize.

Make sure that you get plenty of rest and your diet includes leafy green vegetables. Some people recommend eating seaweed (from health-food stores) to help normal hair growth.

A small number of women have a continuing problem, so if the loss continues after six months, see your doctor, who might suggest a prescription for Rogaine®, a lotion that is applied to the scalp to help regrowth.

Q: My 9-week-old baby has colic. The doctor says she's fine and not to worry, but I'm exhausted breastfeeding her—she's so demanding. Would she settle down better on the bottle?

A: A change to bottle-feeding rarely solves the problem, although it may seem to work for a few days. Breast milk consists of foremilk (more dilute and sweet) and hindmilk (richer in fat and more sustaining). Try to space breast-feeds at least two or three hours apart, so that your baby has room in her tummy for both. Between feeds comfort her by cuddling or rocking her. Give her a pacifier or your little finger to suck (up to the second joint, fleshy side up). Frequent snacks of foremilk may produce gas, so she cries and you give her more foremilk—a vicious circle!

A preparation from the pharmacist may help, but for most parents the answer is patience. She's not crying because you're doing anything wrong; accept this and have patience. Most babies are more settled when they're three to four months old.

Q: As a single parent, I'm not coping very well with motherhood. I love my daughter but I have no energy and I miss my friends. How can I start enjoying my life again?

A: Most mothers feel that they are not coping from time to time! Ask your healthcare provider if she knows a group or another mother whom you could meet. If you do not have any transportation, other moms may be willing to help out.

You might borrow a book of action rhymes from the library to enjoy with your daughter or a pattern book to make something for her.

Even if you don't feel like it at first, making the effort to think beyond chores and to get out and meet people will raise your morale and give you the energy to enjoy life again. Babies are hard work but they are also enormous fun to be with.

APPENDIX

These organizations offer information, support and referral when you are planning a pregnancy, are pregnant or have a baby. Voluntary organizations want their services to be used, so don't hesitate to contact them. Many operate nationwide and can put you in touch with your nearest branch, but some are run by individuals who give what help they can. Often their services have to be fitted in around family demands, so please offer to phone back at a convenient time and enclose a stamped self-addressed envelope if requesting information.

GENERAL INFORMATION

American College of Obstetricians and Gynecologists
Resource Center, 409 12th St., SW, P.O. Box 96920 Washington, DC 20090-6920.
Information about pregnancy, labor, birth or postpartum issues.
March of Dimes Birth Defects Foundation
1275 Mamaroneck Ave., White Plains, New York 10605. Regional offices throughout the United States. 1-888-MODIMES between 9 a.m. and 5 p.m. EST. Or 914-428-7100. TTY: 914-997-4763 URL: http://www.modimes.org E-mail: resourcecenter@modimes.
The Women's Bureau Publications (United States)
U.S. Department of Labor, Women's Bureau Clearing House, Box EX, 200 Constitution Ave., NW, Washington, DC 20210. Toll-free 1-800-827-5335. Information about state laws on family leave.

CONCEPTION, PREGNANCY, AND CHILDBIRTH

American Academy of Husband-Coached Childbirth
(Bradley Method) P.O. Box 5224, Sherman Oaks, CA 91413. Call toll-free: 1-800-423-2397, or call 818-788-6662. Childbirth-educator training and referral.
American Cancer Society
Call toll-free: 1-800-227-2345. Help to quit smoking.
American College of Nurse-Midwives
(ACNM) 818 Connecticut Ave. NW, Suite 900, Washington, DC 20006, 202-728-9860. Information and referral.
American Diabetes Association
Call toll-free: 1-800-DIABETES. Information and referral regarding pregnancy and ordinary diabetes and gestational diabetes.
American Lung Association
Call toll-free: 1-800-LUNG-USA. Help to quit smoking.
American Society for Psychoprophylaxis in Obstetrics
(ASPO/Lamaze) 1200 19th St. NW, Suite 300, Washington, DC 20036-2422. Toll-free: 1-800-368-4404.
Childbirth educator training and referral.
Association of Labor Assistants and Childbirth Educators
(ALACE) P.O. Box 382724, Cambridge, MA 02238-2724. 617-441-2500. Provides information and referral.
Doulas of North America, 1100 23rd Ave. East, Seattle, WA 98112. Fax: 206-325-0472.
Informed Home Birth
313-662-6857. Information regarding home birth.
International Cesarean Awareness Network
(ICAN) 1304 Kingsdale Ave., Redondo Beach, CA 90278. 310-542-6400.
International Childbirth Education Association
P.O. Box 20048, Minneapolis, MN 55420. 612-854-8660.
Midwives Alliance of North America
(MANA) P.O. Box 175, Newton, KS 67114. 316-283-4543.
National Association of Childbearing Centers
(NACC) 3123 Gottschall Rd., Perkiomenville, PA 18074. 215-234-8068. Referral to birthing centers.

Planned Parenthood
Call toll-free: 1-800-230-PLAN.
Information, referral, and clinical services involving fertility, contraception, sexual health, and prenatal care.
Public Citizen's Health Research Group
1600 20th St. NW, Washington, DC 20009; 202-588-1000. Information about C-sections, vaginal births after Cesarean section (VBAC), other pregnancy-, birth-related concerns.
W.I.C. Program (Supplemental Feeding Program for Women, Infants, and Children)
In the United States, call your state or local Department of Public Health.

AFTER THE BIRTH

American Academy of Pediatrics
141 Northwest Point Blvd., Elk Grove Village, IL 847-228-5005, fax: 847-228-5097.
Child Help
Toll-free: 1-800-4A-CHILD (1-800-422-4453).
Child abuse hotline for parents in crisis or children at risk.
Danny Foundation
3158 Danville Blvd., P.O. Box 680, Alamo, CA 94507. Toll-free: 1-800-83-DANNY. Information on crib safety.
Depression After Delivery
P.O. Box 1282, Morrisville, PA 19067. 1-800-944-4773.
INFACT Canada
10 Trinity Square, Toronto, Canada M5G 1B1. Voice: 416-595-9819, fax: 416-591-9355, e-mail: infact@ftn.net Provides breastfeeding information, support, referral.
International Lactation Consultant Association
(ILCA) 200 North Michigan Ave., Suite 300, Chicago, IL 60601-3821. 312-541-1710 or fax: 312-541-1271.
La Leche League Canada
18C Industrial Drive, P.O. Box 29, Chesterville, Ontario K0C 1H0 Canada. 613-448-1842, or fax: 613-448-1845.
La Leche League Canada Francais
Secretariat General de la LLL, C.P. 874 Ville St. Laurent, Quebec H4L 4W3 Canada, 514-747-9127. Fax: 514-747-6667.
La Leche League International
1400 North Meacham Rd., Schaumburg, IL 60173.
1-800-LA-LECHE or 847-519-7730; fax: 847-519-0035.
Medela, Inc.
P.O. Box 660, McHenry, IL 60051. Toll-free 1-800-TELL-YOU. Information, referral for breast pumps, breastfeeding specialists.
Safety Belt Safe USA
123 Manchester Blvd., Inglewood, CA 90301. 310-673-2666. Information regarding car seats and safety belts.
Wellstart
4062 First Ave., San Diego, CA 92130. 619-295-5192. Breastfeeding information.

SINGLE PARENTS

National Organization of Single Mothers
P.O. Box 68, Midland, NC 28107-0068. Call 704-888-KIDS.

MULTIPLE BIRTHS

Center for the Study of Multiple Births
333 E. Superior St., Room 464, Chicago, IL 60611.
Mothers of Supertwins (MOST)
P.O. Box 951, Brentwood, NY 11717. Call 516-434-MOST. Information for parents of triplets or more.
Mothers of Twins Clubs, Inc.
P.O. Box 23188, Albuquerque, NM 87192-1188. Call 505-275-0955.
Triplet Connection
P.O. Box 99571, Stockton, CA 95209. Call 209-474-0885.
Twin Services
P.O. Box 10066, Berkeley, CA 94709. Call 510-524-0863.
Twin-to-Twin Transfusion Syndrome (TTTS) Foundation
411 Long Beach Parkway, Bay Village, OH 44140. Call 216-899-8887.

BEREAVEMENT

Center for Loss in Multiple Birth
c/o Jean Kollantai, P.O. Box 1064, Palmer, AK 99645. Call 907-746-6123.
Perinatal Loss
2116 NE 18th Ave., Portland, OR 97212. Call 503-284-7426 Offers publications on perinatal bereavement.
Pregnancy & Infant Loss Center
1421 E. Wayzata Blvd., Suite 30, Wayzata, MN 55391. 612-473-9372. Offers information on perinatal bereavement.

SPECIAL SITUATIONS

About Face Canada
Call toll-free: 1-800-665-FACE
Information and support for parents of a child with a cleft palate or other facial abnormality.
About Face U.S.A.
Toll-free: 1-800-225-FACE
Allergy and Asthma Network
3554 Chain Bridge Rd., Suite 200, Fairfax, VA 22030. Toll-free: 1-800-878-4403.
American Cleft Palate Foundation
1218 Grandview Ave., Pittsburgh, PA 15211. Toll-free: 1-800-24-CLEFT, or call 412-481-1376.
CARESS
P.O. Box 1492, Washington, DC 20013
Information for parents of children with disabilities.
Direct Link for the Disabled, Inc.
P.O. Box 1036, Solvang, CA 93464. Call 805-688-1603, fax: 805-686-5285 or 805-686-5284, e-mail: suharry@terminus.com
Rare disorders, complicated situations and denial of benefits are information specialties.
ECMO Moms and Dads
c/o Blair and Gayle Wilson, P.O. Box 53848, Lubbock, TX 79453. Call 806-794-0259. Information for parents of premature infants.
Friends' Health Connection
P.O. Box 114, New Brunswick, NJ 08903. Call toll-free: 1-800-48-FRIEND or 908-418-1811, fax: 908-249-9897, Web: http://www.48friend.com, e-mail: fhc@pilot.njin.net
Customized support for individuals and their families with health-related problems.
National Organization for Rare Disorders
(NORD), P.O. Box 8923, New Fairfield, CT 06812.
National Down Syndrome Society
(NDSS), 666 Broadway, New York, NY 10012-2317. Toll-free: 1-800-221-4602.

National Information Center for Children and Youth with Disabilities
P.O. Box 1492, Washington, DC 20013-1492. 1-800-695-0285.
National Reye's Syndrome Foundation
426 North Lewis St., Bryan, OH 43506. Toll-free: 1-800-233-7393. In Ohio: 1-800-231-7393.
Sidelines
Candace Hurley, executive director: 714-497-2265 or Tracy Hoogenboom: 909-563-6199. For women experiencing a complicated pregnancy.

CANADIAN PROVINCIAL, TERRITORIAL HEALTH MINISTRIES

Alberta
Alberta Health, 24th Floor, 10025 Jasper Ave., Edmonton, AB T5J 2P, 403-427-2653, fax: 403-427-2511
British Columbia
Prevention and Health Promotion Branch, Ministry of Health, Main Floor, 1520 Blanshard St., Victoria, BC V8W 3C8. Call 604-952-1531, fax: 604-952-1570.
Manitoba
Manitoba Health, 599 Empress St., Room 259, Second Floor, Box 925, Winnipeg, Manitoba R3C 2T6. Call 204-786-7305, fax: 204-772-2943.
New Brunswick
Department of Health and Community Services, P.O. Box 5100, Fredericton, New Brunswick, E3B 5G8. Call 506-453-2933, fax: 506-453-2726.
Newfoundland
Community Health, Department of Health, Confederation Bldg., West Block, P.O. Box 8700, St. John's, NF A1B 4J4. Call 709-729-3110, fax: 709-729-5824.
Northwest Territories
Child/Family Support Division, Department of Health and Social Services, Government of the Northwest Territories, 5th Floor Precambrian Bldg. 6, P.O. Box 1320, Yellowknife, NWT X1A 2L9. Call 403-873-7054, fax: 403-873-7706.
Nova Scotia
Health Promotion Division, Nova Scotia Department of Health, 1690 Hollis St., 11th Floor, P.O. Box 488, Halifax, NS B3J 2R8. Call 902-424-5011, fax: 902-424-0558.
Ontario
Ministry of Health, 5700 Yonge St., 5th Floor, Toronto, Ontario M2M 4K5. Call 416-314-5485, fax: 416-314-5497.
Prince Edward Island
Health and Community Services Agency, 4 Sydney St., P.O. Box 2000, Charlottetown, PEI, C1A 7N8. Call 902-368-6522, fax: 902-368-6136.
Quebec
Federation des Centres locales de sante communautair, 1801, de Maisonneuve ouest, Piece 600, Montreal, Quebec H3H 1J9. Call 514-931-1448, fax: 514-931-9577.
Saskatchewan
Population Health Branch, Saskatchewan Health, 3475 Albert St., Regina, SK S4S 6X6. Call 306-787-7113 or 787-7110, fax: 306-787-7095.
Yukon
Whitehorse Regional Hospital, #5 Hospital Rd., Whitehorse, Yukon Y1A 3H7. Call 403-667-8700, fax: 403-667-8778.

INDEX

A

abnormalities:
  mother's age and, 14, 55
  testing for, 55-8
aches, 43-4
acupressure, 122
acupuncture, 73, 122
adjusting to pregnancy, 27
AFP tests, 56
afterpains, 174
age, motherhood, 14, 55
air travel, 81
alcohol, 11, 16, 32, 40
alpha-fetoprotein levels, 56
alternative therapies, 73
amniocentesis, 55-6, 57, 58, 59, 60
anesthetic, Cesarean sections, 162-3
anesthetist, 86
animals, disease and, 18
ankles, swollen, 98, 102
announcing the news, 26
antibodies, 96
Apgar score, 140
aromatherapy, 73
artificial insemination, 19
asthma, 17

B

babies:
  abnormalities, 55
  anxiety over, 55-62
  pregnancy, 36-7, 66-7, 96-7
  illnesses, 96
  influencing the sex of, 31-2
  kicking, 69-70, 98, 102
  late pregnancy, 96-7
  mother's lifestyle and, 14, 16-17, 31, 33, 39-42
  movement, 69-70, 98, 102
  newborn, 138
  poor growth, 103
  position, 104-5, 106-7

special tests, 55-8
baby equipment, choosing, 90-1, 93
backache, 12, 17, 44, 46
  during labor, 121, 133
bathing babies, 180
benefits and rights, 46
bilirubin levels, 176
birth:
  after the, 138-40
  at home, 87-8, 140
  breech, 160-1, 171
  Cesarean section, 62, 161-9, 171
  date of, 28, 62, 128
  feelings after, 153
  gentle, 137
  help after, 152
  in birthing centers, 87
  in the hospital, 84-7
  intravenous drip, 147-8
  overcoming a difficult, 153
  partner at, 116-17, 124-5, 155, 171
  preparation for, 110-25
  relatives at, 107
  water births, 88-9
  see also delivery, birthing centers
birthing centers, 87
birthplaces, 118, 119
blood pressure, 53
blood supply, 24
  pre-eclampsia, 102-3
blood tests, 51-3, 56, 60
  fetal-blood sampling 58
body changes, after conception 24-5
bonding, 140
bottle-feeding, 91, 183, 201
bras, nursing 93
Braxton-Hicks contractions, 99
breastfeeding, 91, 167, 180-3, 184, 201
breastfeeding counselor, 86

breasts:
  bras, 93
  enlarging, 93
breathing:
  during labor, 111
  shortness of breath, 98
breech presentation, 104,105, 106-7, 160-1

C

Cesarean section, 62, 161-9, 171
caffeine, 12
carpal tunnel syndrome, 98
cats, disease and, 18,41
checkups, medical, 11
chemicals, avoiding, 41
childbirth-education classes, 79-80
children, informing, 92
chorionic villus sampling (CVS), 57-8, 60
chromosomes, 23-4
  abnormalities, 14
cigarettes, 11, 14, 15, 40
circulation, exercise for, 74-7
classes, prenatal, 79-80
clothing:
  baby, 90, 93
  maternity, 78-9
cocaine, 16
coffee, 12
colic, 201
computer screens, 33
conception, 21-33
  announcing the news, 26
  body changes, 24-5
  calculating the birth date, 28
  ectopic pregnancy, 29
  effect of coffee on, 12
  increasing the chances of, 29
  infertility, 29
  maternity care, 27
  miscarriage, 30
  pregnancy tests, 26

process of, 22-4
relationship with your
partner, 25-6
sex of the baby, 31
congenital conditions, 17
constipation, 72
contraception, stopping, 13
contractions, 128-9, 130, 131-2,
147
Braxton-Hicks, 99
coping with, 132
cordocentesis, 58
couvade, 68-9
cramp, 30, 72
crying babies, 188, 189
cystic fibrosis, 57

D
date of birth, 28, 62, 128
dehydration, 100
delivery, 134-8
episiotomy, 151-2
forceps, 149-51, 156
position, 114-15
vacuum extraction, 149-51
see also birth
dentists, 41
depression, postnatal, 198
diabetes, gestational, 53-4
diapers, 90
changing, 179
diet, 12-13, 14, 18
early pregnancy, 39-49, 62-3
nausea and, 43
vegetarians, 47
disabilities
babies born with, 169-70
mothers with, 17, 92, 171, 188
DNA, 23-4
doctors, when to contact, 54
dogs, disease and, 18, 41
Down syndrome, 57
drink, alcohol, 11, 32, 40
driving, during late pregnancy,
107
drugs, illegal, 16

E
early pregnancy, 35-7
eating habits, 11-13,14,18
early pregnancy, 39-40, 62-3
nausea and, 43
vegans, 47
vegetarians, 47
ectopic pregnancy, 29
electro-acupuncture, 122
embryos, 36-37
employment:
pregnancy and, 78, 98
returning to, 200
rights, 46
epidural, 122, 124,162-3
episiotomy, 151-2, 175
equipment, nursery, 93
exercise, 11, 12, 70, 74-7
postnatal, 194-7
exhaustion, 42, 67
external version, 104, 171

F
fainting, 72
families:
new babies and, 179
preparing toddlers, 92
relationship with, 39
farm animals, disease and, 18
fatherhood, attitude toward, 10-11
fathers, see partners
fear, overcoming, 47
fentanyl, 87, 119, 122
fertilization, 22
fetal-blood sampling, 58
fevers, 32
first-trimester scan, 58
fluid retention, 98, 102
food, 12-13,14,18
early pregnancy, 39-40, 62-3
nausea and, 43
vegetarians, 47
forceps delivery, 149-51, 156
forgetfulness, 81

G
gardening, 41

H
genes, 23-4
genetic problems, 17
German measles, 18-19
gestational diabetes, 53-4

H
hemorrhoids, 72
hair, loss of, 201
HCG, 26
health, planning for
pregnancy, 11-12
heartburn, 73
height, ratio of weight to, 14-15
herbalism, 73
hiccups, baby, 69
high blood pressure, 53
"high-tech" births, 85
HIV tests, 51
home births, 87-8, 92, 140
homeopathy, 73
hormones, 24-5
hospitals:
birth at, 84-7
going home from, 168, 177, 184
labor and, 130
labor suite, 110
husbands see partners
hypnosis, 122
hypoglycemia, 176

I
identical twins, 23
identity bracelets, 138
illness, during labor, 142
incontinence, 72
induction, 146-7
infertility, 29
inner-thigh exercise, 74
intercourse, 69, 191
intrauterine device (IUD), 13
intrauterine growth
retardation, 103
itchiness, 73

J
jaundice, 176

jobs:
 pregnancy and, 78, 98
 returning to, 200
 rights, 46

K
kickcharts, 102
kicking, baby, 69-70, 98, 102

L
labor, 121-133
 active, 131-3
 backache, 121, 133
 birth plans, 118, 119
 breathing during, 111
 contractions, 128-9, 130,
  131, 147
 early, 130
 fast, 133
 help during, 146-52
 long, 133
 monitoring the baby, 148-9
 pain during, 118-23, 141
 partner's feelings about, 116
 positions for, 112-13, 124
 pre-labor, 129
 relaxation during, 110-11
 speeding up, 147-8
laparoscopy, 29
late pregnancy, 95-107
libido, 69
lifestyle, 14, 16, 39-42
lochia, 168, 174
loss of a baby, 169-170
"low-tech" births, 85

M
making love, 69, 191
malformation,
 mother's age and, 14
marijuana, 16
massage, 71
maternity benefits, 46
maternity care, 27
maternity clothing, 78-9
measles, 18-19
medical condition,
 pre-pregnancy, 17

medicines, 16-17
memory, 81
mid-pregnancy, 66-81
midwives, 87
milk, bottle feeding, 91
miscarriage, 30
motherhood:
 attitude towards, 10
 coping with, 188-9, 198-9
 older women, 14
multiple births, 23, 160

N
nausea, 43, 67
neonatal intensive care unit
(NICU), 154, 156-7
newborn baby, 138
 bonding, 140
 caring for, 179-83
 checks, 175-6
 special care, 154
normal pregnancy, 50
numbness, wrists, 98
nursing bras, 93
nutrition, 12-13, 18
 early pregnancy, 39-40
 vegetarians, 47

O
obstetrician, 86
oral sex, 69
osteopathy, 73

P
pediatrician, 86
pains:
 during labor, 118-23, 141
 during pregnancy, 43-4
parenthood:
 adjusting to, 188-9
 attitude towards, 10
partners:
 and the new baby, 178, 190-91
 at the birth, 116-18, 124-5,
  155,171
 attitude to pregnancy, 10-11
 during early pregnancy, 38
 feelings about labor, 116

late pregnancy, 99
 mid-term relationships, 68-9
 prenatal visits, 50
 relationship, 25-6, 31, 38
passive smoking, 16
pelvic floor, 45
pelvic rock, 76
perineum, 136
 perineal massage, 125, 151
pets, disease and, 18, 41
physical condition,
 pre-pregnancy, 17
Pill, 13
placenta, 66, 97, 102-3
 delivery, 138, 139, 155
planning, 9-19
 attitude to parenthood,
  10-11
 getting fit, 12
 medical conditions, 17
 physical conditions, 17
 preparing for pregnancy, 11
 risks in pregnancy, 13-17
 stopping conception, 13
positions:
 during labor, 112-13, 124
 for delivery, 114-15
 posture, 43-4, 46-7, 99
postnatal body, 192-8
 checkups, 196-97
 exercises, 194-6
postnatal depression, 198
posture, 43-4, 46-7, 99
pre-eclampsia, 102-3
pregnancy tests, 26
prenatal care, 27, 49-63
 awaiting test results, 60-2
 classes, 79-80
 deciding about tests, 59-60
 early tests, 58-9
 late pregnancy, 95-107
 notes on, 52
 questions, 54
 special tests, 55-8
 visits, 50-4
preparation for birth, 110-25
 birth partners, 116-17
 birth plans, 118

breathing, 111
making labor easier, 110
pain in labor, 118-23
positions for birth, 114-15
positions for labor, 112-13, 124
relaxation, 110-111
tour of the labor suite, 110
preparation for pregnancy, 11
diet, 11
getting fit, 12
stopping contraception, 13
presentation, 104-5, 106-7
problems:
alcohol, 11, 32,40
drugs and, 16
medicines and, 16-17
mother's age and, 14, 55
mother's weight and, 14
smoking, 11, 14, 16, 40-1

R
relationships:
with your family, 39
with your partner, 25-6, 31,
38
relaxation, 42, 99-101
during labor, 110-111
retroverted uterus, 32
RH factor, 53
rights and benefits, 46
risks in pregnancy, 13-17
avoiding, 41
rubella, 18-19

S
sex, influencing the baby's,
31-32
sexual desire, 69, 191
sharing pregnancies, 81
sheep, disease and, 18
shocks in pregnancy, 107
shoulder rolls, 75
sickness, 43, 67
single parents, 81, 201
sleeping, 98, 100-1
smoking, 11, 14, 16, 40-1
sperm, fertilization, 22

sperm donation, 19
spinal block, 124,162,164
spots, on newborn babies, 185
stitches, 151,164
avoiding, 125
sore, 175
stress, 11, 31
stress incontinence, 72
stretch marks, 63
stretching exercises, 74-7
strollers, 91
support, for new mothers, 189
swelling, 98, 102
swimming, 12
symptoms, early pregnancy, 38

T
Tay-Sach's disease, 17, 57
temperatures, 32
termination, 61-2
testing for pregnancy, 26
tests:
prenatal, 50-4
awaiting the test results, 60-2
deciding about, 59-60
early, 58-9
fetal abnormality, 55-8
reasons for, 59
see also individual tests
tingling wrists, 98
toxoplasmosis, 18
tranquilizers, 16
travel, 81
triple-marker test, 56
triple-plus test, 56
twins, 160
conception, 23

U
ultrasound scans, 51, 56, 60
urine tests, 51
uterus, retroverted, 32

V
vacuum-extraction delivery, 149-
51
vaginal bleeding, 30
varicose veins, 72
VDTs, 33
vegans, 47
vegetarians, 47
vitamin supplements, 18

W
walking, exercise, 12
water births, 88-9
waters, breaking, 129, 130,
141, 147
weight, 14-15
abnormalities and, 14
gain, 62
work:
pregnancy and, 78, 98
returning to, 200
rights, 46
wrists, tingling, 98

X
X-rays, 41

ACKNOWLEDGEMENTS

ILLUSTRATION CREDITS

COVER PHOTO:

SANDRA LOUSADA

Angela Hampton - Family Life Pictures; 60 top, 136 centre, 137 top, 167 bottom, 167 top, 199

Bubbles; 94, 134 top and bottom, 135 top and bottom, F. Rombout 2, 34, 64, 82, Ian West 158

Cleft Lip and Palate Association; 170

Collections; Anthea Sieveking 92, Sandra Lousada 154

Sally and Richard Greenhill; 89, Sally Greenhill 88

Robert Harding Picture Library; S. Villeger 186

HEA Business Unit Picture Library; 12

Image Bank; Anthony A. Boccaccio 84

Sandra Lousada; 6

Lupe Cunha Photography; 144, 180

National Medical Slide Bank; 24, 60 center

Petit Format; Taeke Henstra 172

Rascals; Joanna Mungo 178

Reflections Photo Library; Jennie Woodcock 48, 126, 139 bottom, 139 top, 176, 182 bottom left, Martin Dohrn 163

Science Photo Library; David Scharf 22 center, Petit Format/Nestle 20, 36 top left, 66 top left, Professors P. M. Motta & J. Van Blerkom 23 top right

Tony Stone Images; Andre Perlstein 8

Zefa Pictures Ltd; 108

The publishers would like to thank the parents and babies who were kind enough to model for this book.